PRAISE FOR *WITCH'S WHEEL OF THE YEAR*

"Mankey's scholarship is sound as a bell, his experience rich, and his writing inviting. *Witch's Wheel of the Year* is a helpful and very readable guide to a deeper engagement with the cycle of the seasons often referred to as the Wheel of the Year. This book is good for the novice as well as the experienced Witch, and it's an excellent resource for ritual-makers."

—H. Byron Ballard, priestess and author of *Earth Works*

"*Witch's Wheel of the Year* offers meaning-filled rituals that stir and summon your heart and spirit at the same time that it provides practical guidance on facilitating and experiencing rituals. I particularly enjoyed the way that the history, customs, and folkways of being a witch were dovetailed into the main themes of the book. … A great resource to anyone who celebrates the cycles of nature."

—Ivo Dominguez Jr., author of
Practical Astrology for Witches and Pagans

"A fresh and exhilarating contribution to the literary canon of magick and witch-craft … *Witch's Wheel of the Year* can easily be used by practitioners from a variety of tra-ditions, as its strength lies in Mankey's adept representation of the fundamental patterns of nature itself, the ultimate source of earth-based spirituality. With vast knowledge and charming wit, Mankey delivers a guidebook that every witch, wizard, and shaman should keep at their altar-side."

—Daniel Moler, author of *Shamanic Qabalah*

WITCH'S
Wheel of the Year

About the Author

Jason Mankey read his first book on Witchcraft in the seventh grade, and at age twenty-two dedicated his life to the Craft. Today, Jason is a third-degree Gardnerian High Priest and helps run two Witchcraft covens in the San Francisco Bay Area with his wife, Ari. Jason is a popular speaker at Pagan and Witchcraft events across North America and Great Britain and has been recognized by his peers as an authority on the Horned God, Wiccan history, and occult influences in rock and roll and heavy metal music. He is the channel manager at Patheos Pagan, the world's most read Pagan blogging site, and writes there at *Raise the Horns*, and at the magazine *Witches & Pagans*.

Witch's

Wheel of the Year

Rituals for Circles, Solitaries & Covens

JASON MANKEY

Llewellyn Publications
Woodbury, Minnesota

FIRST EDITION
Third Printing, 2022

Cover art by Kjersti Faret
Cover design by Kevin R. Brown
Interior illustrations by Kjersti Faret, except on pages 59, 60, 114, 258, 300, 330, 331, and 347, done by the
    Llewellyn Art Department

Llewellyn Publications is a registered trademark of Llewellyn Worldwide Ltd.

Library of Congress Cataloging-in-Publication Data
Names: Mankey, Jason, author.
Title: Witch's wheel of the year : rituals for circles, solitaries & covens
    / Jason Mankey.
Description: First edition. | Woodbury, Minnesota : Llewellyn Publications,
    2019. | Includes bibliographical references and index. | Summary: "This
    is a ritual-focused book on the sabbats that make up the Wiccan Wheel of
    the Year"—Provided by publisher.
Identifiers: LCCN 2019030767 (print) | LCCN 2019030768 (ebook) | ISBN
    9780738760919 (trade paperback) | ISBN 9780738760988 (ebook)
Subjects: LCSH: Sabbat. | Wicca—Rituals.
Classification: LCC BF1572.S28 M27 2019 (print) | LCC BF1572.S28 (ebook)
    | DDC 133.4/3—dc23
LC record available at https://lccn.loc.gov/2019030767
LC ebook record available at https://lccn.loc.gov/2019030768

Llewellyn Publications
A Division of Llewellyn Worldwide Ltd.
2143 Wooddale Drive
Woodbury, MN 55125-2989
www.llewellyn.com

Printed in the United States of America

OTHER BOOKS BY JASON MANKEY

Transformative Witchcraft

(Llewellyn, 2019)

The Witch's Altar

(cowritten with Laura Tempest Zakroff, Llewellyn, 2019)

The Witch's Book of Shadows

(Llewellyn, 2017)

The Witch's Athame

(Llewellyn, 2016)

To my Oak Court Witches,
thanks for saving my Craft.

CONTENTS

Figures

INTRODUCTION

My most joyous and spiritual moments as a Witch have generally taken place during ritual. At an early Samhain ritual, I came face to face with the Goddess for the first time when our High Priestess drew down the moon. To have *the* Goddess of the Witches in the body of a friend and peer was life-changing. It was a moment so powerful and fundamental to my development as a Witch that just writing about it brings a smile to my face almost twenty years later, along with a desire to repeat the experience.

While many Witches today try to cultivate an air of mystery and menace about themselves, I've always found Witchcraft to be a bright, sunny, and happy experience (even if we do most of our rituals in the light of the moon). At Yule we toast one another in my coven with alcoholic wassail while weaving magick to ensure a new year full of health and relative prosperity. At Beltane we play absurd games that make us giggle, and at Ostara we eat hot cross buns and indulge the child within.

Ritual has brought me intense spiritual satisfaction and no shortage of good times. It's also a time for *work*, and many of the rituals I've been involved with over the years have been rather serious affairs. Some of them have centered on social justice issues and preserving our environment. For a Witch, ritual is a multifaceted thing, and it's possible to have fun, have an intense spiritual experience, *and* do something super meaningful all in the space of one hour. Many of my proudest moments as a Witch have taken place inside of ritual space, usually when leading a successful rite for and with a large group. When I write or lead a ritual for my extended community, I look upon it as a service, and one I'm happy to provide. Good ritual gets people involved in our local circles, covens, and groves, while a bad ritual experience might drive them away from the Craft forever.

While I don't believe in proselytizing, growing my community and getting people excited about Witchcraft is important to me.

Since the early 1970s, thousands of books full of Witch ritual of varying quality have been published. Witchcraft as we experience it today has really only been around for a little less than a hundred years, and fifty years ago, when we first started putting rituals down on the printed page, we were still trying to figure things out. To put it mildly, a lot of early printed Witch ritual simply wasn't very good. (I'm sure that statement is going to get me into trouble with a few folks, but I stand by it.)

Most early printed rituals were ridiculously short and didn't really offer much to do. There would be instructions for the coven to gather, yell something as a group, and then engage in a guided meditation or short seasonal observance. Reading these types of rituals as a Witchling was especially troublesome to me because they had nothing to do with my Witch experience in those days. I was a solitary, and most printed rituals were designed for groups, and there's a big difference between ritual for one and ritual for thirteen. Even one of the best books on Wiccan-Witchcraft ever written, Scott Cunningham's *Wicca: A Guide for the Solitary Practitioner*, contained very short rituals that didn't resonate with me all that much.

As I grew as a Witch and eventually met and began practicing with other Witches, I often found myself responsible for coming up with our rituals. Many of these rituals were at local psychic fairs and for the college student group we were all a part of then. While trying to put those rituals together, I'd often comb through my rapidly growing Witch library for help and inspiration. Sadly, my books were never much help, and I ended up learning rather quickly that rituals originally written for ten people don't always translate well for groups of thirty or more.

There are fundamental differences between solitary, coven, and circle rituals, and that's a detail mostly absent from Witch literature. (*Circle* is my term here for large groups.) This book is designed to fill in those gaps, all while (hopefully) offering meaningful, involved, and interesting rituals for each *sabbat*, or holiday. What works for ten people may not work for fifty, and what works for fifty people might not work for the Witch alone. I've focused on sabbat rituals in this book because I love them most of all, and because the sabbats are the one common element among the hundreds of Witch traditions today. Most every Witch I know celebrates the sabbats, even if we don't all agree on what to call them.

Because this book is essentially dedicated to sabbat rituals, there's also some good factual information included about all eight of them. However, due to the length of this book, I've kept those overviews brief. I originally wanted to include long, detailed histories of sabbats such as Yule and Samhain, but I often found myself writing instead about Christmas and Halloween, which aren't quite the same thing. Historical context is great, but this book is mainly concerned with how we celebrate the sabbats *today*, not how another religious tradition adapted the rites of ancient paganism(s) to suit their own needs. Those interested in more history are urged to check out the bibliography.

This book contains twenty-four rituals, but that's only a drop in the bucket as to what can actually be done on the sabbats. So in addition to the rituals in this book, I've included other ideas on ways to celebrate our high holidays. My ideas often mention some of the more obvious themes we see in ritual, such as the Oak King/Holly King mythos and the cycle of Maiden, Mother, and Crone. In order to make this work as unique as possible, I made a deliberate decision to try to avoid including rituals that contain themes and ideas that appear with frequency online and in other books. There are lots of books and websites with rituals out there. I hope that the rituals included in this book have something new and/or different to say.

In addition to all the seasonal stuff, there are a lot of tips and tricks included on just how to create effective rituals for both yourself and any group you might be involved in. Ritual scripts are great and all, but they only tell half the story. Knowing how to set up a ritual for the group you're working with (and that "group" might include only you and your gods) is a necessary skill to ensure effective ritual practice.

No book can teach someone how to be an effective ritualist. Learning how to facilitate a powerful ritual can only truly be accomplished through trial and error. Books like this can provide some of the necessary tools, but they are no substitute for actually doing the work. And when that work doesn't go as well as you might have hoped, the only recourse is to get back up and try again. Practice makes perfect, especially when it comes to Witch ritual.

PART ONE
THE MECHANICS OF RITUAL &
THE WHEEL OF THE YEAR

Cast the circle round,

Call to air, fire, sea, and earth.

The rite has begun.

CHAPTER 1

WHY RITUAL?

The Power of Connection

Ask five Modern Witches just what Witchcraft is and you'll probably get six or seven different answers. I'm not always sure myself just how to define Witchcraft in this day and age, but I'm comfortable writing that I know it when I see it. Modern Witches practice in a variety of ways, with many embracing traditions derived from Wiccan-Witchcraft and others exploring traditions more closely related to the disciplines of Conjure and cunning-craft.

There are two elements though that show up in most Witchcraft traditions. The first is magick. Witchcraft is empowering and offers us the means to take control of our lives through spellwork and petitions to deity. The second is ritual, which often goes hand in hand with magickal practice. Much of my spellwork takes place in sacred space, and setting up that space is done through ritual. Anytime we do something magickal in a prescribed order, we are performing a ritual.

As a young Witchling, my first steps upon this path were tentative. I began with prayers to the Goddess, lots of reading, and eventually a smattering of spellwork. After a few months of this, I decided it was time to perform my first ritual. On the Autumn Equinox, I retreated into the most private spot in my basement apartment and lit six candles, one for each of the elements—air, fire, water, and earth—and then one each for the Goddess and the God. I don't remember much about that ritual other than lighting those candles and casting a circle, but it was a start.

Most Witches today, no matter their path or tradition, honor the turn of the seasons, also known as the *Wheel of the Year*. The Wheel of the Year is made up of eight "spokes," with each spoke being a holiday that most of us call a *sabbat*. The sabbats include the earth's annual solstices and equinoxes, along with the days that lie in between them (give or take a few days), which are called the *cross-quarter days*. Not all Witches call these holidays by the same names, but most Witches celebrate or at least acknowledge them in some way.

Since the time of that small ritual in my basement apartment, I've participated in over 250 sabbat rituals. Many of those rituals have been solitary affairs, as I practiced my Witchcraft alone for several years before finding other folks of like mind. There have also been lots of coven rituals, and on several occasions I've presented seasonal rituals for groups of up to 200 people.

Every ritual is different to some degree. The biggest differences involve the size of the rite, when and where the ritual is being held, and the rite's focus. Despite the diversity in the various rituals I've participated in over the years, they all have shared one common attribute: *connection*. What was being connected *to* varied, of course, but all of them connected both myself and those I was with (if applicable) to something greater.

Six Areas of Focus for Ritual

There are six different energies that ritual generally attempts to connect us with, and every ritual in this book is designed to connect its participants with at least one of those. Those rituals may not always succeed in their intended purpose, but that's because we all experience ritual differently (something we'll get into a little bit later on). Many of the energies we connect with in ritual are clear and obvious (the natural world, for instance), while others, such as connection to community, can be a bit more abstract. One of the things that makes Witch ritual so great is that it has multiple points of connection, and all of them are worth exploring.

The Natural World

For many people, Witchcraft is primarily a nature religion or practice. They find solace and comfort in wild spaces and seek to find their place in the natural world. Rituals about the natural world can also be about protecting nature or experiencing just what makes the world divine. I've participated in rituals where I've planted seeds, picked grapes off a vine, stayed up super late to watch a sunrise, and used fallen leaves in spell-work. All of those things are ways to connect with the natural world.

Seasons and the Wheel of the Year

The energy of winter is very different from that of summer. In the summertime I tend to my garden, and by August I begin to enjoy the fruits of my labor. In the winter my garden lies fallow, the rain and cold of the season preparing my garden for what will happen in the spring. There is a cycle and a rhythm to the annual turn of the wheel, and it's one that many Witches choose to connect with during ritual.

The natural energies of certain seasons can also affect our spellwork. Summer spellwork is for the (metaphorically speaking) bright and shiny things we might want or need, like a new (to us) car. Autumn is for letting go of the people and energies that no longer serve us. Winter is about ridding ourselves of bad habits or undesirable traits. Spring is about renewal and new challenges. Connecting to the natural energy of the seasons can change us and charge our magick.

Magick

When Witches create magick in ritual space, we're doing more than just trying to change our circumstances or reach a desired outcome. Magick itself is something we can feel, and when we practice it, we connect in a greater sense to all the magick practitioners the world over and throughout history. The practice of magick allows us to tap into a current that goes all the way back to our earliest ancestors (most likely).

When I engage in magickal practice with my coven, I can feel their energy around me, and I get to share it with them for a few moments. The same type of thing happens when a deity or spirit lends their energy to one of my workings. Practicing magick with another person is an intimate act of connection.

Deity and Other Higher Powers

Many rituals contain more than just calls and invocations to deity; they are specifically about a particular deity (or deities) and focus on interacting with that deity. The name of the god Lugh shows up in the sabbat of Lughnasadh (also called Lammas), so a ritual about connecting with him on that day seems entirely appropriate. Though most sabbat rituals aren't focused on a particular deity, there's no reason they can't be.

By honoring our gods in ritual, we strengthen both them and the bonds between deity and mortal. Sometimes we just feel called to write a rite for a particular deity, too. The Rite of the Three Brigids found in chapter 13 of this book came about because I felt her asking me for a ritual, and who am I to say no to a goddess?

Ancestors, Spirit Animals, and the Fey

Outside of the gods, there are several other entities we often connect to during ritual. Many Witches call to their ancestors in every ritual they do, and for many of us, Samhain in particular is about reconnecting with those we have lost. The fey (or fair folk/fairy folk) have long been associated with Midsummer, and there are also several fair folk who have become a part of modern-day Christmas and Yule celebrations. I've never seen a sabbat ritual built around spirit animals, but it could be done. If something is worth connecting with, it's worth building a ritual around, if time and circumstances permit and it makes sense to do so.

Community

The idea that we should connect to one another gets lost in a lot of Witchcraft circles. If a coven is a chosen family, why wouldn't we want to participate in and craft rituals that celebrate those bonds and bring us closer to one another? Simply doing something enjoyable in a group setting helps connect us with each other.

One of the best rituals I've ever been a part of was a simple rite where we all stood in a circle and took turns throwing around a large ball of yarn. Upon getting the yarn ball, we would share how we were going to contribute to our local community and then throw the ball across the circle to someone else. In the process of doing this, we created a spider web of yarn connecting us all together. What probably made this ritual so memorable was that we were able to physically see the connections that we were attempting to create.

The community we create through ritual often includes more than just the people we share physical space with. When I use the rituals of my tradition, I'm in a sense connecting with every other follower of that tradition who has used those same rituals. Thousands of Witches past and present have read the words of Doreen Valiente's *Charge of the Goddess*, and every time I hear that particular piece of liturgy, I can feel the presence of those who spoke the words of the Goddess long before I was born.

As Witches, we often attach very high expectations to our rites and rituals, and I mostly see that as a good thing. Witches are generally exceptional people, so it stands to reason that our rituals should be powerful and transformative. But because there are so many variables in ritual, not everything we do is going to be earth-shattering. However, even the worst rituals I've attended over the years have still connected me to something.

Most of us who have been around the circle a few times can tell you a story or three about that one Beltane ritual where it rained all day and everyone was soaked and miserable. But once the pain and shock of not having everything go perfectly fades away, such stories usually turn into bonding experiences. "Remember when we were all there together in the rain and how terrible it was? That was awesome!" Ritual is powerful and brings people together, even when it doesn't quite go as planned.

CHAPTER 2

THE ELEMENTS OF RITUAL

What We Do in the Circle

Most Witch ritual today is made up of five components: purification, invitation(s), the working, cakes and ale/grounding, and dismissals. Ritual consists of more than five distinct parts, of course, but the various pieces that make up a ritual can generally be grouped into these five categories. Occasionally you might participate in a ritual that leaves out one of these components, but that's rare. Since these five components are the building blocks of ritual, it's worth spending some time with each of them to look at how they fit into ritual and what roles they serve.

PURIFICATION

Purification rites cover two specific areas: preparing the individual Witch for ritual, and cleansing the space being used for ritual. During the course of a day, our bodies and minds come into contact with all sorts of energies. Often these energies are negative or unwanted. (Think of that frustration you experienced today at work.) Purification rites are designed to remove that bad energy from the body and mind. They help to prepare us for whatever work we are about to undertake in the magick circle and to cast aside our mundane worries and anxieties.

The spaces we use for ritual are also subject to unwanted energies, which is why ritual space is often cleansed and purified before beginning any serious Witch work. If there's been a negative interaction in the space you're getting ready to do ritual in, the energy of that interaction will be a part of your space. Cleansing and purifying the area before ritual will ensure that those unwanted energies don't influence you or your work.

Purification rites also help to rid a ritual area of any unwanted entities. I'm not suggesting that your Witch space is continually full of malevolent spirits, but it's been known to happen from time to time. One of the oldest adages in magick is the idea that "like attracts like." Magickal and ethereal beings are most likely going to be attracted to your ritual space because of this rule (your ritual space should be magickal after all), so it's best to give any unwanted visitors the boot.

There are a whole host of techniques that can be used for purifying and cleansing. Smoke in the form of incense and bundles of sage is extremely common, as is salted water. Using both incense and salted water in tandem is called *censing and asperging*. Other techniques include sweeping away negative energies with a broom, using essential oils, and performing a ritual hand washing. I've also used sound to cleanse a room, and there are covens that require ritual baths or showers before serious workings. All of these techniques (with the exception of ritual baths or showers) will show up in the various rituals included in this book.

The preparation rites involved in cleansing and purification are often a part of the ritual. Many Witches will ceremonially bless, consecrate, and mix together the powers of air, fire, water, and earth (generally represented by incense, a lit candle, a chalice of water, and salt) before using them to purify the ritual participants and space. In my own coven, we ritually bless salt and water and then incense and candle flame before using them for cleansing. It's not necessary to do these things publicly, but I think it can help to create an effective ritual atmosphere.

Unlike the rest of the components we'll be looking at in this chapter, purification rites sometimes happen outside of ritual space. This is obvious in the case of a ritual bath, but sometimes purification rites might only be available for whoever needs them privately before the ritual starts. (This occurs with some frequency at large rituals where there is not a lot of time or space.) My coven uses a blessing bowl before ritual for those who have a lot of negative energy to get rid of. (A blessing bowl is part of the Imbolc solitary ritual in chapter 15.)

In addition, purification rites depend to a large degree on the individual being cleansed. No amount of salt water or incense is going to rid someone of anger if they wish to hold onto it. I think purification rites are essential to a good ritual, but they are not a cure-all. Ultimately, we are all responsible for preparing ourselves for ritual. If we can't get into the right headspace, that's on us, not on the people running the ritual and not on the purification technique that is being used.

The Invitation

The invitation section of a ritual is just that: a series of invitations to various deities, powers, elemental energies, ancestors, and all the Witches who are in attendance at the rite. This is probably the most complicated component of ritual since it's made up of several different pieces, each of which is worth writing about in its own right. In addition, the various rites that make up the invitation section don't all serve exactly the same purpose.

Statement of Intent

Most of my rituals begin with a one- or two-sentence statement summing up the observance and outlining the purpose of the ritual. I think of it like a ritual thesis statement, and when writing ritual, I use the statement of intent as a lamppost. If something I'm thinking about adding to my rite doesn't sync up with the statement of intent, then it probably doesn't belong there.

For example, when celebrating the Winter Solstice, my statement of intent might look like this:

> *Tonight we celebrate the Winter Solstice. We honor the year's longest night and gather to celebrate the rebirth of the Lord of the Sun. Though it is dark and cold, tonight's sabbat is one of joy, for the God has returned and the light is reborn. So mote it be!*

The statement of intent in this case says a couple of specific things. It reminds everyone of just what holiday is being celebrated and why we are all celebrating. Rituals can be both somber and joyful, and everything in between, and in this case the statement of intent let's everyone gathered know that the ritual will be a fun one. It's all pretty simple.

A statement of intent doesn't necessarily have to be verbalized at the beginning of ritual, but I often find it helpful to do so. By letting everyone know the tenor of a ritual beforehand, no one is caught off guard or unprepared for how things will unfold. The statement of intent also serves as a welcome to all the Witches in the circle.

Casting the Circle

Circles are where most Witches do their work. They are human-created sacred spaces where mortals can freely interact with deities and raise magickal energy.[1] Circles serve three purposes in ritual. They are protective places and are designed to keep out negative energy and entities. Circles also contain and store magickal energy until it's ready to be released; this is often called "building the cone of power." And finally, circles are a space between the worlds—a world that exists between our physical reality and what lies beyond. A well-cast circle helps us interact directly with deity, spirits, and various other powers and entities.

Circles are created by Witches using magickal energy, generally channeled through a tool such as an athame,[2] a sword, or a wand (though your finger will work just as well). *Circle* is a bit of a misnomer though, because most Witches actually cast a sphere: the circle goes above and below us, and has a definite top and bottom. Circles are generally cast deosil (clockwise), beginning in the east or the north. Most Witches take them down widdershins (counterclockwise), though I have encountered some who do not. Do what works best for you. Standing in a circle with other Witches is an honor and a privilege. Shared sacred space is something to be treasured.

Calling the Quarters

Most Witches invoke elemental energies (or entities) at each of the four cardinal points of the compass in their circles. The energies correspond to the four elements of air, fire, water, and earth. (Every Witch knows that the universe is made up of more than four elements, but most substances can be classified as a gas, a solid, a liquid, or a flame; hence the four elements.) But "calling the quarters" in the east, south, west, and north is often more nuanced than most Witches believe, because there are several different entities and energies that are often called upon during this part of ritual.

The most common energy associated with the four quarters is elemental energy. These elemental powers are nature in her purest and most primitive form. When a Witch says, "I call to the powers of water," they are requesting that the power of that

---

1. I spend a lot of time talking about circles and their function in my book *Transformative Witchcraft: The Greater Mysteries*, published by Llewellyn in 2019.

2. Another shameless plug: I wrote a book all about athames in 2016 called *The Witch's Athame*, again published by Llewellyn.

specific elemental energy join them in the circle. This energy can then be used to assist in magickal workings.

When a Witch invokes the power of a *watchtower*, they are most often requesting the protective energies associated with an element to join them in the circle. I say "most often" because "watchtowers" originally referred to the angels—Raphael (air), Michael (fire), Gabriel (water), and Uriel (earth)—who were invoked by ceremonial magicians to protect their workings. Though angels are not super common in Witchcraft circles today, there are still some Witches who call them to guard the four quarters.

In addition to angels, some Witches call upon the fey to stand watch at the quarters. There are dozens of different kinds of fey, though the ones I've seen invoked at the quarters the most are sylphs (air), salamanders/dragons (fire), undines (water), and brownies or gnomes (earth). Because both angels and the fey are sentient beings, I recommend using caution when calling them. No matter what Disney might have you believe, the fey have a long history as troublemakers in mortal matters.

The quarters are most often associated with the following directions, energies, and colors, though this can and does vary among Witchcraft traditions.

East/air/yellow
South/fire/red
West/water/blue
North/earth/green

The quarters are typically called in a clockwise (deosil) direction, usually beginning in the east or the north, but since we're working in a circle, there are no true absolutes here. How the quarters are dismissed varies from group to group and tradition to tradition. I know many groups that dismiss their quarters in the order they were called (generally deosil) and others who dismiss them widdershins. I include both ways of doing things in this book, though you should do whatever makes the most sense to you. The same goes for color correspondences. If the color yellow doesn't make sense to you in association with air, pick a different one.

Many Witches light a candle in conjunction with calling the quarters. This is not necessary, though it does add a certain ambience to ritual. In addition, it's acceptable to call upon two different sets of quarters in the same ritual. For instance, my coven invokes the elemental energies of air, fire, water, and earth and then calls to the watchtowers. It's a nice little extra layer of ritual that works for us, though it's not always necessary.

In this book I've included a variety of methods for calling the quarters[3] (the fey, angels, elementals, and watchtowers), so you can pick and choose what resonates most with you. In addition, I've included the creation of the *Witches' Compass* (see the Lammas coven ritual in chapter 30), a technique used by some Witches that combines casting the circle and calling the quarters into one rite. This technique is most often associated with the practice of Traditional Witchcraft, but it can be used by any Witch.

The sky (and the circle) is truly the limit when it comes to calling the quarters, and it's a practice that can be done in a variety of ways. However, I think it's important to know just what you are calling and to do so in a respectful manner. In addition, it's best to call the same types of energies/entities at each of the four quarters. No one wants to see a fight break out between Archangel Gabriel and a dragon in the middle of ritual.

Some Witches invoke a fifth element, generally referred to as *spirit*. This element is honored in the middle of the circle and is most often seen as the cosmic force that binds the elements and the universe all together. It's also sometimes thought of as the original source of energy from which all things come (sort of like a spiritual version of the big bang theory). Spirit is not something I see invoked in very many Witch rituals these days, but it still pops up as a concept from time to time. If it works for you, use it! If it doesn't, then it can easily be discarded.

Ancestors

Not all Witches formally invite their ancestors to every ritual, but some do. My coven has a standing invitation to our Mighty Dead (our Witchcraft influences, known to us both personally and through books), but we don't formally acknowledge them at most rituals. Some Witches call their ancestors only at Samhain or on other specific occasions. The *ancestors* generally refer to our genetic, adoptive, and magickal families from across the centuries.

---

3. "Calling the quarters" is probably a bit too simplistic here, but it's an easy way to categorize things. Always keep in mind that angels, fey, and other sentient beings aren't "quarters" in the way that elementals and watchtowers are.

Deity

While a belief in goddesses and gods is not required in Modern Witchcraft, it's fairly common. Even Witches who aren't believers in deity in the traditional sense often call upon the gods in ritual to symbolize or represent natural forces. The most common way to invite a deity into ritual is with a *call* (also known as an *invocation*). Calls to deity are verbalized invitations to goddesses and gods to be a part of a ritual. Whether or not they show up is entirely up to them.

A call can be a couple of sentences made up on the spot, or something written prior to ritual and more formalized. Simply saying "Great Brigid, join us in ritual tonight" constitutes a call. Calls aren't complex things, though I suggest knowing exactly who you are calling before you do so. In addition, deities like to be flattered, so peppering your calls with compliments isn't a bad idea.

Calls can be addressed to "greater" deity concepts such as the Horned God and the Mother Goddess. They can also be used to attract the attention of specific deities such as Lugh or Isis. This book includes calls at both ends of the spectrum. In many Wiccan traditions, it's commonplace to call to both a goddess and a god at any given ritual, though this isn't a hard-and-fast rule. When calling to more than one deity, make sure those gods actually like one another or are at least compatible in some way. (You can check on this by reading mythology or simply by asking them before ritual.)

Drawing Down the Moon

Drawing down the moon is the process by which a deity enters the body of a willing human being. Most often, drawing down the moon refers to a Witch invoking a goddess into themselves, while invoking a god in the same manner is called *drawing down the sun* (though women can draw down male deities and men can draw down female deities, so don't let anyone tell you otherwise!).

Drawing down the moon is a complex rite and should not be taken lightly. While I think it's one of the central rites of Wiccan-Witchcraft, it's not appropriate for every ritual and it's not a parlor trick. It should be attempted only after establishing a relationship with the deity being drawn down. Since drawing down requires the cooperation of both deity and our physical bodies, it often doesn't work—an important consideration to keep in mind if you plan to utilize it in ritual.[4]

Drawing down the moon can lead to unpredictable results, since it literally involves ceding control of a ritual to a goddess or god. Sometimes a deity will play along with whatever someone has come up with for the ritual, but on other occasions they'll completely throw out the script and take the ritual into weird, wonderful, and different directions. Remember, with drawing down, you've called an honest-to-goodness goddess or god into your circle! Most often a deity will spend a few moments with everyone at the ritual after they've been drawn down, and will perhaps offer the participants some advice or a glimpse into the future. Because drawing down takes a lot of energy from the body, it typically doesn't last very long, usually no longer than thirty minutes to an hour.

When a drawing down doesn't work, many Witches will read the Charge of the Goddess or the Charge of the God (depending on who was called) in its place. Charges function as divine revelations from deity, offering insights into the mysteries of the gods. While charges are of course written by human beings, many of us believe they are divinely inspired. The most famous charge is Doreen Valiente's Charge of the Goddess.

Because most charges are lovely pieces of liturgy, many Witches read them during ritual after calling to their deities. One doesn't have to wait for a failed drawing down to use a charge, as they are a worthy addition to ritual in their own right. Some of my favorite ritual memories are of my wife, Ari, simply reading Valiente's Charge of the Goddess. I get goose bumps just thinking about it!

The Working

The working is the meat (or tofu) of the ritual. After all the cleansing and calling, the working is the ritual's main event. It's also the most difficult part of ritual to write and/or execute. I have been to many rituals where everything was beautifully set up, with stirring calls to deity, powerful summonings of the quarters, and a sturdy circle casting, but then the working involved nothing more than a guided meditation and giving a flower to each participant. Zzzzzzzzzzzz.

The working is the part of the ritual that's supposed to connect us to that thing that is bigger than ourselves. But creating a working that does this is challenging, and some-

---

4. Yet another shameless plug: I spend a lot of time on drawing down the moon in my book *Transformative Witchcraft*. (At least I'm not suggesting you pick up a third book of mine. That will come later.)

times even the best ritual writers (me included!) fail to reach that objective. There are several different types of workings, and nearly all of them show up in this book at some point or another.

A Magickal Act

For many Witches, magickal work is a foundational practice. Because of this, it's not surprising that it shows up in a lot of seasonal rituals. Magickal workings can be complex or simple. They might involve nothing more than building a cone of power (filling the circle with energy and then directing it for a specific purpose)[5] or practicing some candle magick. Some magickal acts are more involved and might utilize something related to the current season, such as a sheaf of grain in the autumn or a bit of snow in the winter.

Sacred Drama

Especially common in large public circles is sacred drama, which functions much like a play and is generally done to illustrate certain truths about the gods or the change of the seasons. Many times the people involved in sacred drama have been touched by the deities they are portraying. I remember one Samhain when I was playing the part of the sacrificial Horned God and I went from simply reading my lines to truly feeling the Horned One in my soul and then experiencing his pain and his love for all of us as the drama unfolded. As I "died," those assembled shrieked and cried over my demise. It was a powerful rite and worked as intended.

However, sacred drama can be hard to pull off. Done right, it involves the audience in some way, either by having them participate in the drama in some fashion or by making sure they are emotionally invested in the story being told. Rituals are not plays, so when one chooses to engage in sacred drama, there has to be a definite hook to get everyone involved.

Divination

A few times a year, my coven throws a deck of tarot cards on our altar and we take turns picking cards for ourselves and our coven. Working together, we create a little energy,

---

5. Another footnote, another plug for *Transformative Witchcraft*. The cone of power is such a cool thing that I wrote 20,000 words about it in that book.

infuse it into the cards, and then take a look at what the next few months might bring us. This may not sound like much of a ritual, but it's always been one of our favorite workings and we look forward to doing it a few times a year.

Tarot cards are not the only way to engage in divination as a working. There are all sorts of divination systems out there that work well in ritual, including scrying, tea leaves, and runes. It's also possible to draw down a goddess or god known for prophecy and then build a ritual around what they might reveal.

Tokens/Gifts/Handouts

Passing out tokens and other small objects as gifts during ritual is a common and popular activity at many large rituals. Such things can work very well in ritual if they somehow fit into the sabbat being celebrated. One of the more common handouts in ritual is seeds, which can be tossed into a cauldron or taken home for planting, usually after being infused with magickal energy.

Most often, gifts are used in combination with some other sort of activity. At a public Beltane ritual a few years ago, we crowned every attendee to illustrate that we were all Queens and Kings of the May. Tokens, especially at large public rituals, can make great keepsakes, though I think giving something away just to do it is rather wasteful.

Energy Raising/Dancing/Physical Activities

Many of the rituals put on by the open circle in my area end with an energy-raising dance around the circle. This is often accompanied by drums or recorded music relevant to the sabbat being celebrated. Oftentimes these dances don't serve any higher purpose than bringing our local community together. Workings that are little more than an extended dance around the altar often feel tired and unimaginative to me, but there's a reason they are commonplace in a lot of circles—they can be a lot of fun!

My friend and coven-sister Phoenix LeFae [6] once put together a Dionysian rite at a festival we were attending built around ecstatic dancing, a bit of drumming, and a drawn-down Dionysus. It was wondrous because the energy we raised while dancing and chanting perfectly complemented and added to the power of Dionysus. Energy raising can be a great working if it fits the purpose of the rite.

---

6. You can check out the blog she writes with her husband, Gwion Raven, called "The Witches Next Door," at https://www.patheos.com/blogs/thewitchesnextdoor/.

Some Witches celebrate the sabbats with games of various types. While these don't always raise a lot of energy, they can help build community. The only downside to activities like this is that everyone at your ritual has to really buy into the idea to make it work. Asking people to engage in a three-legged race to celebrate Ostara when it's barely above freezing is not going to go over well, but it might be fun at Midsummer, provided the weather is nice.

Deity and Other Experiences

Some of my favorite workings revolve around various deities and other entities. At Samhain it's commonplace to welcome the dead into the circle to experience a moment of reunion with those we've lost. This book includes an Imbolc ritual dedicated to the goddess Brigid that offers participants the opportunity to interact and commune with her (see chapter 13). At Midsummer many Witches honor the fey and actively seek them out. Workings built around goddesses and gods and other powers are some of the most powerful ritual experiences one can have.

The biggest downside to building a ritual around an experience with deity is that sometimes the deity decides not to show up. Deities (and beings like the fey) aren't our subjects and aren't ours to command. If Brigid decides not to show up at my Imbolc ritual, that's her prerogative. So if I'm building a ritual around the idea of Brigid showing up, I might want to have a few other activities planned just in case she chooses not to put in an appearance.

Seasonal Observances

Many sabbats are built around experiencing and celebrating the change of the seasons. A coven might celebrate the returning light at Yule or honor the balance between night and day that takes place on the equinoxes. Many Witches at Beltane simply set up a maypole and use that as the focus of their rite. This is a simple idea, but it's a great way to bring a community or coven together through a shared activity.

Seasonal observances can be simple things too. Drinking apple cider or eating a few pomegranate seeds in the autumn is a seasonal observance. I grow closer to the natural world when I eat in a way that takes advantage of where we are right now on the Wheel of the Year. Dyeing eggs at Ostara is fun and connects me to the energy of springtime. When I lived in Michigan, one of my favorite seasonal observances involved melting snow over a candle at Imbolc and often Ostara (though never Beltane luckily). It wasn't the most imaginative thing, but it connected me to winter and my hope that spring would soon arrive.

The various types of workings discussed here are not exclusive either. Oftentimes they are combined and used together in ritual. For instance, a sacred drama might lead to an experience with deity that then leads to a divinatory moment. Many seasonal observances and magickal workings go hand in hand. And at very large rituals, it's common to have several different activities happening at once to allow everyone to participate.

CAKES AND ALE/GROUNDING

After a successful working, many people become a bit overwhelmed and tingly due to the magickal energy coursing through their bodies and around the circle. While this feeling can be rather pleasant, it's probably not a healthy one. (Imagine a battery with too much charge in it.) Getting rid of unneeded energy in order to return oneself to a more mundane state of being is known as *grounding*. Grounding is not a part of every ritual, but it's often necessary if a working has been particularly successful.

There are many ways to ground. One of the easiest is to simply put your hands upon the ground and push any extra energy coursing through your body down into the earth. In our coven, we often "brush off our hands" after a working if there's a lot of residual energy within us. No matter how grounding is done (and there are probably hundreds of ways to ground), the idea behind it is to rid the self of unneeded energy. As long as the technique works, you can do it however you wish.

Grounding rites are often not built into ritual and are simply inserted at the end of a working if the High Priestess thinks it's necessary. (In my own rituals, I leave the decision to do a specific grounding ritual up to my High Priestess wife.) On some occasions, we've also had coven members ask for a bit of grounding. Grounding is one of those little unwritten rules of ritual, and it can take a few years before knowing exactly when it is appropriate and necessary. Leading ritual is a skill that we get better at over time. There are no specific grounding rites in this book because they are not always necessary. However, when grounding is needed, it should be done of course.

Another, less dramatic way to ground is the rite known as cakes and ale (or cakes and wine). Eating and drinking things helps the body to ground naturally, no directions required. But cakes and ale is about more than grounding. It's a celebration of both the earth's abundance and the deities we honor. Shared food and drink also helps to bring a community together. The Pagan group the Church of All Worlds has a saying: "Water shared is life shared." This is true—even if I'm more likely to say "Wine shared is life shared."

The food and drink used during cakes and ale is generally ritually blessed and consecrated, meaning that the powers present in the ritual circle have been added to it. Though wine and bread (or other baked goods) are common defaults for cakes and ale, I like to use seasonally appropriate food and drink when I can. This might mean Santa Claus cookies and hot chocolate for Yule, or fresh strawberries and lemonade at Midsummer. Many Witches use alcoholic beverages for "ale," but anything can be used as long as it resonates with the individual Witch and/or group.

Often during cakes and ale, a bit of food and drink are set aside for the gods, the earth, or other powers. This is known as a *libation*. If the ritual is outdoors, the libation might be poured directly onto the ground or thrown into a fire. Those of us who primarily work indoors often put our offerings into a libation bowl that is then taken outside at the end of ritual.

Many groups perform the symbolic Great Rite before cakes and ale. The Great Rite has a multitude of meanings, but I generally look upon it as a celebration of what happens when different forces join together. To create just about anything in the world or universe, two different energies have to combine in some way. Food and drink are very real, tangible representations of that magick, which is why the Great Rite and cakes and ale pair together so well. The Great Rite also symbolizes the triumph of life over death, as life continually returns to our world no matter how much we humans neglect and abuse it. The cakes we eat and the beverages we drink during cakes and ale are all the result of the earth's fertility and the power of the natural world, and the Great Rite celebrates this too.

In addition to the *symbolic* Great Rite, the act can also be celebrated "in truth," which involves ritual coupling/sex. The Great Rite in truth is rarely if ever performed in front of other Witches and is not done with much frequency in group settings these days. The Great Rite in truth is not a part of this book, but you can read more about it in—wait for it!—my book *Transformative Witchcraft*.

For several decades, the Great Rite was seen by many as simply representing the sexual union of women and men. I've always believed this to be a rather limited way of looking at the world, and one that doesn't reflect the reality we live in. Every coupling produces new energies, and our world wasn't born out of sexual intercourse. Restricting the Great Rite to vaginas and penises restricts the power of the natural world and can be alienating for some Witches. Witchcraft is about inclusivity!

The Great Rite is generally enacted symbolically by joining the athame with the chalice or cup, but there are other ways to celebrate the Great Rite. Some groups use two cups and exclude the ritual knife. If it makes sense to you, it's fair game. I'll admit though that I generally use the athame and cup because that was the way I first experienced the rite. It's also acceptable to simply skip the Great Rite if you're worried it might upset someone.

In my own practice, we generally do grounding rites immediately after the working if necessary. From there we move to the Great Rite and cakes and ale. Occasionally, if our first grounding and cakes and ale didn't quite do the trick, we might lead the coven or circle in a second grounding after finishing up with our food and drink.

DISMISSALS

Dismissals are just what they sound like: a chance to say goodbye and return your ritual space to the mundane place it was before ritual. Just as a good host always says goodbye to their guests, a good Witch always thanks the deities they've invoked, wishes the quarters well on their way, and takes down the circle they've cast. Dismissals sound rather boring, but they're a requirement for good Witch housekeeping.

In addition to dismissals, many groups end their rites with a statement celebrating their community. The most common one is "Merry meet, merry part, and merry meet again!" I often add a hearty "And may the gods preserve the Craft!" as a final coda.

BASIC RITUAL OUTLINE

When these components are all put together, a ritual outline generally looks like this:

- Cleansing/purification
- The invitation/statement of intent
- Circle casting
- Calling the quarters
- Calling to deity

- The working
- Grounding (if necessary)
- Cakes and ale / Great Rite
- Goodbyes to deity
- Dismissal of quarters
- Taking down the circle
- Final statement

While many Witches stick to a ritual structure resembling this one, it is acceptable to move the various pieces around if the rite calls for it. I've started Yule rituals with a working before calling the quarters, and sometimes circumstances require cakes and ale to be done on the way out the door if food and drink are not allowed in the ritual space. (This has happened to me when leading rituals at a local Freemason hall.) Perhaps the gods are even invoked in the middle of a working—it can happen!

I also know many Witches who prefer to call the quarters before casting their circle or to purify ritual participants after the circle is cast. If a change like that makes sense to you, implement it! If you decide to do cakes and ale at the start of ritual, you might want to warn everybody before starting, but most other changes to the general order of things won't bother or confuse anyone very much.

CHAPTER 3

THE SABBATS AND
THE WHEEL OF THE YEAR
A Witch's High Holidays

While the *Wheel of the Year* sounds rather complicated and flashy, it's really just a term for one calendar year. During that period of time, it's possible to watch the world go from life (spring/summer) to decline (autumn) and finally to death (winter), before beginning the cycle all over again. This is probably easiest to see in trees, with their annual shedding and regrowth of leaves, but it also applies to most flowering plants. In addition to life and death, there's also the annual increase and decrease in daylight during one calendar year. (And depending on where one lives, this might be the best way to keep in touch with the turning of the seasons.)

Throughout the course of the Wheel of the Year, most Witches celebrate eight sabbats (figure 1). Those eight holidays include the Winter and Summer Solstices, the Spring and Autumn Equinoxes, and four cross-quarter days, which occur at approximately the midpoint between each solstice and equinox. While eight sabbats are the most common way to divide up the Wheel of the Year, a Witch can choose to celebrate as many sabbats as they wish. If you want more holidays, go for it, and if you want to celebrate fewer holidays, that's fine too. The Pagan tradition of Feraferia, for instance, celebrates a ninth sabbat in the month of November near the US holiday of Thanksgiving.

Figure 1. Wheel of the Year

The word *sabbat* most likely comes from Old French and derives from the Hebrew *Shabbath*, which means "to rest."[7] If the word *sabbat* reminds you of the word *Sabbath*, that's not a coincidence. During the Middle Ages and the early modern period, Witch celebrations were often called *witch's sabbaths*, the term referring to any alleged gathering of Witches. In most English books detailing the activities of Witches printed before the 1950s, Witch gatherings are almost always referred to as sabbaths.

In Dr. Margaret Alice Murray's (1863–1963) highly influential book *The Witch-Cult in Western Europe* (1921), she refers to gatherings of Witches as sabbaths.[8] However, her book includes material from the French Witch trials in French, including the word *sabbat*,

---

7. Guiley, *The Encyclopedia of Witches & Witchcraft*, 283.

8. We don't have the space in this book to do a full overview of history, but Murray's writings on Witches positioned Witchcraft as an organized religion in opposition to Christianity. This was new at the time. Many of the ideas contained within her books were later incorporated into the practices of Modern Witches.

which is where the earliest Modern Witches most likely took the word from. By 1954, Gerald Gardner (1884–1964), the world's first modern, public, self-identifying Witch, was using the word *sabbat* exclusively as a name for the holidays of Witches in his book *Witchcraft Today*. We've been using it ever since.

In *Witchcraft Today*, Gardner lists the four great festivals of Witchcraft as "May eve, August eve, November eve (Hallowe'en), and February eve." He then notes that they correspond to the four Gaelic fire festivals of "Samhaim or Samhuin (November 1), Brigid (February 1), Bealteine or Beltene (May 1), and Lugnasadh (August 1)." [9] Because these four holidays were among the first to be celebrated by public Witches, they are often known today as the *greater sabbats*, though most Witches today don't call them "May eve," "August eve," etc.

The four greater sabbats as we know them today are often thought of as "Celtic" holidays, which is both right and wrong at the same time. There's no evidence suggesting that all of the Celts in the ancient world celebrated the sabbats, but we know that at least the Celts in Ireland did (and possibly those in Wales, since similar holidays are referenced in Welsh mythology and tradition too). Samhain, Imbolc, Beltane, and Lughnasadh were all originally Irish-Celtic holidays and were eventually imported into the rest of the British Isles, where they've been celebrated to varying degrees ever since.

By the close of the 1950s, many Witches had begun celebrating the equinoxes and solstices in addition to the four greater sabbats, but these holidays were generally seen as somehow "lesser" and were often celebrated on the full moon nearest to their actual date. By way of contrast, the greater sabbats were generally celebrated on their actual date and, according to Gardner in his 1959 book *The Meaning of Witchcraft*, were typically occasions for large gatherings of Witches. (He writes that "all the covens that could gather together would do so" at the greater sabbats. [10])

In the late 1950s, the names of the greater sabbats began to evolve as well, with Gardner giving their names as "Candlemass, May Eve, Lammas, and Halloween." [11] Throughout the 1960s and 1970s, those names would continue to evolve, with the Irish-Celtic names becoming more and more common. In 1974 Raymond Buckland used the names

---

9. Gardner, *Witchcraft Today*, originally published in 1954 and available in dozens of different editions today. This information is from the very beginning of chapter 12.

10. Gardner, *The Meaning of Witchcraft*, 18.

11. Ibid.

(and spellings) Samhain, Imbolc, Beltane, and Lughnasadh for the greater sabbats in his book *The Tree: The Complete Book of Saxon Witchcraft*, and as the years progressed, those names became more and more widely used. (Buckland was not the first person to use those names, but having them in print certainly helped popularize them.)

Today the greater sabbats are generally known as Samhain (October 31), Imbolc (February 2), Beltane (May 1), and Lammas or Lughnasadh (August 1), though the names and even dates of the sabbats sometimes vary from Witch to Witch and group to group. It's also worth pointing out that the cross-quarter dates for the greater sabbats are often a little off. October 31 is not *exactly* between the Autumn Equinox and the Winter Solstice. For this reason, there are some Witches who celebrate the sabbats *astrologically*, meaning on the date closest to the actual midway point between the solstices and equinoxes.

The equinoxes and solstices, or the *lesser sabbats*, continued their own evolution. In 1958 a Witch coven wrote to Gardner and asked if the equinoxes and solstices could be moved to their actual dates and given the same level of importance as the cross-quarter sabbats. Gardner agreed and thus ended up creating the standard eightfold Wheel of the Year cycle, and this pattern was later adopted by dozens of Pagan groups around the world.[12] (This change obviously did not occur early enough to affect Gardner's book that would be published the following year.)

By the early 1970s, the solstices were commonly being referred to as Midsummer and Yule by most Witches, and for good reason. Yule is a genuinely old Germanic holiday originally celebrated on the winter solstice, while summer solstice rites can be found in the historical record all across Europe. In England, the Summer Solstice was often called Midsummer, and this made sense to many Witches. (If Beltane is the start of summer, then by extension the Summer Solstice would be in the middle of summer.) Because there are no ancient celebrations of the spring and autumnal equinoxes, those holidays were simply called the Spring Equinox and the Autumn (or Fall) Equinox. (That's right, there were no specific holidays celebrated on the equinoxes, a fact that surprises many people.)

Today, the equinoxes are most commonly referred to as Mabon and Ostara, names first suggested by American Witch Aidan Kelly in 1974. Kelly was looking to do two things with his new names for the equinoxes. The first was to come up with something

---

12. Hutton, *The Triumph of the Moon*, 248.

more poetic than Autumn/Spring Equinox, and the second was to use names that matched up better with the Irish-Celtic names used for the greater sabbats. While working on a Witchcraft calendar that year, Kelly added *Litha* as the name of the Summer Solstice for good measure.[13] (We'll come back to Kelly's names later in this book when we look at the individual sabbats.) Kelly's names were reprinted over the years in various Pagan magazines, and by 1979 (just five years later) they appeared in Starhawk's seminal work *The Spiral Dance*. (Surprisingly, though Starhawk mostly uses the Irish-Celtic names for the greater sabbats, she uses *Brigid* for Imbolc.)

Though there are many Witches today who object to Kelly's terms for the Summer Solstice and the equinoxes, they are impossible to escape. Most every Pagan I know refers to the Fall Equinox as *Mabon*, and while I may not like the name too much myself, people know exactly what I'm talking about when I say it. For that reason, I use the words *Mabon* and *Ostara* in this book generally when writing about the equinoxes, even if there are some Witches who frown upon their use.

As this book progresses, we'll spend a little more time with each sabbat, but that's the evolution of the modern Wheel of the Year in a nutshell. It all happened fairly quickly and it all seems to make sense to a great many Witches around the world.

The Witches' New Year

Ask most Witches when their new year begins and the great majority of them will say at Samhain. There are a couple of reasons for this, the most obvious being that late autumn is a great time for new beginnings. The harvest has been taken in and the world (mostly) lies fallow, waiting for its rebirth in the spring. It's also when many of us begin to turn inward and find ourselves spending more time indoors.

But perhaps the biggest reason so many Witches celebrate the new year at Samhain is because we've been taught that it's the Celtic New Year. This assertion comes up in dozens of Witch books and is a frequent theme at Samhain rituals. However, the idea that Samhain is the Celtic New Year dates back only to the start of the twentieth century. The idea was first put forward by Welsh scholar Sir John Rhys (1840–1915), who interpreted many of the goings-on in early November as being related to the idea of new beginnings. In his book *Celtic Folklore: Welsh & Manx*, Rhys writes that "this is the day when the tenure of land

---

13. Aidan Kelly, "About Naming, Ostara, Litha, and Mabon," *Including Paganism* (blog), May 2, 2017, https://www.patheos.com/blogs/aidankelly/2017/05/naming-ostara-litha-mabon/.

terminates, and when servantmen (sic) go to their places. In other words, it's the beginning of a new year." [14]

Rhys's assertion that Samhain is the Celtic New Year is not one shared by most scholars, but it's an idea that resonates in Witch circles because it simply makes sense to people. (When was the actual Celtic New Year? No one really knows for sure, so in that sense Samhain is as good a guess as any.) However, not every Witch looks to Samhain as the start of their new year. The Wheel of the Year, after all, is a wheel, and that means that its start and end points are rather arbitrary. Any sabbat (or day) could potentially be the start of a new year or a new turn of the wheel.

After Samhain, Yule and Imbolc might be the two most common "other new year" sabbats. They both make sense as the start of a new year because of their focus on the light of the sun. At Yule, the sun is "reborn" and the days begin to grow longer. By Imbolc, the days have become noticeably longer, making this sabbat a great candidate for fresh beginnings. (Imbolc is my personal preference as the start of the year.)

There are a multitude of reasons to consider Ostara the start of the Witches' new year. The astrological year begins at the spring equinox, when the sun enters the constellation of Aries, the first sign of the zodiac. For this reason, Persians celebrate their new year on the first day of spring. Ostara is also traditionally associated with rebirth and new growth, perfect trappings for the new year. For similar reasons, some Witches see Beltane as the start of the year. (When I lived in Michigan, this always made much more sense to me than Ostara, when it was often still very cold!)

There are even a small number of Witches who use Midsummer as the start of their new year. If the longest night works as a starting point, then why not the longest day? I have yet to meet any Witches who celebrate the start of the new year at Lammas or Mabon, but who knows? There might be someone out there doing just that.

Just when a Witch celebrates the new year is up to them. There are no specific rules regulating such things. In fact, the idea of a new beginning or a new year can be used multiple times over the course of the Wheel of the Year. In the fall, I often rid myself of thoughts and tendencies that are holding me back, giving me a clean slate for the new year. Winter is a time for new beginnings, as we start fresh like the reborn sun. Spring is a time to plant what it is we wish to bring into our lives and then see those things grow

---

14. Rhys, *Manx Folklore & Superstitions* (originally published as *Celtic Folklore: Welsh & Manx* in 1901), 9.

as the world around us comes back to life. All or none of these ideas can be part of your rituals, and whatever day you see as the Witches' New Year is worth celebrating.

It's also worth noting that the secular start of the new year, January 1, was invented by a Pagan who worshiped the old gods (just like many of us do!). And there are many Witches who celebrate the start of the year with parties and other goings-on, just like a lot of other people do. I've always believed that the more opportunities we have for milestones and parties, the better it is for all of us!

WHEEL OF THE YEAR MYTHS

Many Witches like to connect the turn of the wheel to specific myths. In these myths, goddesses and gods reenact certain events yearly, and in many cases they age from youth to senior citizen before dying and being reborn. The most common myth cycles among Witches often overlap with one another and in many instances are combined, depending on the need of a specific ritual. Over the course of one year, a Witch might use varying and conflicting myth cycles in order to express particular ideas at their sabbat celebrations.

In many of these myth cycles, the deities being honored, celebrated, or mourned match the energy of a particular season. For example, the Horned God who dies in the fall is mimicking what's happening in the natural world. We often associate the rapid growth common in the springtime with youthful energies, so it's said that the Maiden Goddess presides over that time of year. None of this is meant to imply that only certain deities are around at certain times of the year, but only that we might feel their energies more acutely at certain points of the wheel. The deities we honor and have relationships with are always with us.

MAIDEN, MOTHER, AND CRONE

The most common myth associated with the Wheel of the Year is that of Maiden, Mother, and Crone (MMC). In most MMC stories, the Maiden Goddess emerges near Imbolc and grows in physical maturity as the seasons turn, becoming a Maiden, Mother, and Crone over the course of twelve months. She is then reborn to repeat the cycle. In many versions of this story, she's paired up with a version of the Horned God who progresses physically in a similar manner. There are a growing number of people who find the MMC model incomplete. Not all women will become mothers, for instance. But this model is still commonly used at many sabbat celebrations.

Often the Maiden/Mother/Crone myth is connected to themes of fertility and sexuality. In most versions of this story, the Maiden Goddess becomes sexually aware at Ostara (this sometimes includes flirtation with the young Horned God) and sexually active at Beltane. The two are sometimes said to get married at Midsummer, with the Goddess displaying a very visible "baby bump." The Horned God generally sacrifices himself for the good of the harvest near Samhain, only to be reborn at Yule when the Goddess gives birth. Though rarely articulated as such, this would require the Crone to be the one to give birth, giving the tale one last magickal twist.

While the concept of the Goddess as Maiden, Mother, and Crone feels legitimately ancient, the idea is a relatively modern one and was first completely articulated in 1949 by the poet Robert Graves (1895–1985) in his book *The White Goddess*. Of course, there were Maiden goddesses in ancient paganisms, along with Mother goddesses and Crone goddesses, but in mythology these goddesses weren't reborn annually. Goddesses generally didn't age much past prime adulthood either. It's certainly possible to create a version of the Maiden, Mother, Crone myth by creatively adapting existing mythologies, but that doesn't make the MMC historical.

I have met many Witches who use the tale of Demeter and Persephone to illustrate the MMC story. In the classic version of the tale most familiar to Western audiences, the goddess Persephone, daughter of Demeter, is kidnapped and forced to marry Hades, the god of the Underworld. Distraught over the loss of her daughter, Demeter neglects her duties as the goddess of agriculture, and all fertility in the world ceases. Eventually the Titan goddess Hecate intervenes and persuades Zeus, the king of the gods, to allow Persephone to leave the Underworld and return to Demeter. Zeus then dispatches Hermes, the messenger of the Greek gods, to retrieve Persephone from Hades. Persephone, overjoyed to be leaving the land of the dead, eats between four and six pomegranate seeds before leaving the world of her husband. Sadly, for every pomegranate seed she ate in the Underworld, Persephone must spend one month in the home of her husband each year.

Thus, the seasons are explained by Persephone's eating of the pomegranate seeds. Demeter lets the world whither in the fall and winter while Persephone is away, only to bless it in the spring when her daughter returns to her once more. This myth is super adaptable too. If you live in a cold climate, perhaps Persephone ate six seeds instead of four in your version, while those of us on the California coast can build our myth around the idea that she ate only three seeds.

When using this story to illustrate the MMC myth, the problem is that Demeter is not Persephone; they are separate entities. When Hecate is added to the mix, the story becomes even more garbled. Hecate is not a Crone goddess, and again, is not Demeter or Persephone. There's nothing wrong with creative license, but I'm not sure it's okay to fundamentally alter the very nature of a goddess.

With the often strong emphasis on fertility and reproduction in MMC myths, there are many who feel left out. It's common today to see additional layers being added to the MMC model (such as Warrior or Hunter), along with the removal of some aspects. My wife and I have no children and don't plan on having any. This makes the idea that my wife is a "Mother" rather silly. Women are more than their ability to give birth.

The female-male dynamic in the MMC story also bothers some people. I'm a firm believer that the deities I honor in my circle honor every aspect of human existence, meaning that a Beltane ritual where the Horned God is replaced by a goddess is just fine with me. The most important part of any myth cycle is that it speaks to the people who are using it. If your coven loves the MMC model, by all means use it! And if it leaves people in your group cold, you are free to throw it out.

Despite some people being uncomfortable with the MMC model, it's still one of the most common seasonal motifs in the sabbat rituals of Modern Witches, and because of its flexibility, adaptability, and popularity, it will probably remain so long into the future. Despite its shortcomings, it's still a great starting point for ritual, and much of its language is firmly embedded in many covens as well. (It's hard not to use the term *Mother Goddess* in ritual, for instance.)

Perhaps the most magickal part of the MMC myth is that the Goddess never dies, nor is she ever reborn on a specific date. She simply reappears in the late winter or early spring and resumes her work in this world. In most versions of the MMC cycle, the God is completely dependent on his wife and mother, while the Great Goddess needs no helping hand.

THE DYING AND RISING SACRIFICIAL GOD

Often honored on the Wheel of the Year side by side with the Goddess as Maiden/ Mother/Crone is the *dying and rising sacrificial god*. In this myth, the Horned God sacrifices himself annually for the good of the people and the earth and is then reborn with the sun at the winter solstice. The dying and rising sacrificial god is a mixture of both ancient and modern mythology. Gods certainly sacrificed themselves for the good of others in tales and legends, but the idea of a god dying and being reborn on a yearly basis can only be inferred through ancient myth.

In most myths, gods are either alive or dead; that is, they exist in the realm of the gods and/or earth (alive) or in the Underworld (dead). Periodically souls are allowed to move between the two planes of existence (as was the case with the Greek Adonis), but they do not have to be "reborn" from the womb in order to do so. The idea of the annual rising and dying sacrificial god was made popular thanks to the work of the English anthropologist Sir James George Frazer (1854–1941), who articulated the idea quite explicitly in his multivolume work *The Golden Bough*.

The sacrificial god myth is most often used from Lammas to Samhain, and I've seen the God "die" at both of those sabbats as well as Mabon. Just how the God dies varies from ritual to ritual. Sometimes he's cut down by adversaries, his death enacted in such a way that it parallels the grain harvest. I've been a part of Samhain rituals where it's the Goddess who kills her love, knowing that he must die for the life-giving energy of the world to be renewed. If the God dies before Samhain, he is sometimes honored in late October as the god of death.

THE HOLLY AND OAK KINGS

A clever twist on the story of the sacrificial god is that of the Oak and Holly Kings, originally articulated in Robert Graves's *The White Goddess*. The Oak and Holly Kings are frequent visitors at many solstice rituals. The story of the Oak and Holly Kings is that of two brothers who continually battle for world supremacy.

The Oak King generally rules during the waxing half of the year, from Yule to Midsummer, growing older as every month passes. On the Summer Solstice, the Holly King comes for his older brother's throne and defeats his sibling in hand-to-hand combat. The Holly King then takes the throne, while the Oak King goes off to lick his wounds and be reborn beyond time and space. The Holly King then grows older, and the cycle is repeated over and over every six months.

I've seen some creative uses of this myth over the years. At one especially powerful Midsummer ritual, two of my friends went toe to toe with real swords in an epic battle. When the Oak King eventually fell, it was a grieving Goddess who appeared at his side and drew out her dagger to finish the deed begun by the Holly King. As she killed the Oak King, she said she was doing so in order to ensure the world's continued fertility.

Most of us are probably not skilled enough with a sword to reenact this biannual confrontation between two brothers; however, swords are not really required. A Harry Potter–esque battle involving wands is one way around the use of steel. Other ways of "slaying" one of the brothers might include riddles or even a dance-off. The only real limit here is one's imagination.

My only concern with confrontations between the Oak King and the Holly King at large sabbat celebrations is that they often don't leave much for the other participants to do. The best types of rituals are those that get everyone involved, and that can sometimes be hard to do with this myth.

THE SUN GOD

Many Witches see the annual waxing and waning of the sun as an expression of their God. In this myth, the God of the Sun is reborn at Yule, reaches the peak of his power at Midsummer, and then begins his decline. In some versions of this tale, he might sacrifice himself at Samhain, or simply die of old age at Yule. This myth is usually used in conjunction with others throughout the course of the year, and is especially prevalent at Yule celebrations.

APHRODITE/PERSEPHONE/ADONIS

One of my favorite Wheel of the Year myths is based on one involving Aphrodite and Persephone, who find themselves fighting over the soul of Adonis, a beautiful young man whom Aphrodite is in love with. When Adonis is killed in a hunting accident, Aphrodite asks Zeus to release his soul from the Underworld so that he might live with her on Mount Olympus.

When Persephone spots Adonis in her domain, she immediately falls in love with him and refuses to give up his soul so that he might reside with Aphrodite. Eventually a compromise is reached and Zeus decrees that Adonis will spend six months a year with Aphrodite and six months with Persephone. When Adonis is with Aphrodite, she makes the world bloom, and while he's away, she neglects it and causes it to whither. In a bit of a modern twist, we like to imagine that when Adonis returns to reside with Persephone, the goddess of the Underworld becomes happy once more, thus allowing the dead to be reborn in the world of the living.

Note that it's the goddesses here who hold all the power and not Adonis. It's not his power that transforms the world but that of Aphrodite. When my coven uses this myth, we celebrate the return of Adonis to Aphrodite near the spring equinox, with his return to Persephone thus coinciding with the start of autumn. Though not an extremely common Wheel of the Year myth, it's a fun one and often surprises people.

CHAPTER 4

COVEN RITUALS

Perfect Love and Perfect Trust

In 1951 Gerald Gardner announced to the world that he was a Witch in the pages of the *Sunday Mirror* newspaper. Gardner was the first public, self-identifying Witch, and the Witchcraft he shared with the world was based around coven rituals. For him, Witchcraft was something to be practiced ideally with others. Gardner also thought covens should generally have a maximum of thirteen people, six couples and one High Priestess to oversee the rituals. Gardner even specified the ideal size of a magick circle, nine feet in diameter, a size that severely limited covens from growing beyond the suggested thirteen members.[15]

The system of Witchcraft that Gardner revealed to the world, along with its many variants, became the dominant form of Witch ritual among self-identifying Witches. Anyone who casts a circle, calls the quarters, invokes deity, and participates in some sort of seasonal or magickal working owes a debt to Gardner. The covens of Gardner's time were also choosy too; to join a coven, one had to be accepted by that coven's leaders and then undergo an initiation. Initiated Witches were also prohibited from sharing their coven's rites with outsiders. All of these rules made Gardner's style of Witchcraft very hard to practice for many people, and until the early 1970s there were no readily available books that contained Witch rituals.

There have always been solitary practitioners of Witchcraft, and most of us who practice with others engage in solitary rites as well. Witchcraft is not something that has

---

15. Gardner, *Witchcraft Today*. This information comes from early in chapter 1.

to be experienced with a coven or any other sort of group, and many of the most personal things I engage in as a Witch I do alone. However, the ritual system most of us associate with Witchcraft (circle casting, calling the quarters, etc.) was originally meant to be done with a coven. It's a system designed for four to maybe twenty people (how many people a coven can handle is often debated), which is why solitary and large group rituals are often so challenging.

In addition to being small, covens as articulated by Gardner were also selective to the point of being exclusionary. This does not mean that people were (or are) excluded from covens for homophobic, racist, transphobic, or classist reasons. There are all sorts of legitimate reasons a person might not be admitted into a coven. The members of a successful working coven generally approach ritual and theological ideas in a similar matter. A very loud and proud atheist Witch is probably not going to be a good fit in a coven that makes connection with deity a priority in their work. If the coven calls the watchtowers and a potential covener finds this upsetting, there are bound to be problems. Sometimes certain personalities and people just don't get along, and there's nothing wrong with being honest about that.

Today the word *coven* gets thrown around with a great deal of frequency. Online I often read about people "forming a coven," and there's a group in my area with eighty members who call themselves a coven (at least according to their social media pages). I'm not the coven police, and people are free to use the word coven as they want, but I'm of the opinion that such usages dilute what a coven was originally meant to be: *a chosen family*. I have an intimate bond with my covenmates. In the magick circle, we are free to be our true selves and seek out magick, mystery, and the gods.

There's an oft-repeated phrase in Witchcraft circles in regard to covens: "in perfect love and perfect trust." Perfect love and perfect trust is probably an unobtainable ideal, but at least it's one to aspire to. Is it possible for eighty people to exist as a chosen family in perfect love and perfect trust? Maybe. Can ten strangers operate that way? Perhaps. But I don't think either scenario is likely.

It's the ability to operate in perfect love and perfect trust and exist as a chosen family that makes the coven experience unique. It's also one of the reasons covens sometimes turn down people who want to join them. I have Witch friends who live nearby that I absolutely love, but I know that for whatever reason they just wouldn't be a good fit in my coven. As with most families, there are squabbles even in the best covens, but if people are serious about their work and their commitment to perfect love and perfect trust, they are problems that can generally be solved.

Historically, covens were not just selective and small but also autocratic, and they came with a three-tiered degree system. At the top were the High Priestess and/or High Priest. These individuals generally led the rituals, trained other Witches, and decided who would and would not be initiated. Second-degree Witches followed the High Priestess/Priest, with that degree serving as a training ground for future coven leaders.[16] The first degree functioned as a gateway, introducing people to Witchcraft and the rituals associated with it.

Today there are covens with degree systems and covens without them. A coven can be led by a specific person or persons for years, and some covens elect their leadership, changing who is at the top annually. Some covens are governed by consensus and some are run by "benevolent dictators." There are hundreds of different ways a coven can be run, and they're all acceptable, generally. What's most important is that everyone in the coven is comfortable with how the group is run and every coven member is being respected.

If someone suggests that sex is necessary for coven membership, they are full of shit and should be called out in the community for being a sexual predator. If the people in a coven ask for money beyond what's necessary to pay for ritual supplies, they're also full of shit and trying to take advantage of you. If the members of a coven are emotionally manipulative or threaten others with physical violence, they are not practicing Witchcraft. No reputable coven takes advantage of its members or suggests they do something that might make them uncomfortable.

It's important to understand just what a coven is and how it ideally operates in order to appreciate what makes coven ritual special. I've had amazing experiences with large groups of people in ritual and some extraordinary moments as a solitary Witch. But the best and most consistently rewarding rituals have been with covens, and there are reasons for that.

---

16. Outside of the United States, many second-degree Witches in initiatory traditions act much like third-degree Witches. They lead covens, initiate people, and teach the Craft.

What Makes Coven Ritual Special

Because a coven is a chosen family and its members are generally familiar with one another, its rituals are different from those of large circles and public (open to everyone) sabbat celebrations.

Shared Experience

Many covens use the same ritual structure over and over again. While this might seem boring to some, it's actually a very powerful trigger that makes its own sort of magick. One of my friends once described using the same opening for ritual at most sabbats as a form of trance; familiar words and gestures will transport a person immediately into their ritual headspace.

Even simple things such as using the same type of incense at every ritual can be transformative. When we light our coven's incense, I immediately know that I'm out of the mundane world and in a magickal one. Even when I burn that incense when I'm alone, I find myself drawn into a ritual and magickal state of mind. This type of thing is even more powerful when coupled with the same quarter calls and circle casting at every coven ritual.

A common ritual experience also takes the guesswork out of ritual. By using the same ritual pieces over and over, everyone in our coven knows what's coming up, and everyone feels that much more comfortable participating. It's hard to be active in a rite when no one is sure what's coming next. The same ritual structure remedies that. It also makes writing ritual much easier, because the only thing that really has to be figured out is the working in the middle.

Most covens also develop their own unique quirks and ways of doing things during ritual. Even covens that are a part of the same tradition don't always do things *exactly* the same way. The little idiosyncrasies that develop over time in a coven create bonds and make each group more unique. For many years my coven had a habit of giggling at the start of cakes and ale because I always forgot the words to it (and I wrote it!). This evolved into them starting it for me and eventually reciting the whole thing with Ari and me. I don't know of any other coven that approaches their cakes and ale like this. I love having something that evolved organically and is ours.

No two covens will ever feel the same because a coven is the sum of *all* its parts: rituals, members, energies, and deities. What a group creates together is a powerful shared experience that can't be replicated. A coven's unique energy is what makes it such a treasured and valued part of the Witchcraft experience.

Group Mind

I don't know exactly what everyone in my coven is thinking at every moment, but we work together pretty seamlessly. When we start working with energy, there's no need for long explanations about what we're going to be doing; we simply do it. We don't have to spend time thinking about ritual roles because we all know what we most likely will be doing before the ritual even begins. Often we find ourselves suddenly doing the same thing together without any prompting.

We don't all think alike, but because the coven has its own energy, we get swept up in its individual power and we all know how to best utilize it. We pick each other up without thinking about it, and keep certain people grounded when they need it. Even at public rituals, we sometimes find ourselves falling into the habits and rites of our coven without a second thought.

Familiarity

"Familiarity breeds contempt" is an old piece of wisdom that is sometimes accurate, but I don't think it applies to covens. Knowing what everyone in a group is comfortable with (and doing) makes ritual that much more effective. I've been to rituals where people are forced to speak or act in ways that are awkward or distressing to them, and that energy then often spreads to everyone else in the circle and makes them feel that way too. (Not everyone wants to be in the ritual spotlight.) Knowing what is acceptable (or not) to those around us keeps ritual running smoothly.

Comfort Level

Ever gone to a public ritual and ran into an ex or someone you just don't particularly like? It happens and can make things awkward. A well-functioning coven should be free of such drama. That doesn't mean there will never be coven problems. It happens. Even the best Witches are only human after all, but I find that most coven spaces are free of the drama that comes from break-ups and personality clashes.

With a chosen family, we are also free to be our true selves, something most of us can't do in public. I don't have to be a "guy who writes books" with my coven. I can just be the person who watches football and keeps a mean collection of Scotch whiskies. I feel a responsibility to pick up my house before the coven comes over, but I don't worry about putting away *every* hairbrush in the bathroom. It's also not a complete tragedy if I forget to pick up a piece of dirty laundry in the bathroom. Families share things and families shouldn't judge too much. It's much easier to have the coven over for a night of ritual than knowing my parents are going to visit.

Everyone Is Involved and Knows What's Happening

At public circles and festivals, I often find myself having to explain every little detail of ritual. So instead of just being free to let everything unfold naturally, the rhythm of ritual often gets interrupted by massive amounts of exposition and instruction that would otherwise not be there. This is not an indictment of such situations. Sometimes you simply have to explain what's happening very explicitly. However, when you don't have to worry about those little things, ritual flows a lot more naturally.

Ritual is also not a spectator sport, and things like calling the quarters, calling to deity, and casting the circle require the participation of everyone involved in ritual. This is something that's often either not understood in large group settings or ignored because not everyone gets to speak. The person calling the quarter is verbalizing what's happening, but they aren't alone in the summoning of the quarter. Most people in coven situations are aware of these ritual nuances.

The Doing Options Are Easier

When everyone knows just how a ritual is going to unfold and what the expectations are for each individual Witch, ritual simply becomes easier.

A coven that's been working together for a couple of years doesn't have to fret and worry over who is calling the quarter or casting the circle. People know what there is to do in ritual, and most everyone will know how to do it. Rituals with people worrying about whether or not they are going to have to say something end up generating lots of unwanted nervous energy.

A coven that simply enjoys one another's company doesn't expect a big ritual production at every sabbat and full moon. In fact, at this point our coven often meets without any specific agenda for ritual. We simply set up our container and then do whatever magickal work we need to do. Other times we might just share what's going on in our lives in a magickal environment or do some group divination. We've been doing a lot of the same sabbat rituals for years now, and many of them we can do from memory.

Good covens remember the bits of ritual that work for them and then return to those bits time and time again. Depending on the environment and the circumstances, we know which ways are the easiest for us all to raise the cone of power and just when the coven needs an extra grounding rite. A good coven opens up all sorts of possibilities in ritual practice.

While I'm a big believer in the power of coven rituals, there's also nothing wrong with not ever joining a coven or avoiding them entirely. Despite the rather rosy picture I'm painting here, I have seen my fair share of dysfunctional covens over the years. And for some people, one extremely bad group experience is enough to turn them off from the concept forever.

The definition of a coven is changing today too. I know people who are part of on-line covens that interact with one another in perfect love and perfect trust. I also have friends in groups that shy away from the word *coven* and yet act very much like what's described in this chapter. There are also people who participate in online Witch schools whose study groups end up functioning very close to the coven model. Covens are designed for us, and as our social spaces evolve, covens will evolve right along with them.

CHAPTER 5
SOLITARY RITUALS
The Witch Alone

My first attempt at a solitary sabbat ritual took place during my third month as a Witch, near the fall equinox. I was living in a basement apartment at the time, where my bedroom closet doubled as a storage space for our hot water heater. Because it was a relatively private space (and very much away from my roommates), I thought this would be a good place for my first ritual. I sat down on the ground and lit four tealight candles, placing them in a rough circle around me. I then lit two more candles, one each for the Goddess and the God. This was followed by sitting quietly in the candlelight waiting for something to happen. But nothing did.

I'm sure that I tried to meditate or reach out with my consciousness and explore the energy of early autumn that night, but mostly I just felt stupid. At one point I felt like I heard the Lady nearby, but it was probably just the hot water heater clicking on. The books I was reading at the time made it all sound so easy: just cast a circle, call the quarters, rustle up the gods, and you'll be between the worlds and walking with the Lord and Lady before you know it! But it doesn't really work that way, and in many ways solitary ritual is even harder to do than ritual with a coven or group.

My experience at Samhain a few weeks later was about the same. At Yule I tried again, and this time I decided to read a ritual out loud from one of the books I owned. I was roommate-free that evening and thought that audible verbalization might be the key to ritual success. The moment I started talking, I realized that wasn't the case. To put it bluntly, I felt silly speaking out loud in an empty house and was half-petrified that someone was going to knock on the door, hear what I was doing, and wonder if I was talking to my-self and/or going slowly crazy.

Tips for Solitary Ritual

Over the years, my solitary sabbat rites have improved a great deal (though I still rarely verbalize everything). If you find solitary ritual difficult, the following tips and sugges-tions are for you. If you already prefer solitary ritual to stuff done in groups, you'll probably find everything below rather redundant. The most important thing to remem-ber about solitary ritual is that the only way it can be wrong is if you don't get anything out of it.

Make Sure You Feel Comfortable with Everything You're Doing during the Ritual

This sounds like a no-brainer, but many Witches overvalue the things they read in books and believe that what they do has to be done a certain way. The best Witchcraft is always the Witchcraft that works for you! If you don't feel comfortable speaking out loud while alone, don't do it, and most importantly, don't worry about it.

So many books and teachers speak in absolutes: "Such and such MUST be done THIS WAY and ONLY THIS WAY." That's absolute crap. If what you're doing doesn't make sense to you or makes you feel silly, find a different way to do it. Nervousness and embar-rassment are their own kinds of energy and will get in the way of whatever it is you're trying to do if you let those feelings pollute your rituals.

Use What You Need for You and Just You!

When I'm doing ritual with my coven, my altar is always loaded to the gills with magickal tools. If it's a recognized tool in the Craft, it's on that altar, and often there's more than one. But when I'm alone, I rarely bother with anything more than my athame. Magickal tools are great, but they aren't necessary.

Here's a secret a lot of books won't tell you: the only thing needed to have a ritual is you. Ritual can be done anywhere, and many of the solitary rituals in this book take place in public spaces and can be done in such a way that no one is ever going to notice. If you need sixteen tools, by all means use sixteen tools, but you can probably get by with just a cup of water (or less) if you really want to.

Creative Visualization Can Be Just as Good as the Real Thing

When I'm standing alone in front of my personal altar doing a ritual, I usually imagine myself in a big open space, moving around and verbalizing my intentions with authority. I'm not really doing that, of course, but because I can see and hear myself doing those things in my mind's eye, they become real. You don't even have to stand in front of your altar to make the ritual real. If you can picture the magick and feel it inside of you, it then becomes your reality. Will it be just as effective as a ritual performed in front of a dozen flickering candles? If it resonates with you, then yes, it most certainly will.

Are you living with your parents or with people who make doing Witch ritual impossible? Then just do the ritual in your head before going to sleep. Put yourself in the situation you'd most like to be in and then picture the entire ritual unfolding from the quiet of your bed. To some people this may sound like a cop-out, but it's not. When I was a baby Witch, the rituals that took place inside my head were often better than the ones I did when I had an entire house to myself.

You Really Can Just Stand in Front of Your Altar for an Entire Ritual

My earliest altars were always on bookshelves, and those bookshelves were always against a wall. That meant that when I would work in front of my altar, I'd generally be staring at a wall. However, everything I needed for ritual was right in front of me. I could look in three of the four directions (with the fourth being just a glance over my shoulder away), and my altar always contained representations of the Goddess and the God, so they were always close by too.

When I began doing ritual this way, I worried that it would be impossible to cast a circle in such a small space with a wall, but that fear was unfounded. If the energy used to cast a circle can go under a floor, it can go through a wall! So when I do solitary rituals while facing the wall, I still cast circles when I feel the need to.

There are also times when I don't bother casting a circle at all when I'm working alone. My primary solo working altar is in my office, and I'm about the only person who goes in there other than my cats and the deities I've invited in. And since most days spent writing begin with an offering of incense to a certain goddess, this altar exists in magickal space pretty much all the time. One of the best things about solitary ritual is that we can decide what we want to skip and no one will ever try to "correct" us for doing so.

The Best Solitary Rituals Are Often Spontaneous

I'm something of a ritual planner, but the best rituals are often the ones we do because we feel inspired right then and there. These type of rituals are most often experienced as a solitary practitioner. There is no right or wrong time for ritual. The time to start a ritual is when you feel like it, and the place to do that ritual is wherever you happen to be.

When I visit the ocean, I often find myself drawn to ritual. I'll be at the water's edge and find myself drawing a circle in the sand and calling out to the quarters because the power of that space compels me to. At home I sometimes get sucked into ritual because I hear a favorite song that inspires me to commune with the gods or celebrate the turn of the wheel. Ritual should be meaningful, it should be fun, and it should be something we're capable of doing without a lot of foresight or planning if the moment calls for it.

Intention Is the Key

Solitary ritual is great because it's impossible to mess up. As long as your thoughts are clear, you'll get the results you want. Unlike public ritual, where someone will always make a big deal out of you accidently saying "I call to the spirits of the south" while in the north, no one cares about such things in solitary ritual. The quarters know what's going on, and so do you! Words are important in front of others because they keep everyone on the same page, but they matter much less when you're alone.

What matters most in ritual is *intent*, not how you do (or don't) say or do something. The greatest call to Aphrodite ever written will be wasted if you don't reach out to her with your own personal energy. If you don't truly want her to be there, she's not going to show up. This goes for everything we do in circle. If we aren't serious about our Witchcraft, it won't work for us.

If You're Having Trouble, Find a Ritual Center or Trigger

My solitary rituals improved dramatically once I set up a private altar. Being near my altar, which at the time consisted of a wine glass and a pine cone, made me feel witchy in a way that I did not while sitting in front of my hot water heater in the candlelight. My altar in those early days was nothing more than a two-shelf bookcase, but it quickly became the most magickal place in my house. (Sadly, I gave the bookcase away before I moved to California. I miss it and still think about it now and again.)

Over the years, many of my solitary rituals have been done with music playing in the background, and to this day, simply listening to *The Visit* by Canadian singer-songwriter Loreena McKennitt instantly puts me in a ritual state of mind. My first incense was rose-scented, and for many years the scent of roses immediately called to mind ritual. Notice what makes you feel like a Witch, and incorporate it into your setup for solitary rituals.

When you engage in solitary ritual, you are connecting with the powers and entities that matter most to you in this life. And remember, one of the best things about practicing as a solitary is that you are only really accountable to yourself. Find the methods and tools that work best for you and then use them. The best thing about practicing as a solitary is that the only thing that matters is what works for you.

CHAPTER 6

CIRCLE RITUALS
The Most Challenging Rites

The most difficult kind of rituals to write and execute are large group rituals (what I call *circle* rituals). There are many reasons for this. The first is that Witch rituals just weren't designed to be large. Back in the 1950s, no one envisioned a group of fifty-plus people getting together to celebrate a sabbat magickally. For several decades it's likely that there were only a few thousand self-identified Witches living in the United States and Great Britain. Maybe there were enough Witches in London or New York City for such things (along with just a lot of curious folks), but not in most places.

The second problem with large rituals is that they encourage passivity. Witch ritual is designed to be engaging, not just for the High Priestess and anyone who might be directly helping her but for everyone involved. Witchcraft is not a spectator sport, but in group settings it often becomes exactly that. Witchcraft is not meant to be celebrated by Witches sitting on their hands as if they were in a Christian church; it's meant to be actively celebrated by everyone at a sabbat rite.

Raising energy and engaging in magickal practices requires trust in those around you, and that trust is a multifaceted thing. Generally we are trusting that the people we are celebrating with have some sort of understanding of just how magick works. When someone doesn't know what they're doing while creating the cone of power or calling the watchtowers, that confusion can often be felt by everyone in circle.

There are many Witches who don't have the patience for new or poorly educated practitioners, but I'm not one of them. I love the energy that excited newcomers bring with them, but I'm also aware that as a ritual leader I'm going to have spend some extra time going over the basics before and during the ritual. Trust extends to ritual leadership, and a good leader needs to be able to trust in themselves to explain what's happening during ritual and make up for any shortcomings or confusion that those with less experience might have.

Trust extends to everyday concerns too. Trust means having confidence that everyone in the circle will be treated with dignity and respect. If the young lady next to you is worried about being on the receiving end of leering looks or being inappropriately touched, it will be nearly impossible for her to focus on magick (and rightly so).

Perfect love and perfect trust is a lofty goal and is often unobtainable in large group settings, but no one should worry about being sexually harassed or assaulted at a Witch ritual. Some may think I'm exaggerating a bit here, but make no mistake, I'm not. I have met many women over the years who have been inappropriately hugged, touched, and kissed at public rituals. Many of these people stopped going to public rituals or even engaging in coven practice. "Perfect love and perfect trust" is hard to attain, but we should at least be able to get to "respect and obtain consent" consistently as a community.

While I believe large rituals can be difficult to pull off, the rewards are tremendous. There's a special satisfaction that comes from presenting something to your extended community. Your large ritual might end up being the *gateway* for a seeker new to the Craft, or it might reawaken a seasoned practitioner's love for magick and ritual! There's also the incredible feeling that comes from raising energy with fifty or even a hundred people. Knowing that we can have those types of large communities in the Witching World is something to get excited about.

Large rituals are an example of *service* to the Witch community. We present rituals for others, not for ourselves. The easiest way to ruin a large group ritual is to suffer from the delusion that we are presenting ritual for ourselves. Ritual leaders are the facilitators, not the stars.

There's a person in my local community who loves to present ritual because they turn it into a personal showcase. They dance and sing in the middle of it for no reason other than to dance and sing in front of people. To them, ritual isn't about connecting to the gods, the seasons, or magick; it's about being the center of attention. The end result is a disjointed ritual that doesn't serve the needs of anyone (not even the person who put it together). So remember to keep the focus on everyone in the circle, and not just the people presenting the ritual.

RITUAL SHOULD GIVE PEOPLE SOMETHING TO DO AND KEEP THEM ENGAGED

This might be the hardest part of planning a large ritual. It's not easy to come up with an activity that engages thirty to two hundred people all at once. Many people take the easy way out and create rituals that feature a lot of sacred drama or guided meditations. I understand the inclination, and these things aren't always bad, but most people aren't "doing" very much in those types of situations. And I know several people who tend to tune out entirely when such things are offered in circle.

I think the ideal at a large public ritual is to have two activities of some sort for the working part of the rite. Something that requires a bit of physical activity is good. Just making people walk somewhere makes them a part of the ritual, but the most important thing is connection. Is there an opportunity in the ritual for everyone to connect with deity, the dead, magick, or the Wheel of the Year? Is an environment being created where people feel magickal and engaged?

Ritual should indulge the senses. That's why Witches use incense (smell and sight), chants and bells (sound), salted water (physical touch), and candles (sight). If something looks like Witchcraft, it will in turn feel like Witchcraft on a spiritual level. When a ritual *looks good*, I find myself paying more attention to it. I know how superficial that sounds, but it's true for most people.

My most successful public rituals have been the ones that offered several different types of "doing." At Imbolc, for example, you could have people speak with a drawn-down goddess Brigid, welcome in the reborn light, and then use that light for magickal purposes. All of these things can be done simultaneously by the people in the circle if it's all explained clearly. Some explanation of what you want people to do during a large group ritual is especially important, and it's something I often find myself subtly repeating two or three times during the course of a working.

Don't be afraid to explain things a third or even fourth time. It's better to get things right than to have everyone wander around aimlessly. This is when having a large group to assist you in putting together a ritual can be a major help. Let everyone directly involved in the rite help everyone else out, or have them demonstrate what you want everyone else at the rite to do.

Perhaps most importantly, large group ritual should offer everyone a "moment." Moments don't have to be long. Simply giving everyone a moment to say the name of a deceased loved one at Samhain can be enough. It's the little things that often have the most lasting impact. Part of good ritual facilitation is making sure everyone at the ritual has had a chance to engage in it to some degree. When a person with mobility issues goes to a ritual built around dancing, they may have trouble finding their moment within it, so it's up to you to make sure they do.

Moments and experiences can't always be scripted either. When we put together a ritual, we're setting up a container for the experience. What we can't necessarily dictate is how that experience is going to play out. Everyone experiences magick, the Wheel of the Year, and the gods differently. There are atheist Witches and polytheistic Witches; because of that, a ritual about Brigid will resonate on different levels depending on the individuals.

I'm a bit of a talker, and I sometimes find myself writing overly wordy rituals. This can be problematic. No one wants to be spoken at for thirty minutes, and long, drawn-out monologues often result in people losing a sense of what the ritual is actually about and what their role in it is. I was at an Ostara ritual once where the High Priest spent fifteen minutes explaining the Wheel of the Year to everyone in attendance, and most of us ended up tuning out. No one wants to hear that. If the words are not essential to your ritual, cut them out!

Staging and Theatricality

Coven and solitary rituals generally take place in a limited area, and most of what goes on in those sorts of rituals takes place primarily near or behind the altar. That's not good enough in a circle ritual. To make everyone feel involved and close to what's going on, all of the space in the circle has to be used. A ritual is not a play, and a Witch does not have to be a trained thespian to lead an effective public rite, but what's required for large ritual goes a bit above and beyond what most Witches do in their smaller circles.

The first rule of big rituals is to go "big and slow." Every word that is spoken in the circle should be said loudly and slowly. How it comes out might sound odd to the person saying it, but it will be appreciated by the person standing twenty-five yards away. In ritual, especially when we're nervous, we have a tendency to speak quickly, which makes hearing words at a distance more difficult. In most cases, the Witches leading a public rite can't speak slowly enough. Take time to enunciate each word and really pause between sentences.

Ritual actions should be big so that they can be easily seen. If you're using an invoking pentagram (figure 2) when calling the watchtowers, draw a very large, person-size pentagram. When we're performing the symbolic Great Rite in front of a hundred people, I raise my athame high up over my head and my High Priestess wife raises her chalice and then slowly lowers it so everyone can clearly see what she's holding. Making large, dramatic gestures may sometimes feel foolish, but everyone in the circle will appreciate it.

Figure 2. Invoking Pentagram

Many Witches make the mistake of standing still when conducting a large ritual. Instead of standing behind the altar and reading the Charge of the Goddess, move around the entire circle while reading it. Make eye contact with as many Witches as possible, and share what you're doing with the entire group instead of limiting action to only one part of a large space. When doing public ritual, I rarely stand behind the altar. Instead, I like to be within a few feet of everyone I'm circling with, at least for a few minutes.

The middle portion of the circle is the friend of every High Priestess, High Priest, quarter caller, and circle caster (figure 3). I've been to too many rituals where the people calling the quarters walked to the outside edge of the circle, essentially turning their backs on everyone they were circling with. Not only could no one see what they were doing, but no one could hear them either! If you're calling the spirits of the east, by all means stand in the east, but do so in "center-east," where most everyone will be able to at least hear or see you. The same goes for anyone casting the circle. In coven ritual with thirteen folks, it's easy to simply walk around the outside of the circle, but if that's done with sixty people in attendance, the person wielding the sword will get lost among all of those bodies. Stay in the middle.

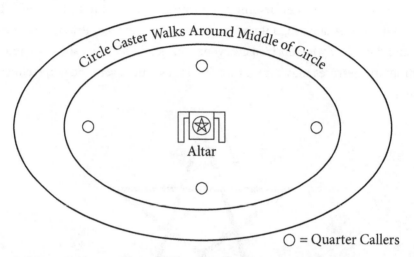

Figure 3. The Middle of the Circle Is Your Friend

I don't rehearse or practice my coven or solitary rituals, but for group ritual it's a must! Everyone who is in the ritual should be familiar with what's happening and aware of what their responsibilities are, and there's no better way to figure those things out than through practice. Even the best set of ritual instructions will leave something out (even those in this book), so the only way to be sure of exactly what might happen during ritual is to do a practice run-through. Since most large public rituals have additional ritual roles that might include people we don't generally work with, knowing how they do ritual and conduct their magickal business can be figured out only through practice.

Rehearsing also allows a group to get a good idea of just how long their ritual will be. I think the ideal amount of time for a large public ritual is about forty-five to seventy minutes. Anything shorter than forty-five minutes and people sometimes feel cheated;

anything longer than that and people start to tune out. There are exceptions though. Samhain rituals will often run long, and perhaps a Beltane ritual with a maypole will too, but most people aren't looking for a three-hour sabbat ritual. Rituals will generally run faster than most practice runs, simply because people tend to speak faster when fifty pairs of eyes are on them.

I know many Witches who believe that everything we say during ritual should be memorized. I'm not one of those Witches, and my memorization skills are absolutely awful. I don't think there's anything wrong with reading during a public ritual. However, having text available during the ritual is no substitute for practicing. Everything that we say should be practiced (out loud!) ahead of time. "Ritual speak" is often very different from how most of us normally talk, and it's easy for our words to become garbled when reading something for the first time. (Also, no one wants to listen to someone struggle to pronounce a challenging or unfamiliar deity name such as Melusine.)

If you do choose to have a script available during public ritual, that script should be presentable. Something fresh off the printer or a few sheets of notebook paper are not good enough; put your script in an attractive-looking book or folder instead. I think it's better to have a script available than to forget one's lines or mess up the meaning of a ritual, which is something I've seen happen several times over the years. If someone's part in a ritual is small (such as someone calling a quarter), decorated notecards are an attractive alternative as well.

Most rituals don't require hard memorization either. Simply knowing what you're going to be doing is often enough for the experienced ritualist, but having a script around in case you get off track can be a real lifesaver. I go off script all the time. Rituals are living, breathing things and sometimes they require slight adjustments instead of exact readings from something put together on a computer.

We tend not to think of things like cakes and ale as staging issues in ritual, but they are. Passing around one chalice during cakes and ale takes what can feel like an eternity during ritual. The easiest solution is to use several chalices, or better yet, pour individual cups of wine or juice and have them on a tray and ready to serve ahead of time. At the public rituals presented by my coven, we have four trays ready to go for cakes and ale, two full of drinks and two full of food. This makes distribution of cakes and ale easy and, most of all, quick. People get restless near the end of a ritual if they stand around for too long, and this is most noticeable at cakes and ale.

Some covens wear robes in rituals, some do things skyclad, and some are "come as you are." I've been in all of those situations, but when it comes to public rituals, I'm almost always in a robe or some other type of magickal dress. When the people running a ritual are dressed up, it shows they care and are trying to create the proper atmosphere. It also helps focus attention on the ritual leaders, which makes giving out instructions in the circle easier.

Even a group that practices and does everything "right" at a public ritual is still likely to stumble now and again. The most important thing to remember about mistakes is that people don't know something is a mistake until you tell them it is. Flub a line? Unless your audience is reading your script as you execute the ritual, no one will ever know. Laughing at yourself is acceptable too. Sometimes people just do things out of order, and it's okay. Don't get flustered!

Keep Control of the Ritual and Avoid Too Many Moving Parts

Nothing derails a large public ritual faster than when the Witch leading the rite loses control of their ritual. I think most of us in the Witch community are nice people, so when someone starts talking out of turn, we don't exactly know how to stop them from doing so or how to tell them that "now is not the time." I've led dozens of large public rituals and this is still something I have trouble with. It doesn't happen with much frequency, but occasionally you will no doubt run into someone who wants to be the "star" of your ritual and will do everything possible to make that happen.

The easiest way to avoid this is not to offer a lot of opportunities for people to talk publicly. There are individuals who will take advantage of a directive as simple as "Say out loud that which you want to be rid of," and turn it into a ten-minute treatise on how terrible their life is. I always feel for such individuals, but it's not fair to everyone else in ritual and changes the energy and dynamics of what the group is building together. When I do allow for people to speak in ritual, I have them do it all at once, or I specify slowly, deliberately, and forcefully that their remarks need to be no more than a couple of words or a short phrase. If someone begins to overstay their moment, it's well within your rights as a ritual leader to cut them off. I know how ruthless this sounds, but your ritual will be better off for it.

Relying on the participants of a ritual to react or behave a certain way is a gateway to disappointment. I have a friend who likes to imagine all of their rituals as beautifully interactive celebratory rites. They plan on people toasting or perhaps engaging in games featuring competitive boasting. Such things often work in a coven situation, but they don't work so well in situations where people aren't familiar with one another. When we create ritual, we set up a container, and how people react in that container will vary from person to person. It's not fair to rely on people at a ritual to behave a certain way or happily engage in things that are far outside their comfort zone just because you think they should.

I generally advise against drawing down (invoking) deities during large rituals. (Of course, I write that knowing there are three circle rituals in this book that call for drawing down deities.) A drawn-down goddess will often change the course of a ritual to *her* liking unless preparations have been made ahead of time, and that's one of the keys. The circle ritual for Samhain in this book (in chapter 37) has the High Priestess drawing down the "Goddess of Death." My wife assures me this is Persephone, but my wife has also had a long relationship with Persephone, so when we draw her down in ritual, certain conditions have been agreed to ahead of time.

Do I recommend asking deities to do (or not do) certain activities when they are invoked in ritual? Not particularly. They are deities after all, but if there's an established relationship between mortal and deity, you probably won't get in too much trouble for asking. Still, even with such an understanding ahead of time, there's always the chance a goddess will change the ritual more to her liking. Even though I know that drawing down a deity is not always the best of ideas, the drama, danger, and excitement of it during public ritual makes it hard to resist.

When deity is drawn down in a group ritual, it's often done in order to let everyone in the circle have an experience with that deity. In the Samhain and Imbolc circle rituals that are a part of this book, there's an opportunity for everyone in the rite to converse with the Goddess. However, when we do that during ritual, we have individuals in place whose job it is to watch over the drawn-down Lady and not let anyone monopolize her time. A few other tips and tricks for managing such situations are included in the individual rituals.

Long pauses and silences are another way to lose control of a ritual. I have seen more rituals get off track during cakes and ale than I can count, generally because people are standing around waiting, with nothing to do. A line of seventy people all waiting to be cleansed at the entryway to a ritual generally makes for a long line of people chatting with each other, whispering, playing with their phones, and telling jokes. If the buildup for a ritual takes twenty or thirty minutes, you're likely to lose everyone at your rite before it even begins.

If you don't take your ritual seriously, no one else will either. Many people who present ritual forget that it's a serious endeavor and, because of nervousness or some desire to be a stand-up comedian, use ritual time for joke telling. Jokes aren't out of bounds at rituals and are even appropriate sometimes, but probably not before calling on your ancestors or trying to draw down the Horned God as the Dread Lord of Shadows at Samhain. If all the people involved in a ritual are telling jokes during the serious part of a rite, why should anyone take it seriously?

I think people like to be surprised during ritual. Doing something new or out of the ordinary creates a heightened sense of awareness. However, adding things to ritual that will likely result in people scratching their heads can ruin a rite and take people out of ritual headspace. The very definition of *ritual* references "a series of actions performed according to a prescribed order," and if you get too far away from that, it's possible that no one will recognize what you're doing as a ritual.[17] Ritual should be familiar enough that people can easily follow along to some extent.

People also expect certain things at certain rituals. Putting together a rite for one's ancestors is perfect for Samhain, but it's a bit out of left field when done at Beltane. It's common to reference Maiden goddesses at Ostara, but less so at Mabon. We shouldn't let such things stifle our creativity too much when creating ritual, but ritual should always have at least a touch of the familiar.

A ritual with too many moving parts is often a disaster waiting to happen. Most people can handle a couple of activities or even three, but seven? There's a point at which participants will simply become overwhelmed and not know what to do. The more moving parts something has, the greater the chances are of that thing breaking. "Keep it simple, stupid" is a commonly repeated piece of advice, and I think it pertains to ritual too.

---

17. *Oxford English Dictionary*, s.v. "ritual," https://en.oxforddictionaries.com/definition/ritual.

"Too many moving parts" can also be an issue in terms of the number of people you have involved in a ritual. Many years ago, a High Priestess friend of mine was putting together a ritual that required drummers and several singers, along with her usual cast of quarter callers, High Priests, and circle casters. The day of the ritual, none of her drummers showed up, she lost her voice, and all of her singers got sick. She doesn't believe in using prerecorded music, so she had no backup plan for the absent singers and drummers. The ritual was obviously a disaster.

When planning a ritual, I do everything with the knowledge that I or a trusted friend might have to step in at any moment. If necessary, I can always call a quarter or pass out cakes and ale or whatever else is required. About the only person I ever have 100 percent confidence in is my wife, and that's only because I know where she sleeps. Keep even the biggest rites simple enough that a ritual role can be adapted or filled in for on the fly, and always have a backup plan just in case.

RITUALS REQUIRE ADAPTATION

Let's say you've written an amazing ritual script and practiced your rite several times and yet it's not quite working. This happens, and the smart ritualist will adapt, roll with the punches, and keep moving forward. Rituals are living, breathing things because they are full of living, breathing human beings. Even the most accomplished ritualist has a tale of two of things not working quite right.

At a large Pagan gathering several years ago, a friend of mine was leading a late ritual, so I went to see what they were up to. Apparently lots of other people did too, and they ended up with a line of about a hundred people waiting to get into the ritual. This person had made the decision to challenge *every ritual attendee* at the door with a sword. Each confrontation lasted at least thirty seconds to a minute.

Even if every challenge was super short, it was still going to result in wait times approaching thirty minutes before the rite even started. I was one of the first people in the ritual space and I immediately found myself having to pee, but there was no way out of space without leaving in a way that some might consider disrespectful. Two hours later, the ritual was finally done, but all I could concentrate on the entire time was not peeing my pants.

Circumstances often require us to change public rituals in order to accommodate the realities we're facing and the expectations of others. If everyone at your ritual is expecting a riotous devotional to Dionysus and the ritual you've prepared is serious and sober, it's going to be problematic. One time, my coven was leading a serious rite at a festival near where we live, and up until then the only rituals I'd presented at that particular festival had been lively and fun affairs. When everyone entered our ritual space, they were expecting a party, and I had to add an opening bit to our ritual to temper those expectations.

I have seen what should have been a good ritual become a miserable failure because no one bothered to check up on where the ritual was being held ahead of time. If your ritual is to be done outside, do you have a backup plan in case it rains? Just because your friend offered to let you use their backyard doesn't mean it's all clear of dog poop, and there's nothing worse than a maypole dance held in an obstacle course. If you're using a public park, make sure to get there early and check the grounds for sticks, trash, and other debris. If your ritual will be indoors at someone's house, make sure the house is picked up and ready for people. These all may seem like things no one would ever over-look, but it happens.

Large rituals require a good amount of preparation and a large degree of flexibility. Nothing worth doing is easy, and that's especially the case with public ritual, but the results are often worth the extra trouble. If you're prepared for the various obstacles along the way and have a plan to get through or around them, everything will work out in the end.

CHAPTER 7

HOW TO USE THIS BOOK
Do What Works Best for You

You're free to use this book in any way you choose, but there are some features within it that I think are worth mentioning. Every ritual in this book is unique. No two circle castings or quarter calls are alike. What resonates most with you might not be what resonates most with me, so you're free to cherry-pick the parts you like the best.

For instance, you might really like how the watchtowers are invoked in the Lammas ritual for covens, and want to use those calls instead of the ones included with an Imbolc rite. That's great! This book is designed for you to mix and match the ritual bits you like best, which is why every section in every ritual is clearly marked.

Though all of the rituals in this book are labeled as being for solitaries, covens, or circles, there's no reason a circle ritual can't be used in a coven setting, or a solitary rite with a large group. With a little bit of adaptation, most of the workings in this book can be utilized for whatever circumstances you find yourself in. Just remember that a ritual designed for twelve people will have to be adjusted a bit if it's going to be used for fifty. In my own practice, I adapt rituals I originally wrote for my coven into larger rites. Use what you think will work regardless of how I (or anyone else) presents it.

Rituals truly come alive only when they are brought to life in a magick circle. Reading a ritual is no substitute for actually engaging with it. I want you to *use* these rituals if they appeal to you, and I want you to feel free to adapt them and change my wording if you need to. The earliest Modern Witches borrowed extensively from a wide range of sources, reassembling and rewriting various bits to serve their needs. I don't see why today's Witches should be any different.

The rituals in this book are generally quite long and wordy. (My magickal name is Verbose, and for good reason.) I really don't expect people to read them verbatim. Think of them more as a starting point than an ending one. I'm also not sure people actually talk with the same tone, cadence, and style that most rituals are presented in. What's most important is that what you're saying during ritual makes sense to you and those you're circling with. Sometimes that might require simplifying some long instructions or moving away from ritual "Witch speak" to something more familiar.

Most of the rituals in this book are written in script format, meaning the person doing the talking is clearly indicated, with their lines following thereafter. Spoken parts are in italics, with actions and movements appearing as standard text. I'm not sure this is the best way to write out ritual, but it works for me and is the most common format in Pagan and Witch books. Generally, how rituals are presented in this book mirrors the way I write them down in my own personal practice.

The majority (but not all) of the group rituals in this book were originally written to be shared with my wife, with the two of us in the roles of High Priestess and High Priest. Because of that, you'll see those two terms pop up in a lot of the rituals. I don't believe that a ritual needs both a female and a male leader to be effective, and two High Priestesses is certainly just as effective as a High Priest and a High Priestess, or just one High whatever. In other words, gender doesn't really play a role, despite it appearing to do so on occasion.

Over the years I've debated ditching the terms *High Priestess* and *High Priest* and replacing them with something like *officiant*, but that just sounds too clinical to my ears. In the Reclaiming tradition of Witchcraft, everyone is a High Priestess and there are no High Priests, which is another great work-around. I know of some traditions that use the term *Reverend* instead of *Priest*, and if people are comfortable with that, great. (To me, it sounds far too Christian.) What's most important is to use terms that appeal to you and those you practice with.

I think ritual is better when as many people as possible are involved, which means I usually have individuals other than the High Priestess/High whatever calling the quarters and casting the circle. Generally these individuals also help out in other ways, perhaps by taking a speaking part during some of the more elaborate rituals or by distributing cakes and ale near the end of the rite. Of course you don't have to conduct your rituals this way, and sometimes circumstances mean one or two people have to do almost all of the heavy lifting during ritual.

The rituals in this book contain several "things left unsaid." In most covens and groups, it's standard operating procedure to repeat certain phrases typically said at the end of pronouncements, invitations, and other forms of magickal work. Phrases such as "Blessed be," "So mote it be," and "Hail and farewell" fall into this category, though instructions to repeat such things are not indicated in this text. Whether a group or coven wants to do that is really up to them, and including those callbacks seemed rather redundant to me anyway. The same goes for instructions like "pass out the cakes and ale." That seems like kind of a no-brainer to me, and just how people distribute such things will vary from group to group. In my coven, we all drink from the same chalice. I'm sure there are other groups that prefer not to do that.

The use or non-use of candles is treated the same way throughout the book as well. I know people who are adamant about lighting candles at every quarter and for every deity they call. In my own practice, I've mostly moved away from this, especially when outside. Unless a ritual specifically calls for the use of a candle, I don't make a big deal out of candle lighting. It's something you can do or not do, and it's not something that *has* to be done in the Craft. Use candles when it's appropriate for you and when you think they'll stay lit.

Many covens use songs and elaborate chants in their rituals, but trying to express musicality on the printed page is difficult and probably not necessary in the era of YouTube. Add songs, chants, and musical circle castings and quarter callings to your rite if you choose! That's more than acceptable. I just lack the ability to convey that in the rituals included in this book.

STANDARD ALTAR SETUP AND MATERIALS NEEDED

I love ritual tools, which is probably why I've written three books about them. I have three athames, eight chalices, and a whole bunch of other stuff I probably don't actually need. When performing a sabbat ritual, I like to have an altar full of ritual tools, even though I know it's not really necessary. Elaborate tools are not required in Witchcraft, and everything a beginning Witch needs is generally already in their kitchen. However, my standard alter setup tends to look like this (figure 4):

- Athame (can be substituted with a wand or your own fingers)
- Chalice or cup (generally containing drink for cakes and ale)
- Something representing air (incense, a bird feather, etc.)
- Something representing water (a bowl of water, a seashell, etc.)
- Something representing fire (a candle, chili pepper, etc.)
- Something representing earth (a bowl of salt or rice, a rock, etc.)
- Statue(s) of the Goddess and the God (or objects or candles representing them)
- Pentacle[18]
- Wand (less necessary if you have an athame)
- White-handled knife (for physical cutting; some people just use their athame)
- Spirit candle
- Libation bowl

These are the tools I tend to always have on my altar, though most of the rituals in this book are simple enough that you can probably get by without most or even all of them. Because there are a variety of rituals in this book, I don't use all of these items for every ritual, and some rituals call for additional tools such as a small cauldron or a bowl and pitcher. When additional materials are required for a ritual, they are listed in the "Materials Needed" section included with each ritual.

Every ritual in this book begins with a brief explanation of the rite, along with the things that make it unique. Sometimes staging information is included with that opening material, and this is especially important with the larger circle rituals since they often require additional preparation. There are also a few instances where I include the history of the working in the rite if it's based on historical sources.

---

18. The pentacle is probably the one tool that can't be readily found in your kitchen or backyard. However, one can easily be made out of a paper plate. I spend a lot of time talking about pentacles in *The Witch's Altar* (co-written with Laura Tempest Zakroff), also published by Llewellyn in 2018.

Figure 4. Standard Altar Setup

There are many types of Witchcraft in the world today, but most of the rituals in this book follow the Wiccan-Witchcraft formula. I have two simple reasons for this style choice. The first is that it reflects my personal practice, and the second is that Wiccan-Witch ritual is the most familiar type of ritual in the modern Pagan and Witch world. It's a ritual language that most of us are familiar with, so it's easily understandable. But fear not, those of you who are tired of Wicca, as there are also rituals in this book in the style of what has come to be known as Traditional Witchcraft.

What's most important are the rituals and sabbats themselves, and it's probably time we got to them.

PART TWO
WINTER
(YULE & IMBOLC)

The sun now reborn,
Winter covers the dead earth.
Life shall come again.

CHAPTER 8

YULE
The Winter Solstice

Name of Sabbat: Yule (also known as Midwinter and the Winter Solstice)
Date: On the day of the winter solstice (which occurs on or about December 21 in the Northern Hemisphere)
Pronunciation: "You'll" (It sounds just like the contraction.)

The winter solstice is the shortest day and longest night of every year. The date of the winter solstice is variable and can occur anywhere from December 20 to December 23 in the Northern Hemisphere. After the winter solstice, the amount of sunlight we receive gradually lengthens until it starts to decline again six months later at the summer solstice. The winter solstice has been celebrated for thousands of years, and many of the traditions associated with it have become part of Christian and secular Christmas and New Year's (January 1) celebrations.

Most Witches refer to the Winter Solstice today as Yule, which is an apt name. Yule was a legitimate Norse holiday commemorating the Winter Solstice and later used as an alternative name for Christmas. The Winter Solstice is also sometimes called Midwinter; if Samhain marks the start of winter and Imbolc its end, then the Winter Solstice is the middle point. The majority of us today use these terms interchangeably. Because many holidays have been celebrated in late December over the millennia, I often refer to this period as *Yuletide*. New Year's Eve, Christmas, and our own Yule can all be traced back to pagan antiquity with some certainty.

For Modern Witches, Yule is generally seen as the rebirth of the sun, and a lot of our rituals are built around this idea. Sometimes the sun is personified as a deity that is reborn on the solstice, and others mark the occasion by lighting candles on the longest night of the year. Because of that long night, the Winter Solstice can be a rather melancholy sabbat if one chooses to approach it that way (it is generally dark and cold that night in many places), but many Yule celebrations are joyous. This is because many of the ancient festivals celebrated near the winter solstice were rather fun and drunken affairs.

The most influential of those ancient holidays was the Roman Saturnalia, celebrated over a period of three to five days beginning on December 17.[19] Saturnalia was generally a celebration of abundance and included feasting and often heavy drinking. It was also a holiday that reversed social norms. The Greek writer Lucian (c. 120–c. 180 CE) wrote of the holiday, "Let every man be treated equal, slave and freeman, poor and rich."[20]

One of the longest-lasting traditions associated with Saturnalia was that of the mock king. Mock kings ruled over individual Saturnalia celebrations, generally encouraging frivolity and issuing absurd proclamations. Though we don't hear or read about mock kings very often today, the practice carried on for centuries. In the Middle Ages, mock kings became "Lords of Misrule" and presided over winter celebrations in manor houses throughout Europe. (If you think the holiday season is long today, the medieval one lasted from about Samhain all the way to Imbolc![21])

Though Kings of Misrule gradually disappeared from most holiday celebrations, what they represented during Yule persisted. Drinking and upsetting social norms became a part of the wassailing tradition. Though often associated today with something akin to Christmas caroling, wassailing was originally a holiday custom focused on food, drink, and sometimes petty vandalism. The poor would visit the homes of the rich and demand food and drink. In exchange, they would often sing, perform plays, and toast to the good health of their host. When wassailers were denied food and beverage, they often retaliated with pranks and violence. (Wassailing is still with us today; we call it "trick-or-treating".) Some historians have argued that wassailing served as a kind of so-

---

19. Forbes, *Christmas: A Candid History*, 8.

20. Forbes, *Christmas: A Candid History*, also page 8. This is a terrific book.

21. Bowler, *The World Encyclopedia of Christmas*, 134.

cial safety valve, allowing the less powerful to gain the upper hand over the nobility and/ or their employers at least for a few days.[22]

In addition to Saturnalia, the Norse Yule also had a tremendous impact on our modern celebration of the holiday (and on the Christian Christmas). Though we don't know a whole lot about how the Norse celebrated Yule, it too seemed to feature feasting and excessive drinking. Animal sacrifice (and the accompanying meat dinner that resulted from it) was a part of the holiday as well, along with some sort of ancestor veneration.[23] Fires and candles were also a part of the holiday, and the custom that eventually came to be known as the "Yule log" also came from the Norse Yule.[24]

Ways to Celebrate Yule

Yule might be my favorite sabbat to celebrate because there are so many different ideas and traditions that can be incorporated into its rituals. Nearly anything associated with Christmas is fair game for Yule rituals, including trees, stockings, mistletoe, or even snow-people if you live in the right sort of climate for it. When our non-magickal friends visit Ari and I's house in December, most of them comment on just how Christmasy it looks. Little do they know that nearly every decoration in our living room has connections to our Witchcraft.

Though Santa Claus doesn't visit every coven, he's long been a guest deity at my Yuletide rites. Despite being known in some circles as Saint Nicholas, Santa Claus has a mixed background and owes just as much to the Norse god Odin (or Woden) as he does to the Christian saint with whom he shares a name. In addition to Santa Claus, Yuletide is full of several other figures with likely pre-Christian origins. Some of these include the Tomte, the Yule Goat, the Yule Lads (or Goblins), the Krampus, and of course the elves that work for Santa at the North Pole. My wife isn't a big fan of the Krampus, but I love working him into our December rituals! One of my other favorite gift givers is probably post-Christian, the Italian *La Befana*, but since she's an Italian Witch, she's worth mentioning here. (She also shows up in the Yule circle ritual in this book.)

Giving has been a part of Midwinter celebrations since the Roman Saturnalia and is a welcome ritual activity among many Modern Witches. Presents can be distributed by

---

22. Nissenbaum, *The Battle for Christmas*, 11.

23. Forbes, *Christmas: A Candid History*, 11–12.

24. Ibid., 12–13.

someone playing the role of Woden or through a Secret Santa gift exchange. Gathering toys and food for those in need is a magickal activity too! Often this is far more satisfying than giving a friend an unneeded trinket.

As a sabbat celebrating the rebirth of the sun, Yule has long been associated with light. It's a time for lighting candles to fight the darkness and for celebrating the rebirth of the sun god. Many Witches celebrate the birth of several different solar deities on or near the solstice, and this is a great idea to build a ritual around. Even the little baby Jesus taps into this theme. Because of the limited light we receive at the start of the winter, many Witches hold solstice vigils on the night of Yule and stay up all night to greet the returning sun.

The story of the Oak King and Holly King is a great way to illustrate the "growing" half of the year that begins at Yule. In many Midwinter interpretations of this myth, the Holly King often looks much like Santa Claus or Father Christmas, making him the "older brother" who is slain on the Winter Solstice. The Oak and Holly Kings are not the only royalty to show up at Yule; Queens and Kings of Misrule are generally welcome guests at Midwinter sabbats as well.

For thousands of years now, Midwinter celebrations have been celebratory. We see this to some degree in our modern world with office Christmas parties and New Year's Eve celebrations, but it was a part of the Norse Yule and Roman Saturnalia too. Toasting to the good health of those around you, playing games, and simply having fun are appropriate ways to celebrate Yule.

For many people, winter is a season that's approached with dread, but it doesn't have to be that way. Winter is when the world is renewed through snow and rain, and the cold weather kills all the bugs that drive most of us crazy. Instead of actively fighting against it, *winter is something that should be embraced*. Bring some snow inside for your rituals, or simply enjoy a cup of hot chocolate or some mulled wine. We should be thankful for the natural world no matter where we are on the Wheel of the Year.

Lights, snow, gifts, battling brothers, wassail, carols, partying, Lords of Misrule, mystical gift givers, the longer days, trees, logs, the sun's rebirth … Yule probably has the longest and most varied list of things to build rituals around. For this reason, it's become a favorite of many Modern Witches. There's something especially satisfying about celebrating a holiday that everyone around you seems to be celebrating too. (And many of them are, even if they don't know it!)

CHAPTER 9

YULE CIRCLE RITUAL

Pine Cones of Yuletide
Past, Present, and Future

Though Charles Dickens's *A Christmas Carol* is not meant to be a witchy or Pagan book, I often think of it that way. It has spirits (the shade of Jacob Marley) and three figures that have to at least be demigods (how else does one explain the Ghosts of Christmas Past, Present, and Future?). Out of those three, the Ghost of Christmas Present always seemed like he'd be the most fun. He's often pictured engaging in a hearty laugh, with a goblet of wine in his hand. For this reason, he's often reminded me of the wine god Dionysus.

Because of that connection I've built a lot of my Yule rituals around Dionysus over the years. The holiday season is the most festive time of year in many parts of the world, and Dionysus is a god who generally wants us to be happy, and usually a bit tipsy. Dionysus has other parallels with Yuletide, though. Although he is usually associated with wine, Dionysus is also the god of ivy and trees, especially pine trees.[25] For this reason, the thyrsus (staff) of Dionysus is decorated with holly and topped with a pine cone. The thyrsus is a symbol of joy, fertility, abundance, and a little bit of decadence—perfect for the Yule season!

Though this ritual doesn't include a thyrsus for every attendee (too complicated!), it does have a pine cone for everyone, and a Yule tree to put them on. It also mentions Yules past, present, and future, connecting it with Dickens's *A Christmas Carol*. In my version of

---

25. Otto, *Dionysus: Myth & Cult*, 157.

the ritual, I've chosen to hang the pine cones that will be given out on a Yule tree, which also means that small pieces of string have to be tied onto each pine cone so they'll hang on the tree. An alternative to this is to simply have the pine cones on an altar. In addition, the pine cones could be decorated with glitter, berries, holly, etc., before or during the ritual, if desired.

In addition to Dionysus, this ritual honors the goddess Diana as *Befana*, an Italian Christmas Witch who acts like a much cooler Santa Claus. Since gift giving is such an integral part of December celebrations, her inclusion feels especially important. Music plays an important part in this ritual, so have either some recorded music ready to go (I suggest some Yuletide jigs) or a couple of drummers. Know also that whoever is leading your ritual is going to have to be loud to be heard over the music.

Ritual Roles

- High Priestess
- High Priest
- Quarter callers
- Circle caster

Materials Needed

- Altar tools and setup
- Two small bowls of water for ritual cleansing, with one or two drops of essential oil (Frankincense is very cleansing and appropriate for this time of year, but you can use whatever appeals to you. Water can be sprinkled using fingers or whisked out of the bowl with an evergreen branch. Water should be cleansed and consecrated before the ritual begins.)
- One pine cone for every attendee
- Yule tree (can be decorated or just adorned with the pine cones)
- Recorded music or drummers
- Thyrsus (for circle casting: optional)

THE RITUAL: PINE CONES OF YULETIDE PAST, PRESENT, AND FUTURE

The ritual environment is bright and cheerful and ideally is decorated with holiday lights and other trappings of the season.

Opening, Cleansing, Statement of Intent

HIGH PRIESTESS: *Beyond our circle, all lies in darkness. It is the longest night, and the air is cold and the winds harsh. But here in our ritual space, the gods watch over us and we celebrate this longest of nights. For Yule is a time of joy and fellowship, because we know that after this night the days will slowly grow longer and the world will be reborn.*

HIGH PRIEST: *On this Yule, we celebrate the goddess Diana, Queen of the Witches, and we celebrate her brother Dionysus, god of wine! For they have always been with us in Yuletides past, are with us now, and will be with us in Yuletides yet to come, spreading joy, gifts, and love!*

The quarter callers step forward, two of them taking bowls of water sprinkled with essential oils and two of them the cleansing incense. As the High Priestess speaks and prepares the attendees for the night's ritual, the quarter callers cense and asperge them.

HIGH PRIESTESS: *Before we begin, let us take a moment to prepare ourselves for tonight's ritual. Close your eyes, relax, and slip inside of yourself for a moment. As you are touched by the cleansing water and incense, imagine all of your cares and worries falling away. Tonight you are among your fellow Witches, free to be yourself and free to celebrate as you will. Allow the sacred smoke to remove the negative energy that often attaches to us, and be cleansed by the waters that take away our troubles, at least for a time.*

Think for a moment about the long night, and the peace and comfort that comes only with the quiet of winter. Imagine the cold cleansing the land and preparing it for what is to come. Think of the Lord and Lady and how they love those who are their children. After you've been touched by the cleansing incense and purifying water, open your eyes and rejoin us in this place, and prepare to celebrate Yule. Blessed be!

Casting the Circle, Calling the Quarters

The quarter callers return the bowls of water and the incense to the altar. The circle is cast using an athame, sword, or thyrsus.

CIRCLE CASTER: *Between the worlds we will stand in a time that is not a time and a place that is not a place. In the confines of our magick circle, we shall see worlds past and worlds yet to come. Let the light and spirit of the season shine in this our sacred space! The circle is cast. So mote it be!*

Candles at all the quarters are optional here, but if they are used, make sure the quarter callers light them after they have invoked the elements.

EAST QUARTER CALLER: *We call to the spirits of the east, spirits of inspiration and knowledge. As the sun rises in the east, we thank you for the rebirth of the light that brings us so much joy at Yuletide. May your light and wisdom shine bright in the dark days ahead. Hail and welcome!*

SOUTH QUARTER CALLER: *We call to the spirits of the south, spirits of passion and desire. We thank you for the gift of the mistletoe, Yuletide symbol of companionship and dalliance. May your longing and intensity warm us in the cold days ahead. Hail and welcome!*

WEST QUARTER CALLER: *We call to the spirits of the west, spirits of love and emotion. We thank you for your gifts of snow and rain. Those gifts blanket the earth, providing sustenance and opportunity for what is to come. May your love wash over us as your power washes over the earth. Hail and welcome!*

NORTH QUARTER CALLER: *We call to the spirits of the north, spirits of foundation and place. We thank you for the gift of the evergreen tree, which reminds us that even in the cold of winter life remains. May your watchful gaze keep us close to hearth and home this holiday season. Hail and welcome!*

Calling Dionysus and Diana/Befana

HIGH PRIEST: *Tonight we call to the great Dionysus, god of passions, wine, transformation, merriment, and mirth! Through the ages you have taken other forms to stay close to the folk, even when they turned their backs on you. In the Middle Ages you were the Lord of Misrule, upending the social order, promoting a fluid sexuality, and bringing happiness to hearts in the depths of winter. It is your torch that is held high this time of year, inviting all with joy in their hearts to celebrate the winter season. Join us in our ritual and revels, O wine god! Be with us as your people celebrate your season. Hail and welcome!*

Light a candle for Dionysus if applicable.

HIGH PRIESTESS: *Tonight we call to the powerful Diana, goddess of Witches, hunting, the moon, and the wild places. You have ever stood beside us, changing your form and face so that you might ever be a part of our worship and celebration. Many know you as Artemis, others Aradia, and in many parts of Italy you are known as Befana, the Christmas Witch, who brings gifts to all the good girls, boys, and Witches. Join us in our rituals and revels, great huntress! Be with us as we celebrate your season. Hail and welcome!*

The Working

HIGH PRIESTESS: *Gifts have been a part of the Yuletide season for thousands of years. The ancient Greeks and Romans passed out gifts as they celebrated Saturnalia. Our Norse ancestors shared presents on the Winter Solstice, as we will tonight.*

Despite what our greater society would have you believe, gifts do not have to cost extraordinary amounts of money, or anything at all. Sometimes the greatest present one can give is a helping hand, a kind word, or some other gesture that comes from the heart. As this circle is a welcoming one, tonight we shall all share some small gifts with one another and, in our own individual way, spread joy as Befana would.

We want you to find someone here you don't know well or at all, and we want you to pay them a compliment. Say something nice to them, make their day, and make all here feel as if they are a part of our community. And it doesn't have to be just one person either. Spread as much joy as you can in the next few minutes, for all who walk the path of the Witch are worthy of compliments and praise!

Everyone is encouraged to step out of their comfort zone for a little bit and greet and compliment those around them. Those running the ritual should watch over the festivities and make sure no one is ignored or left out. Make everyone feel welcome, but respect people's space too. Sometimes too much attention can be a bad thing. You can also play some holiday music in the background so there's no dead air in the ritual space. It can be very unsettling if one voice is suddenly all anyone hears. Once you're satisfied that everyone has been complimented, get your attendees back into a circle shape.

HIGH PRIEST: *So much of this time of year dates back to the paganisms of times past. Our ancient ancestors decorated their homes with holly and evergreen branches, and an old Roman mosaic shows Dionysus celebrating the winter season with an entire tree! The thyrsus, or staff,* *of Dionysus was always adorned with a pine cone to represent the fertility of the god and the earth.*

Since the days of Rome, Dionysus has continued to be a part of the holiday season. His love of the unconventional could be seen in the era of misrule, and what is a holiday party if not a celebration of the joy and laughter given to us by Dionysus? In the nineteenth century, he could be seen as the Ghost of Christmas Present in Dickens's A Christmas Carol, *sharing food and wine while reminding those around him to care for others and watch over them.*

Tonight we are going to create a large cone of power and tap into three parts of our lives: the past, present, and future. We are going to charge the pine cones on this Yule tree with our energy and that of the holiday season. Our magick, the magick of Diana and Dionysus, and the magick of the Yuletide will become a part of these pine cones and we'll all take one home with us! Let these pine cones serve as a reminder of the energy we have created here together, and use that energy when you have need of it, at Yule or whenever it is needed!

Music starts to play. The first song should be mid-tempo, with the songs thereafter getting progressively faster.

HIGH PRIEST: *We need everyone to turn to the right. Your eyes should now be looking at the back of the person in front of you. Raise your right hand and direct it toward the Yule tree in the center of the room, and now step forward in time with the music. As you move, look at our Yule tree and think back on Yuletides past. Imagine yourself as a child opening presents or sitting on the knee of Santa Claus, or imagine yourself delighting in the newborn sun at your friend's Winter Solstice vigil.*

Think good and happy thoughts as we move. Think of cherished memories from this time of year. Imagine New Year's Eve parties or cities all decorated in lights! Whatever it is that has brought you joy in December, picture it in your mind's eye. Feel that energy move through you and out of your hand and into our tree and the pine cones on it. As the energy moves inside of you and our cone of power is raised, chant with me:

> *We charge thee with joy of Yuletides past.*
> *May this festive energy last!*

The moving and chanting continues until it crescendos. The ritual leader should shout over the chanters or otherwise indicate when they want the chant to end. I usually yell something like "One final push, last verse!" so everyone ends together. Let the music fade for a little bit, allowing everyone to catch their breath before starting it back up again for the second push. I usually pick a faster song to start with the second time around.

HIGH PRIESTESS: *We have now charged our circle with Yuletides past, but what about Yuletide present? Move about the circle once more and this time think of your Yuletide celebrations this year. What will you remember most in a year's time? Is there someone you've met tonight that you think you'll get to know better in the future? What are your plans at home for this holiday season? Did you get a bonus at work this year?*

Think about the vibrant energy currently in this room. Feel it around you, circling up and above us in a great cone of power. Reach out toward our Yule tree again, directing your energy at it and filling it with all the positive energy of this holiday season. As we move our energy toward our Yule tree, join me in this chant:

We celebrate Yule today.
With us may this feeling stay!

Just like before, encourage everyone to push their energy toward the Yule tree, building in intensity as the dance and the chant continue. When a crescendo is reached, indicate the end of this part of the ritual and have everyone really push their energy outward. Again, take the music down a bit and give everyone time to catch their breath before beginning the final part of the working.

HIGH PRIEST: *And now, one last time, think about all the Yules yet to come. Envision us being back here in this space next year celebrating on the longest night, or picture being at home with family and friends appreciating the sun's rebirth. As we move one last time around our circle, building our power and energy, think of the happy tomorrows we will have celebrating this holiday.*

Imagine Diana being beside you as you exchange gifts with loved ones or receiving the blessings of Dionysus as you celebrate Midwinter. Reach out to our tree! Reach out to our futures! Reach out to the Yuletide tomorrows and push those visions of joy and happiness into the pine cones, the gifts of Diana and Dionysus for us this night. Chant together:

> *Yuletide joy in the future see.*
> *Happiness to our green Yule tree!*

Lead everyone in one last push. When the energy is at its peak, everyone should release the energy within them out into the center of the circle toward the tree. With one last "So mote it be!" end the chant and stop the music.

HIGH PRIEST: *Now that our pine cones are charged with the magick of the holiday season, the gods, and those of us in this space, let us all spiral forward and take a gift from our Yule tree. Let us all hold hands and be led toward our tree by our High Priestess. Tonight when you get home, place the pine cone you receive here on your own tree or on your altar as a reminder of this night and all the Yules past, present, and yet to come. So mote it be!*

Once everyone is holding hands, the High Priestess should let go of the hand of the person on her left and walk toward the Yule tree, pulling the person on her right forward with her. She should lead a procession up to the Yule tree, letting everyone quickly grab a pine cone before reforming the circle. More music is appropriate here, but choose something a little quieter and less intense. Once everyone has a pine cone and the circle has completely reformed, move on to cakes and ale.

Cakes and Ale

HIGH PRIEST: *Even in the depths of winter, the Lord and Lady bless us.*

HIGH PRIESTESS: *For life's abundance continues in the cold and in the dark.*

The High Priestess and/or quarter callers pick up the ale to be distributed while the High Priest blesses it with the thyrsus.

HIGH PRIEST: *May our days and nights be merry and bright! In the name of the gods and goddesses of Yule, we bless this drink. May you never thirst!*

The High Priest and/or quarter callers pick up the cakes to be distributed while the High Priestess blesses them with the thyrsus.

HIGH PRIESTESS: *Let nothing you dismay, remember that the light was reborn on Midwinter's Day! The light that blesses and grows the grain! In the names of the goddesses and gods of Yule, we bless this food. May you never hunger!*

Cakes and ale are passed around. Since it's Yule, more merriment is welcome if appropriate.

Goodbyes to the Gods

HIGH PRIESTESS: *We thank the great Diana for her presence in our rite this night. We thank her for her many gifts and for our fellowship this night of Yule. May the gifts we have received tonight keep us happy and connected in the cold days ahead. Befana, Diana, Yule Witch, we thank you! Hail and farewell!*

HIGH PRIEST: *Dionysus, god of joy and the spirit of the Yuletide, we thank you for lending your energies to this rite. God of fertility and wine, stay with us in the Yuletide and throughout the year! We thank you for tonight, what has passed, and what is yet to come. Hail and farewell!*

Dismissal of the Quarters/Taking Down the Circle

NORTH QUARTER CALLER: *Spirits of the north, spirits of earth, thank you for joining us in these our rites. We thank you for your gift of the evergreen. May we keep its promise in our hearts in the days ahead. Hail and farewell!*

WEST QUARTER CALLER: *Spirits of the west, spirits of water, thank you for joining us in these our rites. In the days to come, may the snow and the rains fall, renewing our hearts and our lands. Hail and farewell!*

SOUTH QUARTER CALLER: *Spirits of the south, spirits of fire, thank you for joining us in these our rites. May the connections we have with others in this world keep us warm and content over the cold days ahead. Hail and farewell!*

EAST QUARTER CALLER: *Spirits of the east, spirits of air, thank you for joining us in these our rites. In the days to come, we shall look upon the sparkling lights everywhere in our world knowing that they represent the sun that rises anew upon Midwinter morn and grows stronger every day. Hail and farewell!*

Any quarter candles that are lit are blown out at the conclusion of each farewell. And now the circle caster steps forward, picks up the thyrsus, and takes down the circle, beginning in the east and moving counterclockwise.

CIRCLE CASTER: *I cast this circle as a place of joy, merriment, and mirth. It has served us well, and now we leave this place between the worlds, where Yules past, present, and future have met. We return to our waking world secure in the knowledge that we will carry our joy from this Yule forward. The circle is open but our fellowship never broken. So mote it be!*

HIGH PRIESTESS: *And now our rite is at an end. To you all, a joyous Yule, and merry meet, and merry part, and merry meet again!*

FIN

CHAPTER 10
YULE COVEN RITUAL
Cheers to You

This is the "fun" ritual, perfect for the coven that truly wants to celebrate the holiday season. It features something akin to traditional wassail, an English drink generally associated today with door-to-door carolers. Most wassail is made with a base of apple cider (nonalcoholic), but some recipes also call for wine. I use apple cider in my versions of this rite, but feel free to substitute something else if that doesn't work for you.

The major working of this ritual involves adding several different ingredients to the cider, with each ingredient representing an idea or a wish for the new year. Coveners should infuse the ingredients they add to the cider with their own personal energy. In my coven, we generally add rum or whisky while making our wassail, but make a second nonalcoholic batch too. I've included ten ingredients in this ritual, but more (or fewer) can be used. The only limit is your imagination.

I like to use ingredients that are readily available, so my list includes a lot of spices that are probably already sitting on your spice rack. In addition to traditional spices, our coven also uses dimes and clear quartz crystals. Since they sink to the bottom of the bowl, there's no chance that anyone is going to swallow one. I've listed some common correspondences associated with each ingredient, but my listings only scratch the surface. Many of us have our own personal ideas about magickal properties, so feel free to use your imagination.

The second act of the ritual involves "Christmas crackers," which can be picked up in many department stores. Christmas crackers aren't particularly old, dating back only to the nineteenth century, but they are fun and make a satisfying "pop" sure to frighten your cat. Christmas crackers always contain small toys and gifts, and when someone from the coven uses one of those toys in a certain way, we generally crown them the "Queen or King of Misrule." In this ritual, we do this when someone puts one of the paper crowns on top of their head (and nearly every Christmas cracker manufacturer includes crowns with their wares).

We have a fancy court jester hat we use to honor our Queen of Misrule. Tradition-ally, Kings of Misrule would instruct their "subjects" to do silly things, but since many people are uncomfortable ordering others around, we just make sure our Queens of Misrule take their cakes and ale first and then lead the passing out of our coven's Secret Santa presents. If misrule doesn't appeal to you, it can easily be dropped from the ritual. The wassail part is usually more than enough for everybody.

This ritual includes a "lighting of the temple" that welcomes the elemental energies of earth, air, fire, and water. I like this variation particularly at Yule because it takes the ritual space from darkness to light very quickly. The quarters are later welcomed in the more traditional manner after the circle is cast.

Ritual Roles

- High Priestess
- High Priest
- Circle caster
- Quarter callers

Materials Needed

- Altar tools and setup
- Two Crock-Pots or two large bowls capable of holding the wassail
- Coffee mugs (one for each covener)
- Two ladles for the wassail
- Rum or whisky (representing adventure, warmth, joy, and truth)
- Vanilla (representing calm, love, and soothing)
- Orange slices (representing joy, energy, and sunshine)
- Cloves (representing good health and protection)

- Cinnamon (to add spice to your love life, good luck, and new beginnings)
- Nutmeg (representing good luck and divination)
- Sugar (representing happiness, a full cupboard, and joy)
- Allspice (representing healing and overcoming adversity)
- Dimes (representing prosperity and deflecting negative energy)
- Clear quartz crystals (representing clarity, divination, and connection)[26]
- Christmas crackers (one for each covener)
- Bowls or cups for all the wassail ingredients
- Court jester hat for the Queen/King of Misrule

The Ritual: Cheers to You

All is dark in the ritual space, with no lights and no candles lit. The coven gathers quietly in a circle. The Crock-Pots full of cider are placed safely out of the way, with the ingredients to be added later sitting near them. In the darkness, the High Priestess approaches the altar and lights a candle in its center.

Opening, Cleansing, Statement of Intent

HIGH PRIESTESS: *We light this candle to represent the hope that resides within all of us on this night. Darkness envelops the land, but we know that in the darkness the light is once more reborn. Tonight we celebrate that light and the joy it brings to us in the Yuletide season. Hail the light! Hail the coven! Hail the Yule!*

The High Priestess picks up a small container of diluted cinnamon oil and anoints each covener on the forehead with it, drawing an invoking pentagram as she does so.[27]

HIGH PRIESTESS (TO EACH COVENER): *With this oil, I anoint and welcome you into our ritual space. Blessed be!*

---

26. It's tempting to throw all sorts of stones into your wassail, but many of them can be poisonous! Clear quartz is safe, which is why I use it here.

27. Cinnamon oil is very strong, and it's easy to use too much. Try using one drop of cinnamon essential oil to two or more cups of a carrier oil, such as olive, almond, jojoba, or sesame oil. Never rub or massage cinnamon oil directly on skin unless it's diluted with a carrier oil. Cinnamon oil doesn't mix with water.

The High Priest lights a stick of evergreen or pine incense from the center candle and cleanses each covener with its smoke.

HIGH PRIEST (TO EACH COVENER): *With this purifying smoke, I cleanse and welcome you into our circle. Blessed be!*

HIGH PRIESTESS: *May love and joy be present with us tonight in our sacred space, for upon this longest night we celebrate Yule and the bonds we have formed as a coven. Let us now invoke the powers of the elements and cast our circle. So mote it be!*

Lighting the Temple, Circle Casting, Calling the Quarters

EAST QUARTER CALLER: *May the element of air bring to us the light of inspiration. So mote it be!*

The east candle is lit.

SOUTH QUARTER CALLER: *May the element of fire bring to us the light of life. So mote it be!*

The south candle is lit.

WEST QUARTER CALLER: *May the element of water bring to us the light of love. So mote it be!*

The west candle is lit.

NORTH QUARTER CALLER: *May the element of earth bring to us the light of chosen family. So mote it be!*

The north candle is lit. The circle caster picks up a sword or athame and casts the circle, beginning and ending in the east.

CIRCLE CASTER: *I cast this circle to be a place of joy, happiness, and truth. May it shine like a beacon and cast the darkness of this night away, for within the circle there is hope and light for all who are the children of the Lord and Lady. In their names do I bless and consecrate this circle. So mote it be!*

HIGH PRIEST: *We shall now summon the spirits of the quarters to guard and bless this circle.*

EAST QUARTER CALLER: *We call to the spirits of the east, spirits of air, to bless and watch over our circle as we celebrate on this Midwinter night. Hail and welcome!*

SOUTH QUARTER CALLER: *We call to the spirits of the south, spirits of fire, to bless and watch over our circle as we celebrate this Midwinter night. Hail and welcome!*

WEST QUARTER CALLER: *We call to the spirits of the west, spirits of water, to bless and watch over our circle as we celebrate this Midwinter night. Hail and welcome!*

NORTH QUARTER CALLER: *We call to the spirits of the north, spirits of earth, to bless and watch over our circle as we celebrate this Midwinter night. Hail and welcome!*

Calls to the God and the Goddess

HIGH PRIEST: *We call to the Great God this sacred night of the winter solstice. We call to Jack in the Green, he who runs across snow-laden forests, protecting the life within so that it may awaken in the spring. We call to the Lord of the Underworld, caretaker of the land of death, whose hand has touched much of this world at this bleak time of year. We call to the Sun, he who is reborn this night, he who gives us light and life. We welcome the Great God in all of his forms and with all of his faces this blessed night. Welcome and blessed be!*

The High Priest lights the God candle if applicable.

HIGH PRIESTESS: *We call to the Great Goddess this sacred night of the winter solstice. We call to the Crone, she whose wisdom in the face of difficulty keeps us here and in good health. We call to the Lady of the Moon, she who casts her spell across the snow-filled plains, her reflection glistening like silver and melting our hearts with its beauty. We call to the Great Mother, who magickally brings forth life in this time of death. We welcome the Great Goddess in all her forms and in her many roles this blessed night. Welcome and blessed be!*

The High Priestess lights the Goddess candle if applicable.

The Working

HIGH PRIEST: *For thousands of years, people have been celebrating on or near the winter solstice. Generally, those rites have been joyous, full of laughter, merriment, and mirth. People ate and drank, welcomed the returning sun, prepared for the coming year, and toasted to their good health. Tonight we shall do as our ancestors did and celebrate a most joyous Yule!*

HIGH PRIESTESS: *Wassail has been a part of Midwinter celebrations for hundreds of years now. People drank Yuletide wassail, generally made of apples, to ensure an abundant harvest in the coming year. Right now our wassail lacks any extra ingredients, but as Witches we shall brew our wassail and infuse our drink with powers and energies to ensure a happy new year!*

HIGH PRIEST: *Here near our bowls of wassail are several ingredients: dimes, crystals, orange slices, nutmeg, cinnamon sticks, allspice, vanilla, sugar, cloves, and rum. Pick the ingredient you want to add to our wassail and infuse it with your energy before adding its power to our drink. When we are done, we shall toast and drink in the wealth, health, and whatever else has been added to our brew!*

Each covener goes forward and puts something into the wassail, making sure no alcohol goes into the nonalcoholic wassail bowl! Coveners are free to say whatever they want, of course, but I've included some examples below. Each person can go once or multiple times, depending on what the coven wants to do. People are also free to add the same ingredient twice. The rum is always very popular in our circle.

COVENER 1: *To our drink I add this rum. May it keep us warm in the cold nights to come.*

COVENER 2: *In our wassail I place these dimes, as I wish you all a prosperous new year with no money worries. So mote it be!*

COVENER 3: *Wishing you all joy and the energy to do all of the things you wish as the sun grows in the sky. So mote it be!*

COVENER 4: *I add this crystal to our Witch's brew. May it bring us all clarity in the coming days, weeks, and months. Blessed be!*

COVENER 5: *May this vanilla bring all of you the sweetness of love and passion during these winter months. So mote it be!*

COVENER 6: *To our wassail I add this allspice. May all of your dreams for the coming year manifest in your life. Blessed be!*

COVENER 7: *It is my wish that the cupboards and pantry of you, my chosen family, always remain full and plentiful with many good things to eat! For that I add this sugar to our drink. So mote it be!*

COVENER 8: *A happy and healthy new year to you all, which is why I add these cloves. To our good health!*

COVENER 9: *With this cinnamon stick I bring to all of you the spice of life! May it be passionate and fiery. So mote it be!*

COVENER 10: *To you all, I give good luck with this nutmeg. So mote it be!*

Once everyone has added their ingredients, they all should grab a coffee mug and pour themselves a glass of warm wassail and then reform the circle.

HIGH PRIEST: *And now is the time we toast. To good health, wealth, and all our dearest desires manifesting in the coming year! Blessed be!*

Everyone in the coven can now lead a toast to whatever it is they wish to celebrate. Be sure to clink your mugs, too. That's the best part of the toast and a great way to share energy. When the toasting is done, the mugs should be safely put away.

HIGH PRIESTESS: *For thousands of years, people have been exchanging gifts at this time of year. So tonight we give all of you the gift of this cracker. May its joyous noise bring happiness to your heart, and may the gift inside amuse and delight you. Though our ancient pagan ancestors did not have such devices, many of our ancestors did. As they celebrated this time of year, so do we.*

Christmas crackers are passed out clockwise, and once everyone has received one, they are "cracked." The first person to put a paper crown on their head is crowned the Queen of Misrule and is then allowed to "rule" over the rest of the rite. If no one puts a crown on their head (which is unlikely; people always put them on!), simply inquire as to what everyone in the circle received. You can then ask someone to "try on" the crown. In our coven, the moment someone becomes the embodiment of misrule, my High Priestess wife and I will often drop to our knees and begin yelling, "Queen (or King) of Misrule! Queen of Misrule!"

Once the Queen of Misrule has been chosen, they can lead the coven in games or carols or simply instruct everyone that it's time to end the ritual. As mentioned earlier, we then let the King of Misrule "rule" over the coven during our post-ritual fellowship.

Cakes and Ale

The High Priestess and High Priest stand before the wassail bowl with the coven's ritual chalice or cup. The High Priestess holds the cup while the High Priest ladles some wassail into it.

HIGH PRIESTESS: *The bounty of the earth keeps us warm and fed even on the year's darkest night.*

HIGH PRIEST: *We thank the earth and the gods for their gifts, gifts that are freely shared with all who walk in the Old Ways.*

The High Priest pours the wassail into the ritual chalice, then the High Priestess holds the cup aloft.

HIGH PRIESTESS: *Lord and Lady, please bless this drink. May it keep us happy, healthy, and warm in the days ahead. Blessed be!*

The High Priest picks up a tray of ritual cakes/bread/cookies and holds it aloft.

HIGH PRIEST: *Lady and Lord, please bless these cakes. May our bellies and our hearts be full this Yuletide. Blessed be!*

Cakes and ale are passed around to everyone in the coven, with some of each reserved for the libation bowl.

Goodbyes to the Gods

HIGH PRIEST: *We thank the Great God for being with us tonight in our circle. As we look up in the sky and see the days grow longer in the coming weeks and months, we will think of you and say thanks for your presence in our lives. Hail and farewell!*

HIGH PRIESTESS: *We thank the Great Lady for being with us tonight in our circle. Each time the gift of new life visits us this winter season, we will think of you and your continual presence in our lives and thank you for your love. Hail and farewell!*

Dismissal of the Quarters/Taking Down the Circle

NORTH QUARTER CALLER: *We thank the spirits of the north, spirits of earth, who have watched over our circle and blessed our rites with their presence. Hail and farewell!*

WEST QUARTER CALLER: *We thank the spirits of the west, spirits of water, who have watched over our circle and blessed our rites with their presence. Hail and farewell!*

SOUTH QUARTER CALLER: *We thank the spirits of the south, spirits of fire, who have watched over our circle and blessed our rites with their presence. Hail and farewell!*

East Quarter Caller: *We thank the spirits of the east, spirits of air, who have watched over our circle and blessed our rites with their presence. Hail and farewell!*

The quarter candles can be blown out with each dismissal at the discretion of the coven. Once the quarters have been dismissed, the circle caster steps forward and takes down the circle with the sword or athame, beginning in the east and moving widdershins.

Circle Caster: *I cast this circle as a place of joy, happiness, and truth. It has served us well, but now the time has come to take down our sacred space and return to the world of mortals. In the names of the Lord and the Lady, I release this circle but ask that the joy raised within remain in our hearts to keep us warm in the dark and cold days ahead. The circle is open but never broken. So mote it be!*

All in the circle join hands.

High Priestess: *With our rite now at an end, I say to you…Blessed Yule! And merry meet, and merry part, and merry meet again!*

FIN

CHAPTER 11

YULE SOLITARY RITUAL

Grow with the Light

For me, Yule rituals with the coven and my extended family of Pagan friends have always been boisterous and full of good cheer. But when doing ritual alone, Yule becomes more introspective and often focused on my personal deficiencies as a Witch.

With the end of December, the rebirth of the sun, and all the talk of New Year's resolutions, I find the Winter Solstice a good time to work on personal growth. The waxing half of the year has traditionally been a time for manifesting change and bringing new things into our lives. This ritual attempts to harness the growing powers of the Goddess and God so that we can progress as Witches.

Because this ritual deals with the winds of change in our lives, the quarter calls are to the four winds. In this ritual, I was looking for them to blow away the things that have limited me and my potential in Witchcraft. When I call to them, I envision them entering my ritual space as a slight breeze, bringing their different energies with them. Even the cold north wind brings cleansing energy. There's good to most everything if you know where to look.

Tools Needed

- Regular altar tools
- Two good candles, one each for the Goddess and the God
- A notecard or piece of sturdy paper
- Pen/pencil

The Ritual: Grow with the Light

Cleansing, Statement of Intent

If you happen to live in an area where it snows or you get winter rains, collect some before your ritual, placing it in a bowl or cup on your altar. If snow or rain is not possible, tap or spring water is also acceptable. Take your athame and dip it in the water and say:

> *As the winter rain / snow cleanses the land and prepares it for what is to come, I too use this water to cleanse myself and prepare for the rite to come. I cleanse and consecrate this water for use this night in my Yule ritual. So mote it be!*

Standing before your altar, dip your dominant hand in the water and use it to anoint yourself, starting at your feet and moving up to your head. After saying each of the following lines, lightly touch that part of your body with the water.

> *Blessed be my feet, which have brought me before the gods.* (touch feet)
> *Blessed be my knees, with which I kneel before the glory of the earth.* (touch knees)
> *Blessed be my sex, source of passion and longing.* (touch sex)
> *Blessed be my heart, font of power and strength.* (touch heart)
> *Blessed be my lips, which shall speak only truth in the circle.* (touch lips)
>
> *On this night of Yule, I celebrate the rebirth of the sun, the light in the darkness, and the promise of the Lord and Lady that all will be reborn. So mote it be!*

Casting the Circle, Calling the Quarters

Using your athame or sword, slowly cast the circle clockwise, saying:

> *In the names of the Lord and the Lady, I cast this circle. May it serve as a boundary and a protection from all that might wish me harm, and as a place of warmth, light, and truth. So mote it be!*

Starting in the east, call upon the four winds to bless and protect your rite. If you like, you can light a candle to represent each of the winds.

> *I call upon the winds of the east that turn the seasons and bring us rain. Lend your power and energies to my rite this night! Hail and welcome!*

I call upon the winds of the south that warm the land and bless the earth.
Lend your power and energies to my rite this night! Hail and welcome!

I call upon the winds of the west that bring us ripe fruit and the promise of new tomorrows.
Lend your power and energies to my rite this night! Hail and welcome!

I call upon the cold winds of the north that bring us the winter's quiet breath and cleanse the
land. Lend your power and energies to my rite this night! Hail and welcome!

Calling the Lord of the Sun and the Mistress of the Moon

Now say:

> *This night of the Winter Solstice, I call to the Great God, he who is reborn as the Lord of the*
> *Sun! Where once your power in the sky waned, now you grow in power and in strength.*
> *Though the nights ahead will still be long, you are a bringer of hope, and with it the promise*
> *that all things in this world eventually begin anew. What once was shall be again. Blessed be!*

Light the God candle on your altar. As you do so, imagine it as the Lord of the Sun, who grows from humble beginnings to the powerful sun of the summer. Feel him in the power of the candle. As the light of the God candle fills your ritual space, think of it as *his* light bringing you illumination and clarity.

> *This night of the Winter Solstice, I call to my beautiful Lady, she who is the Mistress of the*
> *Moon and the source of all beauty and joy. Even in the depths of winter, I know that you*
> *watch over me and those I love, filling us all with courage and strength, even in the darkness.*
> *Shine your light upon my rite this night and lend your energy and blessings to my work!*
> *Through you all begins anew. Blessed be!*

Light the Goddess candle on your altar. As you do so, reach out to her in your ritual space and feel her power and her presence. Feel her love, which exists even when the world is dark and cold. Feel her energies of growth and abundance, energies that exist even in the winter. Imagine her sharing those energies with you on your journey as a Witch.

The Working

The Winter Solstice is a wonderful time to begin new projects. As the sun's waxing energy slowly fills our skies from Yule until the Summer Solstice, it can also help us fill our cauldrons as Witches. Think of what it is that you most want to work on as a Witch over the next six months. Are you looking to deepen your relationship with the earth? With magick? With the gods? Perhaps you need to spend more time on your Witch work. In that case, imagine a future where you spend a few minutes each day communing with the powers and energies that give your life purpose as a Witch.

Once you've contemplated whatever it is that you want to grow over the next six months, write it down (or draw it) on a notecard or piece of paper. Be as specific as you can, using words or pictures, whatever feels most specific to you. As you put your intentions down on paper, imagine them moving through you and into your pen, then out onto the paper. Clearly visualize what it is you want. Imagine your relationships growing stronger, your practice becoming more focused, your magick growing stronger, etc. Also picture yourself taking whatever actions are necessary to make those things so.

After you've written down your intentions, take the God candle from your altar and drip the wax onto your paper in the shape of an invoking pentagram. As you drip the wax, say:

Great Lord, as your power grows in the sky, may my power grow in this world. Bless the undertaking I've begun this night. As you are reborn on this night, let my desires come into this world and manifest. So mote it be!

After setting down the God candle, pick up the Goddess candle and draw one more invoking pentagram while saying:

Lovely Lady, powerful Goddess who watches over us all, lend your energy and power to my endeavor. Share your magick and might so that I might grow as a Witch and accomplish all of my goals. May I be all you want me to be and all I know I can be. So mote it be!

As you're drawing your invoking pentagrams with the wax, imagine the Lord and Lady helping you with your task. Reach out into the darkness of your ritual space and feel them around you. As you pour the wax, see yourself doing the things that will help you accomplish your goal, and see yourself doing just a little bit more each day, mimicking the growth of the sun in the sky.

Cakes and Ale

Pick up your athame with your dominant hand, and a cup or chalice of wine (or other beverage) with your other hand. Touch the athame to the lip of the cup and say:

May this drink ever serve as a reminder that the gifts of the Lord and Lady are always with me, even in the depths and darkness of winter. Blessed be!

Drink deeply from the cup, pausing to reflect on whatever it is that is good in your life. If it's really good, raise the glass up to the gods, toasting them and then sharing a bit of your drink with them by pouring it into the libation bowl.

Next take your athame and bless the cakes, cookies, or bread that you've brought to your rite, touching each cake with your knife while saying:

Though the earth lies fallow, the gods are always with us. Lady and Lord, bless these cakes that I might have joy and prosperity in the longer days ahead. Blessed be!

Consume one or two cakes, enjoying the quiet and darkness. During this part, I sometimes reach out to feel if any of my deceased kin have joined me in my rite. Relatives always like to visit during the holidays. Be sure to put a cake in your libation bowl to share with the gods later on.

Goodbyes to the Gods

Now say:

Great Lady, Mistress of the Moon and source of all joy and abundance, thank you for being with me in my rite tonight. Continue to walk with me so that I might manifest my desires and grow as a Witch. Blessed be!

Now blow out the Goddess candle upon the altar. After this I usually blow her a kiss, placing my middle and index fingers upon my lips and then kissing them and raising my hand upward.

Lord of the Sun, giving God, he who is reborn upon the Winter Solstice, thank you for being with me in my rite tonight. As you grow in the sky, I pledge to also grow as a person and a Witch. Blessed be!

Blow out the God candle upon the altar. Notice the growing darkness around you and say:

> Though short in time, the light kindled this night will only grow longer and stronger! So mote it be!

Dismissal of the Quarters / Taking Down the Circle

Starting in the east and moving deosil, dismiss the four winds standing guard in your circle.

> I called upon the winds of the east to be a part of my rite and I now release them from that service. Thank you for blessing my work and standing guard in the darkness. Hail and farewell!

> I called upon the winds of the south to be a part of my rite and I now release them from that service. Thank you for blessing my work and standing guard in the darkness. Hail and farewell!

> I called upon the winds of the west to be a part of my rite and I now release them from that service. Thank you for blessing my work and standing guard in the darkness. Hail and farewell!

> I called upon the winds of the north to be a part of my rite and I now release them from that service. Thank you for blessing my work and standing guard in the darkness. Hail and farewell!

Blow out each quarter candle as the winds are dismissed if applicable/desired. Then pick up your athame or sword and take down the circle, beginning in the east and moving deosil.

> On the longest night, this circle has brought me closer to the Lady, the Lord, and the power of the returning sun. Now I release the power gathered up here and take down this boundary between the world of mortals and that of the Mighty Ones. All in this room shall be as it once was, but I shall be forever changed by the power of the gods! So mote it be!

As the ritual concludes, feel free to thank the Lord and Lady once more or to let out a hearty "Hail the Craft!" Be sure to put the notecard or piece of paper with the invoking pentagrams of wax in a prominent place on your altar as a daily reminder to grow as a Witch. When you look up at the sun over the next six months, think of your pledge and feel it growing within you as the sun grows in the sky. Feel free to burn the card you created this night when you feel as if all the magick has manifested.

FIN

CHAPTER 12

IMBOLC

Brigid's Night

Name of Sabbat: Imbolc (alternative spellings include Imbolg and Óimelc; also sometimes called Candlemas, Brigid, and February Eve)

Date: February 1 (also sometimes celebrated on January 31 or February 2)

Pronunciation: "Im-BOWLK" (most Americans), "Im-MULG" (silent *b*, Ireland)

We know very little about the ancient Irish-Celtic celebration of Imbolc, but it was most certainly a real holiday, and the goddess Brigid undoubtedly played a major role in its celebration. The word *Imbolc* has been linked to two different activities, the first of which is milking, which is not surprising given the time of year. In Ireland, early February is when sheep would have been giving birth and, by extension, lactating. Imbolc has also been linked to purification, a popular activity in the early spring. In Ireland, Imbolc was also seen as the start of spring, though in many other places it was the height of winter.

Brigid was most certainly a part of early Imbolc celebrations, but just how much of a focal point is hard to say with any certainty. Much of that has to do with how little we know about the Celtic goddess of that name. She might have been a near-universal deity among European Celts, and there are others who believe her worship was confined mostly to the area around modern Kildare in Ireland. It's also possible that there were several different Brigids worshiped throughout the British Isles. Those different Brigids might all be connected in some way, or each of them might be completely separate deities simply sharing the same name.

What can't be questioned is that it was Brigid the goddess, and not a person of that name, who became a Catholic saint. There are no historical records pointing to a real-life Brigid, and her myths are so garbled that if there was a person behind the saint, that person had a life span of hundreds of years. In mythology, Saint Brigid was the wet nurse of the infant Jesus and is said to have died in the year 525 CE.[28] Catholic mythology has an abundance of Saint Brigids, most of whom get lumped together by people who honor the saint today.

Many of the things we associate with the goddess Brigid today come from Christian celebrations of the saint (Brigit) who shares her name. The tradition of building a bed for Brigid (usually called Brigid's bed) first shows up in Ireland's Christian era, though it's a custom that is part of many Witch rituals today and could theoretically go back to pagan antiquity. Even Brigid's cross, a popular symbol for the goddess, dates back only to the seventeenth century in the historical record, but since the saint evolved directly from the goddess, I think it's fair for us to use it.

Imbolc is associated with three different dates, and it's up to each individual Witch to decide which one to use (or you could make it a three-day celebration!). The Celts began the next calendar day at sundown instead of midnight, meaning that Imbolc probably originally ran from the night of January 31 to sunset the following day. For this reason, the Catholic Church made February 1 the feast day of Saint Brigid. In his book *The White Goddess*, poet Robert Graves (he's someone we'll see a lot of in this book) gives the date of Imbolc as February 2, which is the date I most associate with the holiday.

February 2 is a popular date for holidays too. It's the date of Groundhog Day in the United States and Canada. As with many old traditions, the origins of Groundhog Day are rather obscure but come to us from the Pennsylvania Dutch (the Amish are one example of the Pennsylvania Dutch, for those unfamiliar with the term), who most likely used a badger as their weather prognosticator in Germany and then switched to the groundhog upon arriving in America. It is said that winter will last six more weeks if a groundhog sees its shadow on February 2, and that an early spring will arrive if it doesn't. In other words, cloudy or stormy weather on Groundhog Day is usually hoped for.

Groundhog Day is often associated with the Christian holiday of Candlemas, and throughout Europe, February 2 was seen as a bellwether of whether or not winter would

---

28. Date from Catholic Online, "St. Brigid of Ireland," https://www.catholic.org/saints/saint.php?saint_id=453.

be ending sooner rather than later. A Scottish poem sums up the day's powers of prognostication:

> If Candlemass Day be dry and fair,
> The half o'winter's to come and mair [more];
> If Candlemass Day be wet and foul,
> The half of winter's gane [gone] at Yule. [29]

Though Candlemas sort of shares a date with Imbolc (depending on what day you celebrate it), and many early Witches used the name *Candlemas* in place of *Imbolc*, the two holidays are not related. Candlemas began in Greece in the fourth century CE (far away from Ireland) and was later adopted by the Catholic Church in the seventh century. Candlemas celebrations in the Christian tradition often include purification rituals and candle blessings.

Candlemas, though not related to Imbolc, is probably still related to ancient paganism in some way. The word *February* comes to us from the Latin word *februa*, which signified purification, and there was even a holiday with that name in ancient Rome in the middle of the month of *Februarius*. February has long been associated with both spring cleaning and candles, two popular ritual activities at Imbolc.

Ways to Celebrate Imbolc

Just how a person celebrates Imbolc will most likely depend on where they live. For many, Imbolc might truly be the start of spring. In Northern California, where I currently live, flowers bloom, trees bud, and the grass turns a lovely shade of green every February. It's not always super warm here, but there are usually several signs of what most people would call spring. When I lived in Michigan, early February was the height of winter, and searching for signs of spring with a foot of snow on the ground was largely a fool's errand (though we tricked ourselves into doing this for years).

The Wheel of the Year is not about what the Celts did two thousand years ago; it's about where we are as individuals and groups. If it's winter outside, use some melted snow in your Imbolc rites and decorate your altar with bare branches and other signs of

---

29. From Snopes, "What Are the Origins of Groundhog Day?," https://www.snopes.com/news/2017/02/02/where-groundhog-day-from/.

the season. If you live where it's green in February, decorate with flowers and other seasonally appropriate items. Instead of dreading winter, celebrate it!

For many of us, Imbolc is about the return of the light. It's a ritual theme this sabbat shares with Yule, but unlike in December, the increase in daylight is now easily visible. The sun sets a whole forty minutes later in February than it does in December. That may not seem like a lot of time, but it's most certainly noticeable. Because of the return of the light, candles are a frequent sight at many Imbolc rituals. Candles can be used magickally to drive away any darkness in our own lives, and they make great reminders of the sun's growing power.

Taking a page from Candlemas, Imbolc is a great time to renew ritual items. Over the course of a year, many of us go through multiple candles or we might break a chalice or other tool. Imbolc is a great time to dedicate new tools and retire old ones. My coven does an every-other-year ritual for this, which is included in this book in chapter 14.

Winter is also a time when the earth renews itself. Underground, all sorts of things are happening that we can't see that are preparing the way for spring. February is also the time of year when many animals give birth to their young, renewing their herds. The very word *Imbolc*, with its ancient links to animals milking, has honored this part of nature's cycle most likely from the earliest beginnings of the holiday.

Even though most rituals include some sort of purification rite, sometimes it's beneficial to go a bit deeper than incense and salted water. At Imbolc, my wife likes to get out her athame and cut away any negativity or bad energy attached to those in her chosen family. A little extra cleansing and purification of your house or ritual space is another great idea to build an Imbolc ritual around. Get your broom out and sweep away any bitterness, resentment, or jealousy that might be plaguing your sacred space.

Most sabbats aren't generally reserved for specific deities, with two exceptions: Lughnasadh (which contains the name of the god Lugh) and Imbolc (which is associated with Brigid). As we have seen, Brigid is such an important part of Imbolc that some Witches use her name for the sabbat! Devotions, thanks, and any other rite in honor of Brigid that you can think of are appropriate at Imbolc. For a lot of Witches, Brigid is the very reason for the season.

CHAPTER 13

IMBOLC CIRCLE RITUAL
The Rite of the Three Brigids

The goddess Brigid (also spelled Brigit, Bride, and Brig) is an Irish-Celtic goddess and later became a Christian saint. She has been linked to other goddesses over the centuries, most notably Britannia and Brigantia, and she is also honored in New Orleans Voodoo and Haitian Voudun as the loa Maman Brigitte. This ritual plays into her many roles throughout history and includes drawing downs of the Irish-Celtic Brigid but also the Christian Saint Brigid and the goddess Brigantia. Had I known a Voodoo priestess in my area when I wrote this ritual, it would have ended up being called the Rite of the *Four* Brigids.

This main focus of this ritual is Brigid, and after she is drawn down into her three Priestesses, everyone participating in the ritual will have a chance to ask her a question and receive a gift from her. Because Brigid is often associated with wells, we had her give coins to everyone who asked her a question and set up something resembling a well to receive those coins. This ritual also celebrates the return of the light and allows participants to share that light on one of three different altars. The three altars are each dedicated to one aspect of Brigid and represent community (Brigid), healing (Saint Brigid), and justice (Brigantia).

The setup for this ritual requires a great deal of floor space, three comfortable chairs for the Priestesses drawing down the Brigids, four altar spaces, a large bowl (or better yet, something resembling a well), and candles and coins for everyone in attendance (we used electric tealights and pennies from Ireland, respectively). We placed all of our electric candles in an adjoining room next to our main ritual space and kept that room dark (minus the candlelight) to represent the lack of sunlight in the winter. If an extra room isn't possible, simply putting all the candles in a corner of the room will work just fine. Because we had access to a small circular stage, we placed the three Brigids and their chairs on top of that, about a foot up off the floor. Because of all the extras required for this ritual, this is probably not the easiest rite to put together, but it's worth the effort.

This ritual also has a lot of roles. In addition to the three Brigids, each Brigid Priestess should have an attendant to watch over them during the ritual and help with the drawing down the moon portion of the rite. There's also a narrator/master of ceremonies, a circle caster, four quarter callers, and ideally some sort of "wrangler" to manage the line of ritual attendees wishing to talk to Brigid.

The group I put this ritual together for has a tradition of having everyone in attendance say their name out loud at the start of the ritual (one at a time, clockwise in the ritual circle). I've always thought this was a pretty cool little ritual addition, so I've kept it here. In addition, since Saint Brigid is a part of the rite, instead of the usual quarter calls to elemental energies or watchtowers, I've added calls to the four angels traditionally associated with the four cardinal points of the compass. I address the angels individually as "they" during their invocations because I'm not quite sure if angels identify with a certain gender.

I suggest playing some sort of music during the middle part of the ritual to avoid any awkward silences or conversations between ritual goers and Brigid. When my group did this ritual, we had each of the three Brigids choose a color representative of the goddess they were drawing down, with their attendants dressing to match. This is obviously not necessary, but it looks impressive. In addition, each Brigid needs a veil, even better if it's color coordinated with each High Priestess's outfit. Instead of cleansing with incense (fire and air), we cleansed with sound using two small cymbals. This was done mostly because we were in a ritual space that didn't allow fire or incense, but also because it's one of my favorite uncommon ways to do a cleansing.

Ritual Roles

- Narrator/master of ceremonies
- Brigid (the goddess)/High Priestess
- Brigid (the goddess) attendant

- Saint Brigid/High Priestess
- Saint Brigid attendant
- Brigantia/High Priestess
- Brigantia attendant
- Four quarter callers
- Circle caster
- Line attendant

Materials Needed

- Standard altar setup
- Altar representing community (decorated accordingly)
- Altar representing healing (decorated accordingly)
- Altar representing justice (decorated accordingly)
- Two bowls of water
- A well or large bowl
- Three chairs for the three Brigid High Priestesses
- A veil for each High Priestess
- Pair of cymbals or a bell
- A coin for each participant
- A candle for each participant
- Cakes and ale

Hashtags

- #Deity, #WheeloftheYear, #Community, #NaturalWorld, #Angels

The Ritual: The Rite of the Three Brigids

Ideally the three High Priestesses embodying Brigid should be seated in throne-like chairs that sit above the floor. (When I first led this ritual, the chairs of our Brigids were placed on a small stage six inches off the ground.) If that's not possible, their chairs could all be placed on a special rug or carpet in the ritual space. What's important is designating that these three individuals are somehow different from everyone else at the ritual. The three Brigids should each have a veil over their face, with each veil a different color.

A small room off from the temple space is filled with small electric candles but is otherwise devoid of light. The candles will probably have to be set on some tables or pedestals. This room is kept hidden from all the participants until later in the ritual.

At one end of the hall sits a wishing well, and at the other end, three altars, each one dedicated to a different thing: community, healing, and justice. The Brigid attendants stand near their respective goddesses, with the narrator, quarter callers, and circle caster in the center of the ritual space (figure 5).

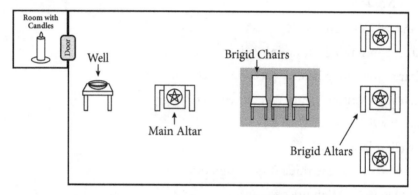

Figure 5. Imbolc Circle Ritual Setup

Saying of the Names/Statement of Intent

NARRATOR: *Tonight we gather to celebrate the sabbat of Imbolc. Imbolc represents the returning light and the opening of the earth, that we might transition from winter into spring. But it's also a holiday and a date sacred to the goddess who has always been with us, Brigid-deity, saint, protector, healer, and patroness of sovereignty. On her night, we now say our names so that she might know us as her own when the time is right.*

Going deosil, everyone says their name out loud in the ritual space.

Cleansing of the Participants

NARRATOR: *Before we can enter sacred space and commune with our Lady, we must all be cleansed and readied by the power of the four elements.*

The narrator puts two bowls of water upon the altar pentacle and then puts their athame into each bowl. Any type of water will work here, but melted snow is great if it's available, as is rain or spring water.

NARRATOR: *I cleanse thee, O water, and cast out from thee all that might hinder our work. In the names of the Lord and the Lady, so mote it be!*

The narrator takes a dish of salt and places it upon the pentacle, then places their athame into the dish.

NARRATOR: *I cleanse thee, O salt, and cast out from thee all that might hinder our work. In the names of the Lord and the Lady, so mote it be!*

The narrator takes their athame and removes three measures of "earth" (salt), placing it in the water. The salted water is then presented to the west and north quarter callers, who sprinkle it upon the participants, each one cleansing half the circle. As they sprinkle the participants, the narrator places a pair of cymbals (or a bell) upon the altar.

NARRATOR: *I cleanse these cymbals and cast out from them all that might hinder our work. In the names of the Lord and the Lady, so mote it be! And now let the powers of air and fire wash over you, and may the purity of this tone cleanse and prepare you for the journey to come. So mote it be!*

The cymbals are handed to the south quarter caller, who rings them at each of the four cardinal points. When done, they are placed back on the altar.

Casting the Circle

To cast the circle, start in the east and proceed deosil three times using a sword or an athame.

CIRCLE CASTER: *I conjure, cast, and create this circle as a sacred space to be filled with love and the magick and wonder of the Lady Brigid. This circle is a vessel to a place between the worlds, where mortal and goddess might dwell among one another. It shall contain the magick we raise within it and share the light we will manifest. Wherefore do I bless thee and consecrate this circle in the names of the Lord and the Lady. The circle is cast. So mote it be!*

Calling the Watchtowers/Angels

EAST QUARTER CALLER: *We call to the archangel Raphael, who dwells in the east and controls the winds that change the seasons. Join us in our rites this night and lend your blessings to our work. Hail and welcome!*

SOUTH QUARTER CALLER: *We call to the archangel Michael, who dwells in the south and controls the power of fire and that of the growing sun. Join us in our rites this night and lend your blessings to our work. Hail and welcome!*

WEST QUARTER CALLER: *We call to the archangel Gabriel, who dwells in the west and controls the waters of river and sea. Join us in our rites this night and lend your blessings to our work. Hail and welcome!*

NORTH QUARTER CALLER: *We call to the archangel Uriel, who dwells in the north and controls the waking earth beneath our feet. Join us in our rites this night and lend your blessings to our work. Hail and welcome!*

After each angel is invoked, that direction's quarter caller should draw an invoking pentagram in the air in front of them with their athame, wand, or finger.

Call to the God and to the Three Brigids [30]

NARRATOR: *This night of Imbolc, we call to the Great God. Lord of the Sun, Horned One of the wild places, join us in our circle! Let us feel and see your growing power. Stand with us tonight as the world's light is renewed. Help us to walk with the goddess as we celebrate the power and legacy of the great Brigid! Be with us as we work our will! Hail and welcome!*

Slight pause here before Brigid is welcomed to the rite.

NARRATOR: *Brigid is the goddess who never left her children. She was with the Celts in Great Britain and those upon the Emerald Isle of Ireland. She is a Pagan goddess, and her name means "exalted one"! But when the invaders came, she became a Christian saint so that she could remain with her people and hear their prayers, and she is also Maman Brigitte of the loa. Brigid*

---

30. By default, I usually call to both a goddess and a god at most of my rituals, but his presence is not particularly vital or necessary at this ritual. He can be left out of this rite if that makes more sense to those presenting the ritual.

can be found in the rites of Witches, the prayers of Catholics, and the dances of Voodoo, and on the lips of anyone who has ever invoked justice.

Imbolc has always been her sacred night. To the Celts, it was the start of spring and the return of the light. On Saint Brigid's Night, she visited those who loved her and left them gifts. She is a goddess who wants us to be happy and endeavors to bring her followers hope and joy.

Tonight we celebrate Imbolc and the Exalted Goddess! Soon you shall be able to visit with her, where she will give you a coin. That coin can be placed in her well, along with a wish spoken in her name.

Brigid also brings with her the returning light of Imbolc. Through the darkness, through that door, is her light and the light of this earth. Walk through it and back into this world and into your heart. That light can then be placed upon one of her three altars. Our Lady is a giving goddess, and as she gives to us, we can also give of ourselves. Our first altar is for the light you shall shine in our community. The second altar is dedicated to healing: to healing hearts, bodies, minds, and the earth. And finally the third altar, which carries the light of justice. Place your light there for those who are oppressed and need their voices heard.

And now we will call the Great Lady to join us in her many guises.

BRIGID (GODDESS) ATTENDANT: *Tonight we call to the goddess Brigid, goddess of the forge, healing, creativity, and serpents! O Exalted One, be with us in our circle tonight! Let your love and light shine down upon us so that we might know your mysteries and connect with those who have gone before us. Great warrior goddess Brigid, prepare us for the battles ahead that we all must face, both alone and together.*

O Exalted One, we thank thee for the gifts that will be bestowed upon us tonight. You are a giving goddess, and tonight we will receive your blessings in the form of a coin. As you want us to be happy, we will take that coin and place it in your well, making a wish in your name. Grant us our boon if possible, and let us feel your love all around us!

Brigid, Pagan goddess of the Celts of Ireland, be with us in this sacred space! Hail and welcome!

SAINT BRIGID ATTENDANT: *This night we call to Saint Brigid, she who would never forsake her children. When the New Religion forced its beliefs upon our ancestors, you stayed with them and then with us, transforming into something else so that you could remain among us unhindered.*

Your sacred fires were never snuffed out, even during those dark times. And now at Imbolc, you offer your light to us once more. The days remain short and the nights long, but the promise of light calls to us. This night we will venture into the darkness and reclaim your light, the light of truth and spring, and share it with those who need it most.

Great Brigid, walk with your children once more and be with us in this sacred space! Hail and welcome!

BRIGANTIA ATTENDANT: *And now we call to Brigid as Brigantia, goddess of justice and the righteous! Goddess of nations, we ask that you be with us tonight, to light our way in these dark times! Shine your truth upon us and the hearts of this nation that need it most! O High One, raise us up that we might do your work!*

We yearn to reach the lofty ideals you offer to those who would listen! Let us take your light and share it with those who need it most. May that light heal this nation, those hurting and those in need of healing. May your light rekindle the passion and desire that fuels our collective will!

Lady Liberty, be with us, and may those who ignore your call suffer the consequences! Shine your light in our sacred space! Hail and welcome!

Drawing Down Brigid(s)

The Brigid Priestesses leave their chairs and walk down from the raised platform/stage (or move off from the special carpet their chairs are sitting on) to stand near their attendants. Their attendants stand next to them and perform the following drawing down ceremony while it's read by the narrator. The attendants should kiss each body part of their Priestesses when indicated.

NARRATOR: *Blessed be thy feet, which have walked the sacred earth.* (The attendants all kiss their Priestess's feet.)

Blessed be thy knees, which kneel to tend the fields. (All kiss knees.)

Blessed be thy womb, from which all life grows. (All kiss womb.)

Blessed be thy heart, which tends to your children. (All kiss heart.)

The attendants remove the veils from the faces of the Brigid Priestesses.

Blessed be thy lips, which share truth and knowledge. (All kiss lips.)

Then the Brigid attendants assume the "adore" position, which is on their knees, with their head near the chest of their Brigid Priestess. They stay in this position until the end of the invocation. When the invocation is finished, the Brigids are led back to their chairs.

NARRATOR: *We invoke and call upon thee, O Exalted One, Great Brigid, she who has never left her children! Come to us so that we might understand your mysteries. Rise up and fill the bodies of your servants and Priestesses here. See through their eyes, speak with their lips, let us be close to you on this sacred night of Imbolc! From distant shores you have arrived to be here with us this night!*

> *Hail Brigid, fair from the Celtic shore.*
> *Allow us to pass through your door*
> *To the world of enchantment and magick fair,*
> *For it is you we adore with both grace and care.*
> *Come by leaf and bud and by branch and bough,*
> *Goddess of healing, magick, wells, and plow.*
> *Be with us in this most holy and sacred space,*
> *For it is you, fair Brigid, that we seek to embrace.*
> *Hail Brigid! Blessed be!*

There should be a brief pause here as the three Brigids are reseated.

NARRATOR: *Now go forth, all who have assembled. Find the light of Imbolc and share it with those who need it most! If you wish to speak to fair Brigid, gather here and form one line. When you speak to her, you may ask her a question, listen to her wisdom, receive her coin, and then visit her fountain. Discover the mysteries of the returning spring and our Lady Fair!*

At this point in the ritual, all the participants should be encouraged to participate in everything that's going on and explore all the space in the ritual room. They should visit the room set up with candles and then set one of those candles upon the altar of their choice, pledging to spread their light for that particular cause or idea. They should speak to the goddess Brigid, receive her gift, and then visit her well.

In order to avoid a long line forming around one particular aspect of Brigid, I think it's best to have everyone who wishes to speak with her form one line. At the front of that line should be the "Brigid wrangler," who sends people to the first available Brigid. You'll have some people who want to visit a particular aspect of her, but this way of doing things works much better. Trust in the power of the goddess to lead people where they most need to be. Seriously, I've been to rituals where two goddesses sit around with nothing to do while a third goddess has a line thirty people long. You want to prevent that sort of thing from happening.

In addition, have the narrator, circle caster, and quarter callers mill around the ritual, making sure everyone knows what's going on.

When to end an open-ended rite such as this is mostly a judgment call, but when people start chattering among themselves and there are no more lines, the rite can probably come to an end. Whoever is in charge of calling an end to things should let everyone working on the ritual know ahead of time so they can be ready when things wrap up.

NARRATOR: *And now our rite has neared its end. The goddess Brigid has been among us, and the light of Imbolc guides our way forward this turn of the wheel. To our ladies upon the dais, it is near time for you all to rejoin us. Blessed be the goddess! And blessed be we the people who hear her call! Until we meet again, Great Brigid!*

Goodbyes to the Brigids

Let people return to their original places in the circle. Everyone helping with the ritual should do the same.

NARRATOR: *Before all can be as it once was, we must bid our Lady a fond farewell and return those who served as her Priestesses to us and this, our waking world. Look one last time into the eyes of our Lady before she goes. We start with Brigantia.*

Before each attendant reads the words dismissing their Brigid, they should replace the veil that was originally on their Priestess's face at the start of the rite.

BRIGANTIA ATTENDANT: *To Brigid Brigantia, we thank you for joining us tonight in our rite! Shine your light of truth and justice so that all may see! Hail and farewell!*

SAINT BRIGID ATTENDANT: *Saint Brigid, whose light at Kildare still burns, we thank you for joining us tonight in our rite. Thank you for sharing your light with all of your children! Hail and farewell!*

BRIGID (GODDESS) ATTENDANT: *Fair Brigid, Exalted One, you have been with us since the beginning and will be with us until the end! Long may your light shine and the flames of your forge be lit! Hail and farewell!*

Cakes and Ale

EAST QUARTER CALLER: *Even in the depths of winter, the wheel continues to turn. All that has died will be reborn by the powers of the sun, wind, rain, and earth! Hail the coming spring!*

SOUTH QUARTER CALLER: *At Imbolc, we thank our Lady Brigid for her many faces and her many gifts.*

The west quarter caller approaches the altar and raises the chalice there.

WEST QUARTER CALLER: *Great Brigid, we thank you for this gift of drink. May it warm our bodies and warm our spirits and remind us of the promise of longer days to come! So mote it be!*

The north quarter caller approaches the altar and raises a plate of cakes up in the air for all to see.

NORTH QUARTER CALLER: *Brigid, goddess of forge and plow, we thank you for these cakes. May we be well fed and not know hunger in these days before spring truly comes! So mote it be!*

The quarter callers should distribute the cakes and ale as quickly as possible, letting the Priestesses who called Brigid eat and drink first. As mentioned in Chapter 6: Circle Rituals, the easiest and fastest way to distribute cakes and ale is to use large trays with individual portions already prepared.

Goodbye and Dismissing the Angels/Watchtowers

NARRATOR: *To all the powers that have joined us in our rite this night, we say thank you. Horned One, thank you for allowing us to see Lady Brigid in all her glory. We thank the newly powerful sun, whose light shall shine down upon us all! We thank the earth for the wonders of the springtime. And we thank Brigid, who shall ever dwell in our hearts. Blessed be!*

After each angel is dismissed, a banishing pentagram can be drawn.

EAST QUARTER CALLER: *Great Raphael, archangel of the east, we thank you for lending your energy and power to our rite. Hail and farewell!*

SOUTH QUARTER CALLER: *Great Michael, archangel of the south, we thank you for lending your energy and power to our rite. Hail and farewell!*

WEST QUARTER CALLER: *Great Gabriel, archangel of the west, we thank you for lending your energy and power to our rite. Hail and farewell!*

NORTH QUARTER CALLER: *Great Uriel, archangel of the north, we thank you for lending your energy and power to our rite. Hail and farewell!*

Starting in the east and walking widdershins, the circle caster releases the circle using their sword or athame.

CIRCLE CASTER: *I conjured, cast, and created this circle as a place to be filled with love and the magick and wonder of our Lady Brigid. It has served us well and allowed us to walk between the worlds. Now I undo this place between goddess and mortal, so that we might stand once more in our waking world. But know that our Lady ever walks with us, and where she walks our light shall manifest. In the names of the Lord and the Lady, the circle is open but never broken. So mote it be!*

Encourage everyone in the circle to hold hands and recite the "merry meet" part below as a group at the end of the rite.

NARRATOR: *We have journeyed to the boundary between winter and spring. There we took the light of Imbolc forward and met with our lady Brigid. The earth stirs and prepares to wake! And now I say to you, merry meet, merry part, and merry meet again, and may the gods preserve the Craft!*

FIN

CHAPTER 14

IMBOLC COVEN RITUAL
Preparing the Temple

I've always looked at February as a time for spring cleaning. I realize that it's not truly spring at Imbolc in many places in the Northern Hemisphere, but it's an idea I have trouble letting go of. Even when I lived in Michigan and Imbolc usually meant freezing temperatures and lots of snow, I still tried to clean up both my house and my altars and the room I generally practiced the Craft in.

It usually takes our coven about two years to go through a candle set aside to honor one of the four elements. Because of that, every two years at Imbolc, we bless and consecrate new candles for our temple and strive to put a little bit of our own personal energies into them. I doubt most covens have rites to dedicate new quarter candles, but it makes sense to me, and I think the idea plays very well into the idea of light returning at Imbolc.

For this ritual you'll need five candles, one each for earth, air, fire, and water and a fifth for the element of spirit, which my coven keeps on its working altar. You'll also need a statue or an object representative of the goddess Brigid. Though this ritual is not all about her exclusively, I find it hard to leave her out of Imbolc rites since she's such a significant part of them. In our circle, we lay a statue of the goddess on a soft towel and place that in a basket, resulting in an easy-to-make version of Brigid's bed. Creating a bed for Brigid to lie upon is a very old tradition and a way to pay your respects to the goddess (or to the saint, in some cases).

My coven's call to spirit at the start of most rituals is more like an opening blessing than a call to an element or a deity. We look at it as a summary of our beliefs as Witches in the broadest strokes possible. This opening rite can easily be added to all of the other rituals in this book if desired.

Every coven has their own preferences when it comes to cakes and ale, but Imbolc has long been connected to the lactating of sheep. Because of that, I've been known to use milk (and cookies!) in my cakes and ale rites at Imbolc. In my coven, we begin most rituals with a ceremonial hand washing as a way for coveners to cleanse themselves. If you choose to do this, you'll need a very large bowl and a pitcher. I usually scent the water for the hand washing with a few drops of rose or ylang-ylang oil. The person carrying the bowl in the ritual is advised to wrap a small towel around one of their arms so coveners can dry their hands with it.

Materials Needed

- Regular altar setup
- A Brigid statue (or an item representing her; corn dollies work well here and are traditional)
- A bed for Brigid and something for her to lie on, such as a blanket or some straw (I suggest a basket)
- Five new candles
- Cakes and ale
- Pitcher of water
- Bowl
- Towel

Ritual Roles

- High Priestess
- High Priest
- Quarter callers
- Circle casters

THE RITUAL: PREPARING THE TEMPLE

The rite should begin with the altar in the middle of the circle, with the coven standing around it in a circle. The candles to be blessed should be either on the altar or perhaps under it, depending on space limitations.

Statement of Intent/Cleansing

HIGH PRIESTESS: *We gather this night to celebrate the sacred festival of Imbolc. We welcome the return of the light and the Lady Brigid, goddess of healing and forge. This evening we prepare the coven for the warmer and longer days to come. Long may the light of our circle shine! Blessed be!*

HIGH PRIEST: *And now in order to prepare for our rites, we shall cleanse all those gathered here.*

The High Priestess and High Priest take the pitcher and bowl (generally placed somewhere other than on the main working altar) and move around the circle, pouring water over the hands of each covener. Most coveners will probably touch their head and heart with the water on their hands, but people can do as they wish. The person pouring the water should say something like "We cleanse and bless you in the names of the Lord and the Lady!" or "In the name of Brigid, I cleanse and bless you this night of Imbolc." This is generally followed by a "Blessed be!" once the covener has touched the water to their face or chest. The phrase is then repeated by the covener.

When the last covener has been reached, the High Priestess or the High Priest should take both the pitcher and the bowl and pour water over the other's hands, and then exchange roles. When everyone has been cleansed, the pitcher and bowl should be placed out of the way of the rite.

HIGH PRIESTESS: *All have been readied for our rite this night. Hail Imbolc!*

Call to Spirit/The All

In my coven, we begin many of our rites with a call to the element/concept of spirit, or the "all." We see it as the magickal energy that holds the universe together and the original source of all that is a part of the universe. We generally welcome it in with a prayer shared by the High Priestess or High Priest and recited by the rest of the coven. At the start of the prayer, a central candle is lit on the altar. We often use this candle to light every other candle in ritual, including the ones at the quarters, by utilizing a taper or a much smaller candle.

HIGH PRIEST: *From thee, spirit, all things come and all things proceed.*
   Thou art the first source, the beginning, the all of the universe,
   For thou art the source of both life and death.
   This world and that which also lies beyond.
   Earth, air, fire, and water are encompassed within thee,
   As are our Lady and Lord and all that lies in between.
   And now in their names, we begin our rite.
   Blessed be this place, this time, and all who are now with us.

Casting the Circle/Lighting the Temple/Calling the Quarters

The circle caster should cast the circle beginning in the east and moving clockwise, using their sword, athame, or wand to do so.

CIRCLE CASTER: *I conjure thee, O circle of power, that thou may serve as a gathering place for truth, love, and joy. By our will, your walls shall keep out all evil and negativity and serve as an entryway between the worlds where we might walk with the gods. Wherefore do I bless thee and consecrate thee in the names of the Lord and the Lady. So mote it be!*

The quarters should be summoned beginning in the east and proceeding clockwise. In this instance, candles are lit at each of the four quarters, candles that will be retired during the ritual.

EAST QUARTER CALLER: *I call to the spirits of the east, spirits of air, and the winds that turn the seasons. Spirits who rule the realm of intuition and inspiration, yours is the creative soul of nature. Join us tonight as we celebrate new beginnings and the coming of spring. Blessed be!*

SOUTH QUARTER CALLER: *I call to the spirits of the south, spirits of fire, and the light that guides our way. Spirits who rule the ecstasy of the spirit, yours is the cup of the wine of life. Join us in our circle tonight as we celebrate the return of the light and the coming of spring. Blessed be!*

WEST QUARTER CALLER: *I call to the spirits of the west, spirits of water, and the gifts that give us life. Spirits who give the blessings of rain to the parched and hungry land, yours is the promise of life renewed. Join us tonight as we celebrate the rain and the coming of spring. Blessed be!*

NORTH QUARTER CALLER: *I call to the spirits of the north, spirits of earth, you from which all things proceed and to which all things return. Spirits who are the beauty of the green earth, yours is the peace and serenity for which we long. Join us tonight as we celebrate the growing green and the coming of spring. Blessed be!*

Calls to the God and the Goddess

HIGH PRIEST: *This night of Imbolc, we call to the Great God. Lord of the Sun, Horned One of the wild places, join us in our circle! Let us feel and see your growing power. Stand with us tonight as we renew the light of this coven. Be with us as we work our will! Hail and welcome!*

Candles can be lit for the Goddess and God as desired by the coven. If they are lit, this ritual provides a great opportunity to replace them if needed.

HIGH PRIESTESS: *This night of Imbolc, we call to the Great Goddess. Mistress of the Waters, Lady of the Moon, and Mother of all, join us in our circle! Let us feel the awakening earth in the ground beneath our feet and upon the breeze that touches our cheeks. Be with us as we renew the light of this coven and help guide us ever forward in your name. Hail and welcome!*

Welcoming of Brigid

In our coven, we usually have our main devotional statue of Brigid already placed in a basket to signify Brigid's bed. Alternatively, she can be ceremonially placed in her bed at this time if she's sitting on the altar.

HIGH PRIEST: *Once more, we welcome the goddess Brigid to her rightful place in this temple. Tonight, upon her night, we honor her once more. We present her to you so that you might know her and honor her mysteries. For the last year she has watched over us and she will continue to do so on this turn of the wheel.*

HIGH PRIESTESS: *Great Brigid, join us in our rites this night and in the nights to come! We salute you, unconquerable goddess! When the invaders came and drove out the old gods, it was you who stood by your folk. You donned a different cloak but remained our goddess, a goddess of the people and the earth. We are honored to have you as a part of our rites! Hail and welcome!*

Brigid's bed is carried around the coven so that everyone might pay homage to the image of the goddess. After she has traveled the length of the circle, she is put in a place of honor upon the altar or in other sacred space used by the coven.

Candle Blessing

HIGH PRIEST: *As the days grow longer, this is now the time to renew our temple and prepare it for the rites and rituals yet to come. That this temple room may ever be a space of love, joy, and truth, we must replace the candles that give us light in the darkness. As these candles represent not just the power of the elements but also the power of this coven, together we should charge and bless them.*

HIGH PRIESTESS: *Before we bless the candles that shall light this temple, we must properly prepare and cleanse them for use in ritual. To do that, we call upon the powers of the elements and the tools of our Craft.*

Before the candles can be blessed, burning incense and salted water should be prepared. As in many of the other rituals in this book, the blessing of the salted water and the lit incense can be done at the beginning of the ritual. But for this particular rite, I decided to move it to the middle of the ritual. In ritual, most everything is flexible, and you should do what makes the most sense to you.

The High Priestess begins this part of the ritual by lighting the incense, using the flame of the spirit candle in the middle of the altar. What type of incense you use here is up to you. For cleansing, I prefer sandalwood, lavender, and copal.

HIGH PRIESTESS: *I light this incense using the power of our sacred flame. May this creature of air and fire bless, consecrate, and cleanse the light we add to this temple space. So mote it be!*

The High Priestess sets the incense down, and the High Priest picks up his athame and scoops three measures of salt into the water, mixing them together.

HIGH PRIEST: *May this creature of earth and water bless, consecrate, and cleanse the light we add to this temple space. So mote it be!*

The candles being blessed should now either all be placed on the coven's pentacle to be cleansed or be cleansed one at a time. In this ritual, I've chosen to cleanse the four quarter candles all at once upon the pentacle.

HIGH PRIESTESS: *I cleanse these candles with the powers of water and earth. I remove from them all negativity and darkness. May their light shine brightly in this coven!*

The High Priestess sprinkles the candles with the salted water.

HIGH PRIEST: *I cleanse these candles with the powers of air and fire. I remove from them all negativity and darkness. May their light shine brightly in this coven!*

The High Priest carries each candle through the incense smoke.

HIGH PRIEST: *Before these candles can be placed around our circle, they must all represent the chosen of this coven. In order that we should mark these candles as our own, I offer you a chance to add a Witch mark to the bottom of each candle. May your movements be precise and quick and help us make these candles ours.*

When I mark a candle, I tend to use a pin or needle. Some like to use their athame or a white-handled knife, which is traditionally the tool dedicated to the task of cutting during ritual. Marks on the candle should be small: a rune, a symbol, and no more. Pass each candle around the circle and let each member of the coven mark it. When everyone is done, return the candles to the pentacle on the altar.

HIGH PRIESTESS: *Four candles, four quarters. Four directions, four points of light. These candles each represent a different element and a different emotion. In the east is air and knowledge, to the south is fire and desire. The west brings us water and the mysteries of initiation, and the north gives us earth and strength.*

HIGH PRIEST: *So far this night we have cleansed and marked our candles, but now is the time to put a bit of our will into each one. When the eastern candle comes to you, share with it the knowledge you hope to gain in our rites over the coming years. The candle in the south is a place to put your Craft desires, and with the western sentinel, share your wonder of the mysteries that are our Lady and Lord. Finally, to the north, lend a bit of strength to our guardian and this coven. So mote it be!*

When the candles have all gone around the circle, they should return to the altar and from there should be picked up by each of the four quarter callers. Starting in the east, have each of the quarter callers, one by one, take a taper and use it to transfer the flame currently burning to the newly consecrated candle. Once the flame is transferred to the new candle, the old candle should be blown out. As they transfer the light, each quarter caller should call out a salute to that element.

EAST QUARTER CALLER: *May our light and that of the gods ever shine in the east.*

COVEN: *Hail the east!*

SOUTH QUARTER CALLER: *May our light and that of the gods ever shine in the south.*

COVEN: *Hail the south!*

WEST QUARTER CALLER: *May our light and that of the gods ever shine in the west.*

COVEN: *Hail the west!*

NORTH QUARTER CALLER: *May our light and that of the gods ever shine in the north.*

COVEN: *Hail the north!*

The old candles should be gathered up and placed in a secure place. Our coven is lucky enough to have a ritual space with several altars, but even a basket will work just fine.

HIGH PRIEST: *While these candles will no longer bring the elements to us, they may still be of service to this coven. I place them here upon this shrine that they may continue to add their light to our rites. So mote it be!*

Our coven works entirely by candlelight, and as a result, we have a few candles that we light before ritual starts. Those have almost always been old quarter candles. As many of those have died in the last year, our now decommissioned quarter candles will take their place.

HIGH PRIESTESS: *And now we come to the center, the place from which all hope springs. Before we can dedicate our new spirit candle, it must be cleansed and readied.*

The new center candle is placed upon the pentacle and sprinkled with salted water by the High Priestess before being cleansed with the incense by the High Priest.

HIGH PRIESTESS: *May the light brought to us from spirit ever shine upon this coven and those who walk the path of the Witch. Connected to all are we, and that connection is symbolized and made manifest here upon the altar. Ever-shining light, renew yourself this night of Imbolc.*

The High Priestess uses a taper to transfer the light of spirit from the old candle to the new one. When the light has been established in the new candle, the old one is blown out. The old candle is moved to another place in the temple space if it remains usable. I'm always weirdly sad when we have to decommission a spirit candle, which we generally then offer a place of honor in our ritual room.

HIGH PRIEST: *And for your service these last two years, O candle, I shall set you in this place of honor so that your light may continue to be a part of this coven. So mote it be!*

The Great Rite/Cakes and Ale

The High Priest picks up their athame or wand, and the High Priestess picks up the coven's chalice.

HIGH PRIEST: *This world and all that has been given to us is sacred.*

HIGH PRIESTESS: *As Witches, we honor that gift by thanking that which made it possible.*

HIGH PRIEST: *The athame is to the sun and sky,*

HIGH PRIESTESS: *As the cup is to the land and sea.*

BOTH: *And when they are united, all is born.*

The High Priest plunges the athame into the chalice and then uses it to bless the bread for cakes and ale, preferably with a drop or two of liquid still upon its blade.

HIGH PRIEST: *In the names of the Lord and the Lady, we bless this bread.*

The High Priest touches the athame/wand to either the bread or the plate it is being served upon.

HIGH PRIESTESS: *In the names of the Lord and the Lady, we bless this drink.*

The High Priestess picks up her athame and touches the lip of the cup with it. The drink is then passed around first, with the bread following.

Goodbyes to the Lady and Lord

HIGH PRIESTESS: *We thank the Great Lady, goddess of the skies and seas, for joining us tonight in our rites. Look over us as the light grows and change manifests itself in our lives. With love and devotion, we walk this road with you. Blessed be!*

HIGH PRIEST: *We thank the Eternal Lord, god of the earth and the wild places, for joining us tonight in our rites. We will feel your touch with our every step upon this world. With love and devotion, we walk this road with you. Blessed be!*

Dismissing the Quarters/Releasing the Circle

Starting in the north and proceeding counterclockwise, the elements are dismissed. Each of the newly installed candles should be blown out at "Hail and farewell!"

NORTH QUARTER CALLER: *Spirits of the north, spirits of earth, thank you for being with us this sacred night. We thank you for all of your gifts: the green grass, the fertile soil, and new life. And now we say to you, hail and farewell!*

WEST QUARTER CALLER: *Spirits of the west, spirits of water, we thank you for being with us this sacred night. We thank you for all of your gifts: the rains that make all possible and the ocean that calls to us. And now we say to you, hail and farewell!*

SOUTH QUARTER CALLER: *Spirits of the south, spirits of fire, we thank you for being with us this sacred night. We thank you for all of your gifts: for the longer days, the return of the light, and the passions that burn within us. And now we say to you, hail and farewell!*

EAST QUARTER CALLER: *Spirits of the east, spirits of air, we thank you for being with us this sacred night. We thank you for all of your gifts: for the winds that turn the seasons and the ability to feel joy and happiness. And now we say to you, hail and farewell!*

Beginning in the east, the circle caster releases the circle using the athame, sword, or wand, moving deosil.

CIRCLE CASTER: *I conjured thee, O circle of power, to serve as a meeting place of truth, love, and joy. By our will, we shaped your walls to keep out all evil and negativity, and you have served us well in that purpose. We have journeyed between the worlds and walked with the gods. All* is now as it once was, and all that has joined us this night has been dismissed in the names of the Lord and the Lady. So mote it be!

HIGH PRIESTESS: *We have journeyed to the boundary between winter and spring. There we have prepared our coven for the rites to come and met with our lady Brigid. The earth stirs and prepares to wake! And now I say to you, merry meet, merry part, and merry meet again, and may the gods preserve the Craft!*

FIN

CHAPTER 15

IMBOLC SOLITARY RITUAL
Preparing the Way

I've always loved the quiet nature of Imbolc. As someone who first discovered Witch-craft in the American Midwest, early February was always a time of cold, snow, and at least another month of winter. But despite the cold, Imbolc always spoke to me of pos-sibilities. The longer days always felt like a reminder that warmer days were ahead, and even on the coldest and darkest nights, hope and life seemed to fill the air.

There was one particular Imbolc night in Michigan I remember more vividly than the others. We had a foot of snow on the ground and the mercury hadn't gotten up above freezing in over a month, but as I opened my bedroom window that night, the breeze was wet and warm. It was just enough to remind me that the Maiden had begun making her rounds upon the frozen earth and saved me from the usual despair that's often a part of the Midwestern winter experience.

For many of us, Imbolc is a time of transition, existing in a space and time between the seasons. Winter is still a reality for many of us, yet there's something we can feel that lies just beyond what we're experiencing. Imbolc is a great time for getting rid of the unwanted things we've carried forward into this new turn of the wheel and for preparing for the gifts we might yet receive. This ritual is about getting rid of the unwanted while preparing for what's to come. In that sense, it's much like the earth in winter. In the winter, things die, yet those deaths prepare for the new life that is to come.

To honor the Goddess and God and their reemergence into the world at Imbolc and to bring new blessings into our own lives, we'll be melting snow or ice cubes during this ritual. If you live where there's snow, you're in luck. Right before you begin the ritual, take some of that snow and make two snowballs. In one, place a coin of some sort to represent the God, and in the other, place a flower petal for the Goddess. If there's no snow where you are, simply put these items in an ice cube tray and let the water freeze, then fetch your ice cubes before the ritual starts.

I've chosen a coin to represent the God in this ritual because many gods of the earth, such as the Gallic Cernunnos, were also gods of commerce and money. I chose a flower petal for Persephone because the flower petal reminds me of her imminent return to most of North America at the spring equinox. If a coin or flower petal doesn't represent the gods to you, don't use them, and come up with something else. For magick to be truly effective, it should always resonate with you personally.

In order to melt snow or ice cubes, I suggest using an oil diffuser powered by a candle. Since the amount of snow you'll be melting is small (as is an ice cube), a diffuser is usually just the right size. If that's not something you have, a small ceramic or metal bowl placed near a few low-burning candles (such as tealight candles) should do the trick. If your ritual space is warm, both snow or ice will most likely melt pretty quickly.

You'll also need a broom for this particular ritual. If you have a ritual broom, great! If you don't, a normal broom will work just fine. We'll be sweeping away the disappointments and despair of the past turn of the wheel, and any sort of broom will do the trick for this particular work. The ritual itself calls for simply sweeping your ritual space, but if you want to sweep everything in your home, that's perfectly acceptable too!

The Blessing Bowl

One of my favorite ways to begin ritual is with a blessing bowl. Many Witches like to take a ceremonial shower or bath before entering ritual space, but I find a blessing bowl much more effective. In order to create a blessing bowl, all you need is a big bowl filled with water and a few drops of essential oil or perhaps a measure or two of salt. I use either cleansing oils, such as ylang-ylang or tea-tree, or an oil that reminds me to love myself, such as rose.

I like to set up my bowl in a dark corner of my house, preferably near a mirror so I can try to remind myself that I am worthy of the gods' love. Around my bowl I place several candles (or electric candles—my wife worries about me burning down our house) and the following prayer. After reading each line of the prayer, I anoint that part of myself with the water in the bowl, visualizing it removing any negativity from my body and reminding myself that ritual is a place to meet and interact with greater powers.

Though this book doesn't call for it, I will often set up a blessing bowl before coven rituals, or use it before I engage in a solitary rite. It's a great way to remind yourself (and others) that what we do as Witches is magickal, holy, and divine, and that we ever walk with the Lord and Lady.

Blessing Bowl Prayer

Lady and Lord, may your love wash over me this night.

Blessed be my feet, which have brought me to your ways (anoint feet).

Blessed be my eros,[31] *which brings me closer to your mysteries. (anoint eros)*

Blessed be my heart, which shall always be true to you. (anoint heart)

Blessed be my lips, which shall utter your sacred names. (anoint lips)

Blessed be my eyes, that I may see your beauty. (anoint eyes)

Blessed be my ears, which have heard your call. (anoint ears)

Blessed be my soul, that I may know you. (anoint forehead)

May I ever be blessed be!

Materials Needed

- Regular altar setup
- Snow or ice cubes with a coin and a flower petal
- Extra bowls/candles or a candle-powered oil diffuser(s)
- Besom/broom
- Cakes and ale

THE RITUAL: PREPARING THE WAY

Start the ritual knowing you are cleansed and refreshed from the blessing bowl prayer performed before the start of the ritual. Then take a centering breath and give your statement of intent:

---

31. I've always liked the term *eros* as a substitute for *phallus, vagina,* or *reproductive organ.* It just sounds elegant.

I come this night before the Lord and Lady to celebrate the sabbat of Imbolc. May this be a time of new beginnings and for ridding myself of things unwanted and collected over the last turn of the wheel. I celebrate winter's height and spring's soon return. So mote it be!

Circle Casting/Calling the Quarters

Starting in the north, cast your circle with a sword, athame, or wand.

Within this circle, only love, power, and transformation! With the blessings of the Lord and Lady, I cast this circle and create this magickal space. So mote it be!

Again starting in the north, call to the elements to be a part of your ritual. If you have candles to light for them, be sure to do so.

Spirits of bone and earth, I call you to attend this circle and stand watch over my rites. Blessed be!

Spirits of change and breath, I call you to attend this circle and stand watch over my rites. Blessed be!

Spirits of passion and flame, I call you to attend this circle and stand watch over my rites. Blessed be!

Spirits of womb and rain, I call you to attend this circle and stand watch over my rites. Blessed be!

Calling to the Lord and Lady

Visualize the deities you serve. Picture them in your mind's eye and reach out to them with your heart and spirit as you call to them. Light any candles you might have for them at the conclusion of your calls.

Great Lady, be with me tonight as we welcome the growing light. May this turn of the wheel bring love and understanding into my life, and may I reciprocate those feelings with those around me. May the world awaken with your returning presence and take its first steps toward spring. Bless your child this night of Imbolc. Hail and welcome!

Great Lord, be with me tonight as I celebrate the longer days that have now arrived. May this turn of the wheel find me healthy, happy, and able to provide for myself in life. May I share those blessings with those I love and choose to call family. As your hooves touch the ground, may they bring us closer to the return of the green! Bless your child this night of Imbolc. Hail and welcome!

The Working

Light the candles to place under your oil diffuser (or near the bowls in which you will melt your snow), then ask the Goddess and God to be a part of that light.

I light this candle to bring forth the power of the Lord and Lady. As the heat of the sun shall soon melt away the snow and death that surround this earth, I ask that the heat of this candle melt away the obstacles that keep me from obtaining all that I wish for in my life. Let me be happy, healthy, wealthy, loved, and giving of my own love. Bestow your blessings upon me so that I might share them with those I care for. So mote it be!

Place your snow/ice cubes in your bowl or dish and imagine the Goddess and God walking upon the cold earth. Visualize their steps bringing life to the world, and those gifts bringing you happiness and security.

As that picture begins to fade in your mind, stand up in the center of your ritual space and begin dusting off your hands. As you do so, imagine all the setbacks and disappointments of the last twelve months falling away from them and onto the ground. If a memory is especially painful or troublesome, don't be afraid to let those emotions escape and manifest as tears or a cry of pain. The point of this exercise is to rid yourself of negative and painful memories. Don't hold back!

When all the bad and unwanted things have left your body and soul, take your broom and begin sweeping those feelings away and out of your circle. If you're in a position to sweep those things outside, do so, through either a door or a window. If that's not possible, at least sweep those energies out of your circle and away from you. As you begin to sweep, say:

I sweep away the pain and heartache of the past year so that I may start the spring born anew. I am like the earth, reborn yet again in the closing days of winter and the opening of spring. I rid myself and my life of these things, and may they not trouble me again unless it is by my will! In the names of the Lord and the Lady, so mote it be!

I find that when I'm using a broom dedicated for magick, I can easily sweep things out of my circle. However, if the broom is not enough, cut a small gateway in your circle and sweep through that, repairing the circle when you're done. If dealing with your own pain has left you hurt and vulnerable, go back to the blessing bowl and remind yourself that you are a much loved Witch, a child of the Goddess, the God, and the earth itself.

By the time you're done sweeping and ridding yourself of negative things, your snow/ice cubes should be melted. Take the coin and flower petal out of your dish and hold them in your hands for a moment. Feel the love of the Goddess and God flow through them. When you're done, place them on your altar as a reminder of this Imbolc night, or carry them with you for good luck and to attract the things you desire and wish for.

Before moving on to cakes and ale, blow out the candles you lit to melt what was frozen, saying:

> The days are not yet long and the light is not quite yet strong, but what was begun here tonight shall only grow. So mote it be!

Cakes and Ale

Take your chalice of wine/drink and hold it aloft, asking for the blessings of the Goddess.

> Even on the coldest night, my Lady walks with me and would warm my heart and soul.
> I gladly accept this blessing and gift from her. Blessed be!

Have a generous sip of wine/drink, making sure to pour some into your libation bowl. When that's finished, thank the God for the food you're about to eat.

> Here in the darkest winter, the Lord stands with me and fills my belly and my spirit. I gladly accept this gift and blessing from him. Blessed be!

Eat some of your cake, reserving a bit for your libation bowl. I like to sip and nibble in the silence of Imbolc for a bit, thinking about what is to come and letting go of the past. When you're satisfied that your ritual has come to an end, begin by saying goodbye to the Lord and Lady.

Goodbyes to the Goddess and the God

> Great Lady, Great Lord, I thank you for being a part of my circle this night. May your blessings grow alongside the waxing days, and may I be free of that which keeps me from happiness. Walk with me as you walk over this earth, sharing your power, wisdom, and grace. Blessed be!

If you've lit candles for the Goddess and God, now is the time to extinguish them before closing up your circle.

Dismissing the Quarters/Releasing the Circle

Starting in the west, dismiss the quarters. If you've lit candles for them, blow those out at the end of each quarter call.

Spirits of womb and rain, I called you to attend these rites, and for your presence I thank you. Blessed be!

Spirits of passion and flame, I called you to attend these rites, and for your presence I thank you. Blessed be!

Spirits of change and breath, I called you to attend these rites, and for your presence I thank you. Blessed be!

Spirits of bone and earth, I called you to attend these rites, and for your presence I thank you. Blessed be!

Take your athame, sword, or wand and release the circle you cast for Imbolc.

This circle has been a place of love, power, and transformation, and now in the names of the Lord and the Lady, I release the energies created here and return once more to mundane space. So mote it be!

Standing before your altar, signal an end to your rite.

Winter behind, spring ahead, I walk forward upon the path of the Witch! May the gods ever preserve the Craft!

If you can still feel the energy you swept up earlier, throw some salted water upon it or break it up using some cleansing incense until it is truly no more.

FIN

PART THREE
SPRING
(OSTARA & BELTANE)

Bright flowers blooming,
Our Mother Earth awakens,
Hearts renewed again.

CHAPTER 16

OSTARA

The Spring Equinox

Name of Sabbat: Ostara (also called Eostar and the Spring Equinox)

Date: On the day of the spring equinox (which occurs on or about March 21 in the Northern Hemisphere)

Pronunciation: "Oh-STAR-uh"

Along with its cousin Mabon, Ostara is a bit of an outlier when it comes to the sabbats. The four cross-quarter (or greater) sabbats, along with the solstices, are all associated with very real holidays that were once celebrated (and in most cases continue to be celebrated) in Europe (and later North America and other places), but the sabbats we celebrate today as Ostara and Mabon lack those links. To put it simply, there was no great ancient pagan (or Witch) celebration of the spring equinox, at least in Europe.

This can be rather frustrating to many Witches because it most certainly *feels* like there should have been some sort of ancient spring festival, but alas, it just doesn't exist. Many Witches look to Easter for the ancient spring festival that should have been, and it's possible that Easter absorbed several pagan elements, but we'll never know for sure. What's always most important with a sabbat celebration is that what we're celebrating makes sense to us today as Witches, and in that sense Ostara is certainly just as real and as valid as any other sabbat. Even without a historical parallel, Ostara has always been one of my favorite sabbats.

This doesn't mean that the spring equinox has been completely ignored around the world. There are several monuments in the Americas (both North and South) built to align with the spring equinox, including the famous Mayan El Castillo at Chichen Itza. Cambodia's Angkor Wat, built about nine hundred years ago, also aligns with the sun on the spring equinox.[32] The Persian (or Iranian) new year, Nowruz, has been celebrated on the first day of spring for at least three thousand years, which is absolutely amazing. So there are and were some events associated with the spring equinox, but I'm unaware of any traditions from those celebrations becoming a part of Modern Witchcraft.

Ostara has only been used as the name of the Spring Equinox sabbat since 1974. That's when American Witch Aidan Kelly settled upon the name when designing a Witch calendar (see chapter 3). It was a divinely inspired choice because Ostara certainly sounds like the name of an ancient sabbat celebration. Ostara (or Eostre) is the name of a Germanic fertility goddess who was first written about by the English historian Bede (c. 673–735 CE) in the eighth century. In his *The Reckoning of Time*, Bede writes that Britain's Anglo-Saxons named the month we now call April in honor of Eostre, and eventually began using her name to refer to Christendom's biggest spring holiday, the day we now call Easter.

It's worth noting that *Easter* as the name of the day when Jesus allegedly returned from the dead is known as Easter only in Germanic languages (*Easter* in English and *Ostern* in German). In the rest of Europe, the holiday is not in any way linked to the goddess Eostre, making the idea that Easter is some sort of corrupted Germanic holiday much less likely. Bede's pagans who worshiped Eostre did do a lot of feasting during her month, so there's probably a holiday in there somewhere. It's just been lost to history.

In Germany, the folklorist Jacob Grimm (1785–1863) worked backward from the holiday of Easter to reconstruct the goddess Ostara. His version of the goddess is the one most of us know today from internet photos and memes. She's a goddess of eggs, rabbits, and most everything associated with both Easter and the spring. The problem with this is that there's no physical evidence to support any of his ideas about Ostara.

However, many of the trappings we now associate with Easter play directly into pagan themes that are generally welcome in the circles of Witches. Bunnies, eggs, and plastic grass have absolutely nothing to do with Jesus and everything to do with the natu-

---

32. Jessie Guy-Ryan, "5 Ancient Sites Built to Align with the Spring Equinox," Atlas Obscura, March 20, 2016, https://www.atlasobscura.com/articles/five-ancient-sites-to-celebrate-the-spring-equinox.

ral world in late March and early April. Eggs have been used in a variety of cultures for thousands of years for a myriad of purposes, so it's impossible to say just why they were inserted into the Easter holiday. But as a symbol of life and its renewal, they are perfect for Ostara.

Rabbits, who are known for fornicating, are another symbol of life's renewal in the springtime.[33] Rabbits generally bear between four and eight litters a year, with the average litter consisting of six baby rabbits. (Did you know that one mama rabbit and her offspring are capable of producing 95 billion rabbits in seven years?[34] Rabbits are amazing breeders.) Though we'll never know if the ancient Eostre had a hare as an animal companion, many other pagan goddesses had hares serving them, most notably Hecate and Freya. Many people have long thought that the Easter Bunny is some sort of relic from pagan antiquity, but the first time he shows up in the historical record is in the early 1600s, and he wasn't alone as Europe's gifting mammal: the Easter Fox was once nearly as popular.[35]

For many of us, spring is a time of new beginnings, and in that sense Eostre might be the perfect goddess for the holiday. *Eostre* contains the root word *eos*, which translates as "beginnings" and was the word most often used to describe goddesses of the dawn (such as the Greek Eos) among Indo-European groups. A sabbat with such linguistic connections is fine by me.

Ways to Celebrate Ostara

One of the things I love most about Ostara is that there are many ways to celebrate it. Because I'm mostly a child at heart, I like to start with the Easter decorations I find at the local grocery store. I'm a big fan of eggs and bunnies at Ostara, despite their use in the Christian Easter. Both eggs and rabbits are steeped in fertility symbolism, and fertility is exactly what's going on outside my front door in late March. Dyeing, hiding, and burying eggs are all great Ostara ritual ideas. I've yet to bring the Ostara Bunny into my circle, but I'm sure it will happen sooner or later.

---

33. I use the word *rabbit* out of laziness, but Europe lacks rabbits. Europe is home to the hare, which is a completely different, though related, species from the American rabbit.

34. Forbes, *America's Favorite Holiday*, 100.

35. Cavalorn (Adrian Bott), "Eostre, Ostara and the Easter Fox" (blog), Feb. 27, 2014, https://cavalorn.live journal.com/587630.html. Bott has written extensively about Ostara on his LiveJournal account. It's a weird thing to cite, but his history is good.

Celebrating the feelings of childhood has been a part of many of the Ostara rituals I've participated in over the years. I remember spending one delightful Ostara evening surrounded by friends, crayons, and coloring books as we all tapped into our inner third grader. Simply trying to approach the world with a renewed sense of awe and wonder is a great Ostara activity. The longer we do Witchcraft, the easier it is to become a bit jaded toward the practice. So actively trying to push past that to reclaim a sense of excitement ties into the themes of springtime renewal and rebirth.

My wife and I have always associated Ostara with the Maiden goddess. We've often used our own relationship to tell the story of the Wheel of the Year, and it's at Ostara that the rather silly (and sometimes smelly) Goatboy (young Horned God, though our name for him is better) finally gets to kiss his beloved, the rather demure but wise-be-yond-her-years Maiden. Of course it's equally fine for the Goatboy to kiss another Goatboy, or no one at all, but it's hard to resist the opportunity to see our own lives playing out in the Wheel of the Year myths we honor.

If you are someone who has trouble balancing your work life and Craft life, Ostara might not fix the problem, but it's a good time to start working on it. As much as we might like to totally immerse ourselves in Witchcraft, most of us aren't given that opportunity. We can use the balance of night and day at Ostara to try and magickally swing our inner pendulum toward finding time for all the things we care about and need to do to pay the bills.

Planting seeds might be the most obvious of all Ostara-related activities, but it's an effective one. Some spring planting, whether indoors (most likely) or out, is a great activity for the solitary Witch and the coven. I've long looked at gardening as a magickal act, and March often finds me laying the groundwork for planting in April and May. (Not all of our rituals need to be in front of an altar.) "Seeds" can be metaphorical too. At Ostara, my coven usually begins planning for the rest of our calendar year and especially the summer. With its focus on new beginnings, Ostara is an especially potent time for magick dealing with money or a new job. Plant a magickal seed and grow some wealth and abundance!

I've long associated the spring with initiations, perhaps because it was then that I was first initiated into a specific Witch tradition. Not every coven or Witch needs an initiation ritual, but I believe initiation rites can be powerful tools when executed effectively. They may not be entirely appropriate for Ostara, but the energy around the spring equinox enhances them a great deal.[36]

Hot cross buns have been eaten for good luck in the spring for several centuries and are a welcome (and often warm) addition to any Ostara rite. And perhaps even more welcome, especially in cold climates, is that first real hint of spring that comes in late March. If there's anything close to a warm breeze blowing, open a window or go outside to take advantage of it, and if such a thing is still far away in your corner of the world, be sure to melt some of that pesky snow to let it know that it should be on its way.

Even though she has a sabbat named after her, Eostre is not nearly the presence in Ostara circles as Brigid is at Imbolc ones. Much of that is because Eostre lacks the extensive mythology and documented history we often associate with Brigid, but she's still worth inviting to your festivities. Despite its shortcomings historically, Ostara offers a wide variety of ways to celebrate.

---

36. I write about initiations extensively in my 2019 book *Transformative Witchcraft*, and my coven's initiation rite is included in my 2016 book *The Witch's Athame*. Thank you for reading this footnote.

CHAPTER 17

OSTARA CIRCLE RITUAL

The Gifts of Eostre
and the Green Man

Many sabbats are interchangeable. Depending on where one lives, a sabbat originally designed for Imbolc might make more sense at Ostara. Many of the Lammas rituals I've attended over the years feel more appropriate near the fall equinox than in early August. Much of the ritual I'm including here was originally written for Imbolc, which for Northern California is certainly appropriate but for most people probably makes better sense at Ostara.

We know very little about the goddess Eostre from the historical record. She doesn't appear in any mythology, and we don't have any statues featuring her face. She features most prominently in the work of the English historian Bede, who wrote in *The Reckoning of Time* that she's the source of the word *Easter* and that the Anglo-Saxons once named an entire month after her. Linguist Philip Shaw, in his work *Pagan Goddess in the Early Germanic World*, links Eostre to the Germanic matron goddess *Austriahenea*, and while doing so makes a strong case for the historical existence of Eostre.[37]

What makes Shaw's connection of Eostre to a matron goddess interesting is that I've never experienced her in such a way. For the Spring Equinox one year, my coven hosted a large open-house type of ritual for friends and family where we called down Eostre. The goddess's way of speaking and acting was that of a young girl, not an older goddess.

---

37. Shaw, *Pagan Goddesses in the Early Germanic World*, 61.

She was fairly self-possessed but also unsure of what exactly she should be doing. Despite her confusion, her presence filled our circle with an incredibly joyous energy. It was something all thirty of us felt that night, and ever since I've had a desire to fit Eostre into as many rituals as possible in March.

In addition to Eostre, this ritual features the Green Man in a costarring role. Late March and early April often mark the first time many of us see green grass in the new year, so his inclusion here seems appropriate to me. Much like Eostre, the Green Man lacks a mythology, and the name we use for him dates back only to the start of the twentieth century. However, since that time he's been imagined as the power of the rolling hills, the fertile countryside, and the earth beneath our feet.

Because drawing down deity can lead ritual in all kinds of different directions, the High Priestess and High Priest do not call down Eostre and the Green Man into themselves. Instead, each of those deities has their own Priestess/Priest to serve as their container. The calls to deity in this ritual are also staggered. The Green Man is called to and drawn down and then leads a working. The process is then repeated for Eostre. As an alternative to drawing down, you could have people simply play the roles of Eostre and the Green Man, and even in such scenarios you'll find that the energy of the deities being "played" will show up. However, there's something exciting about a real drawing down that adds to the overall energy of a ritual.

One of the main workings in this rite is a spring cleansing of the self, which is why this is one of the few rituals in this book that skips an opening purification of ritual goers. Opening with such a thing and then performing one later in the ritual just feels redundant to me. There are many groups who feel lost without a cleansing. If yours is one of those, you should add one from the many in this book or your personal practice, or set up an area to do a cleansing of individuals before the ritual.

This ritual doesn't require much in the way of props, but it does require some containers of loose soil, a few small slips of paper (along with accompanying writing instruments), and most likely a couple of containers or small bowls for the cleansing water used at the end of the rite. For those of you who like to be elaborate with the staging, creating costumes for both the Green Man and Eostre adds a great deal to the rite, though it's not necessary. When I'm calling down the Green Man, I often wear a leather face mask designed to look like leaves, and when Ari calls down Eostre, she often wears a springlike dress.

Ritual Roles

- High Priestess
- High Priest
- Eostre Priestess
- Green Man Priest
- Four quarter callers
- Sweeper

Materials Needed

- Regular altar setup
- Pot of loose soil that can be either comfortably held or placed on a small table in front of the Green Man
- Slips of paper (with pens/pencils)
- Extra bowls/dishes of water for the cleansing
- Besom/broom
- Cakes and ale

The Ritual: The Gifts of Eostre and the Green Man

The rite begins with a ceremonial sweeping of the ritual area. The goal of the sweeping is to get rid of any negative or unwanted energies that might be in the ritual space. Sweeping should be done in a clockwise manner, proceeding in a spiral pattern from the middle of the circle outward. As the area is being swept, the High Priestess opens the ritual.

HIGH PRIESTESS: *This night we prepare ourselves for the spring to come. We will cast away that which no longer serves us and be cleansed by the gifts of Eostre. Tonight we celebrate the time of equal light and night and prepare for the mysteries of the spring. So may it be!*

Circle Casting/Calling the Quarters

HIGH PRIEST: *Tonight we shall cast our circle using the power of our voices. As we tone together, imagine our energies uniting and creating a sphere. Our circle will be below, above, and all around us. Project clear protective energy from within you and out for all to share in. See it form and shape into our circle this night. Together, "Ehhhh."*

Toning is a way of raising energy using the voice and our will, which exists within. Toning generally utilizes a vowel sound, and whoever is leading the toning to cast the circle can choose whatever vowel sound they wish. The idea here is that the energies projected outward from all in attendance will be used to raise the circle. It's best that whoever leads the toning has an ear for music, as a flat initial tone is not good for circle building. When the toning has reached a crescendo, the High Priest should signal everyone to stop.

HIGH PRIEST: *Together, our circle is cast! So mote it be!*

Call the quarters beginning in the east and moving clockwise. Candles can be lit for each of the quarters, and invoking pentagrams drawn.

EAST QUARTER CALLER: *We ask this night for the blessings of the east! Spirits of air, join us in our rite and bring to us the breath of life and the power of clarity. Be with us!*

SOUTH QUARTER CALLER: *We ask this night for the blessings of the south! Spirits of fire, join us in our rite and bring to us the spark of life and the power of transformation. Be with us!*

WEST QUARTER CALLER: *We ask this night for the blessings of the west! Spirits of water, join us in our rite and bring to us the promise of life reborn and the power of new beginnings. Be with us!*

NORTH QUARTER CALLER: *We ask this night for the blessings of the north! Spirits of earth, join us in our rite and bring to us the touch of life renewed and the power of your wisdom. Be with us!*

For the Green Man

HIGH PRIEST: *We call to the Lord of the Earth, god of the wild places, god of the soil and the green growing things. We call to the Lord who joins with the Lady when the spring rains come. Take away our hurts and fears, and let them be swallowed up by the very earth that is you! Join us in our circle tonight as we purify ourselves and cast away that which we no longer wish to carry with us. Let us feel your presence in our rites! And so that we may truly feel your power, we ask that he who would be your vessel step forward.*

The person who will be drawing down the Green Man steps forward and stands next to the High Priest.

HIGH PRIEST: *Are you ready to contain the power of the Green Man this night for our rite?*

GREEN MAN: *Yes, I am.*

HIGH PRIEST: *Then we shall draw him down into you so that we might meet with him and be in his presence!*

The High Priest begins the fivefold kiss upon the servant of the Green Man, kissing each part of his body as he moves upward from feet to lips.

> *Blessed be thy feet, which walk upon the green grasses.* (kisses feet)
> *Blessed be thy knees, which shall kneel upon the sacred earth.* (kisses knees)
> *Blessed be thy eros,*[38] *which may bring forth life.* (kisses eros)
> *Blessed be thy heart, which loves this world.* (kisses heart)
> *Blessed be thy lips, which speak the ancient truth.* (kisses lips)
>
> *I invoke and call upon thee, O god of the green growing places! Come down from your perch upon the high church walls and join us in our rite, for you have always loved and cared for us and this earth! We ask that you might descend into this, the body of your Priest and servant, so that we might know you and celebrate your gifts. Speak with his tongue, hear with his ears, touch with his hands, and love with his heart. These things we humbly ask, great god of rebirth and spring!*

Anytime a deity is drawn down, a coven or circle is opening itself up to the unknown. Most often the deities will play along with whatever you have scheduled, but sometimes they'll take control of your rite and lead you into strange pastures. Allow the Green Man to get his bearings for a bit before proceeding with the ritual, and ask him if he has anything specific to say. When all is clarified, ask him to participate in the ritual.

HIGH PRIEST: *My Lord Green Man, will you bless the soil we have gathered tonight for our rite?*

The Green Man should be led to the container of soil set aside for the ritual. When we do this ritual publicly, we keep the container on a large table that is not our altar but is

---

38. The term *eros* is a substitute for *phallus, vagina,* or *reproductive organ.*

still accessible. The Green Man should pick up his athame, or perhaps a trowel, and bless the soil for the ritual.

GREEN MAN: *I exorcise thee, O creature of earth, and cast out from thee all the impurities and uncleanliness. May you serve those gathered well this night as a place to cast out that which they no longer want. In my sacred soil, may it be transformed into something that serves this world. By my power, I say so mote it be!*

The athame (or other tool) is then placed into the container of soil and blessed by the power of the Green Man. The Green Man should then be directed to stand at the end of the table, where he can either hold the small bowl of soil or have it set directly in front of him. The High Priest then explains the rest of this part of the ritual before it proceeds.

HIGH PRIEST: *Tonight you have the opportunity to meet with the Green Man and cast out whatever in your life is negative. We shall form a line, and when you reach the table, write down whatever it is you wish to cast away. Once you've decided what it is that you would rid yourself of, focus on it as you draw closer to the dirt of the Green Man. When you approach the earth he has blessed for us, picture him rising up from the soil and swallowing and taking those negative things away, cleansing you as we prepare for the spring. Bury whatever it is you wish to rid yourself of in his fertile soil. Let it be taken into the earth, where the Green Man will carry it far away from you and from us. When you give your burdens up to him, take a moment to verbalize the process. Say "Gone!" or "Be rid of this!" to make the magic stronger.*

Ideally, everyone should move through the line rather quickly. It's probably best to have a few people near the table containing the soil to make sure everyone is moving through quickly. I suggest having music in the background here to cover up any restless energy as people stand in line. (Can I suggest the song "Green Man" by the band XTC?) If you have lots of room for your ritual, you can set up a writing station and a separate station for the Green Man and his soil. Spreading everything out gives people more things to do or at least anticipate.

The Green Man may talk to people, but in my experience he's not much of a talker. When everyone is done, the High Priest should thank the Green Man and the earth.

HIGH PRIEST: *Hail the Green Man! Hail the earth! Blessed be!*

The Cleansing by Eostre

HIGH PRIESTESS: *Tonight we call upon Eostre, the goddess of the dawn and new beginnings. We call to her, she who pours out her blessings upon the earth so that life may be renewed and all made sacred. It is your rain that purifies all that it touches, preparing us and this world for the spring and summer ahead. Lady of the Heavens, join us in our circle tonight! Purify your children for the year to come. Great Goddess, smile down upon us and truly join us in our circle tonight! Is there one here tonight who would channel the power of our Lady?*

EOSTRE: *I would.*

HIGH PRIESTESS: *Then we shall draw down the Goddess into you so that we might meet with the Maiden of the springtime.*

The High Priestess begins the fivefold kiss, moving up the body of Eostre's servant.

Blessed be thy feet, which awaken the earth. (kisses feet)
Blessed be thy knees, which help tend to this world. (kisses knees)
Blessed be thy eros,[39] from which life emerges. (kisses eros)
Blessed be thy heart, full of love and kindness. (kisses heart)
Blessed be thy lips, which shall utter the sacred truths. (kisses lips)

I invoke and call upon thee, O mighty Eostre, eternal goddess of the spring! Join us in our rites and renew our bodies and spirits as you renew the earth around us. Descend into this, the body of thy Priestess and servant, so that we might receive your love and blessings. Speak with her lips, touch with her hands, and see with her eyes. These things we most humbly ask of you who brings to us the spring!

As always when a deity is first invoked, be prepared, since they might do just about anything. When Eostre is firmly situated in the body of her servant, she will most likely ask you what you want her to do, or you can ask that she read a blessing (which is below).

HIGH PRIESTESS: *My Lady, will you read this blessing for us?*

EOSTRE: *Ostara is the dawn of spring, the entryway to summer. At the spring equinox, the earth stands fresh and renewed. Let us all be like the earth. Let us cast away the darkness of winter and embrace the wonder of green growing things. May we find delight in that which blooms*

---

39. The term *eros* is a substitute for *phallus, vagina,* or *reproductive organ.*

around us, and let us never forget our responsibility to this place we call home. This world is a magickal place. May my power and the beauty of nature remind us of that every day we draw breath.

 Tonight I shall journey among you so that you might receive my blessings. May my touch stir your heart and remind you of the magick and wonder inside us all. Put away your cynicism and doubt and embrace me, who gives the blessings of the spring. May my presence be a reminder of the power of the earth and of me, who is your Lady.

HIGH PRIESTESS: *My Lady, will you bless the salt and water we will use for our cleansing?*

Eostre takes her athame and sticks it into the bowls of water and blesses and cleanses them.

EOSTRE: *I exorcise thee, O creature of water, and cast out from thee all impurities and uncleanliness. By my power, you shall serve us well this night!*

Using her athame, Eostre adds a measure of salt to each bowl of water.

EOSTRE: *By my power, I exorcise thee, O creature of salt, and cast out from thee all impurities and uncleanliness. I now join together water and salt, earth and rain, so that my children can be renewed by my power and that of the spring! So mote it be!*

HIGH PRIESTESS: *We stand here with past negativity already taken away. We now renew ourselves with the gifts of the Lady. Visualize yourself newly reborn, clean, and whole, made pure by the light and love of our Lady. Let the touch of her gifts and power take away any lingering feelings of doubt or pain and be born anew by her magick.*

The quarter callers should walk up and pick up the bowls of salted water, which are then sprinkled upon everyone in attendance. To make this move more quickly, I suggest using four bowls of salted water, one for each quarter caller, so that all can be cleansed in an expedient manner.

HIGH PRIESTESS: *Tonight I walk this circle with our Lady so that you might honor her and thank her for her blessings.*

The High Priestess leads Eostre around the circle. All present should bow or curtsy (she is a goddess after all!), and they may touch or squeeze her hand. If there aren't a lot of people there, the goddess could conceivably speak with everyone, but if there are, then not so much unless you want a three-hour ritual.

When all have been cleansed and have met with the Lady, you'll want to publicly devoke the gods before moving on to cakes and ale. If your Eostre and Green Man are wearing masks or crowns of some sort, publicly removing them is a great way to indicate that the deity that was once inside of them has left. Start by devoking Eostre and welcoming back the person the goddess inhabited.

HIGH PRIESTESS: *And now we must thank those who have served us this night. My Lady, it is time for you to leave us in your current state and return our friend to us. We thank you for your presence and now welcome back our friend and fellow Witch. (Name of person), return! (Name of person), return!*

While speaking the name of the person who has drawn down Eostre, grab their hands and push some energy into their body. As you push the energy inward, think of the person you know and imagine their consciousness rising to the surface, with them being in control of themselves. If you're not quite sure if the deity within has left, a little salt on the tongue will go a long way in restoring a person to their regular state. Once the goddess has left, move on to the Green Man.

HIGH PRIEST: *And now you, my friend, thank you for your service. Great Green Man, it is time for you to leave the body you inhabit and return our friend to us. Great Lord, we are grateful for your presence, but we must welcome our fellow Witch back. (Name of person), return! (Name of person), return!*

Once the Green Man has left the body of his servant, escort him and the person who drew down Eostre to a comfortable chair and thank them once again for their service. Drawing down is hard work!

Cakes and Ale

HIGH PRIESTESS: *At Ostara, all stands in balance as the world is reborn.*

HIGH PRIEST: *We now celebrate that rebirth with the feast of cakes and ale.*

The High Priestess holds up a chalice of drink.

HIGH PRIESTESS: *The chalice and its contents are symbolic of the potential that exists within all things. In the spring, almost anything feels possible.*

The High Priest holds up a plate of cakes.

HIGH PRIEST: *And these cakes represent the abundance that is all around. Even when the world seems bleak, we know that we are blessed.*

BOTH: *Through the love of the Lord and Lady, all things are possible. Blessed be!*

Cakes and ale are distributed to everyone in the circle.

Goodbyes to the Gods

HIGH PRIEST: *Green Man, lord of the wood, keeper of the wild places, thank you for being with us in our rite this night. As the trees bud and the sun shines stronger, we will feel you close to us and know that you are watching over this world. Hail and farewell!*

HIGH PRIESTESS: *Eostre, goddess of the spring, Maiden of the equinox, thank you for being with us in our rite this night. Thank you for letting us receive your blessings and feel your magick. You are the power that makes the grass grow green and the flowers blossom. Continue to walk with us in the springtime and beyond. Hail and farewell!*

Dismissing the Quarters/Releasing the Circle.

Beginning in the north, dismiss the quarters, moving widdershins. If there are candles lit for any of the quarters, blow them out at the conclusion of each dismissal.

NORTH QUARTER CALLER: *We called for the blessings of the north and received them! Spirits of earth, thank you for joining us in our rite and blessing us with your great wisdom. Go if you must, stay if you will. Blessed be!*

WEST QUARTER CALLER: *We called for the blessings of the west and received them! Spirits of water, thank you for joining us in our rite and blessing us with fresh opportunities. Go if you must, stay if you will. Blessed be!*

SOUTH QUARTER CALLER: *We asked for the blessings of the south and received them! Spirits of fire, thank you for joining us in our rite and blessing us with your powers of transformation. Go if you must, stay if you will. Blessed be!*

EAST QUARTER CALLER: *We asked for the blessings of the east and received them! Spirits of air, thank you for joining us in our rite and blessing us with your powers of clarity. Go if you must, stay if you will. Blessed be!*

HIGH PRIEST: *As we brought our circle into existence together, we shall now release it together. As you tone outward, let the energy flow from within you and out into our circle, dissolving the power that has protected us and provided refuge for our rites.*

The High Priest should make a vowel sound different from the one used to build the circle, and instead of letting the energy peak, he should direct it downward, letting it fade out slowly. When satisfied that the circle has been released, he should indicate that the toning should stop.

HIGH PRIEST: *The circle is now open but never broken. Blessed be!*

HIGH PRIESTESS: *We have been blessed and cleansed by our Lady and Lord. Together we have welcomed in the spring and joined once more in fellowship and community. As we leave this place, take with you this fresh start and put it to good use. Until next we meet, remember that we are Witches all! Blessed be!*

FIN

CHAPTER 18

OSTARA COVEN RITUAL

Eggs and the Outdoors

When I lived in Michigan, Ostara often marked the first opportunity of the year to go outside and engage in ritual without being *too* uncomfortable. Since the average high temperature was only about 44 degrees Fahrenheit (or 6 degrees Celsius), our rituals would often start inside before transitioning into some sort of outdoor working and then returning to our indoor temple space. Just the idea of being able to go outside and do *something* usually made everyone a bit giddy with anticipation.

This ritual uses the inside / outside / inside formula and also requires a good bit of pre-ritual planning. The working in the middle utilizes decorated Easter eggs, and you'll need every participant to decorate their own (hard-boiled) egg before the ritual starts. I usually set things up in my kitchen and allow people to decorate their egg in the hour or so of pre-ritual socializing my coven generally engages in. In addition to decorating an egg, every coven member should write on their egg whatever it is they wish to grow in their lives as the world transitions from winter to spring.

If you've never boiled an egg for decorating before, it's surprisingly easy. Lay a single row of eggs on the bottom of a large saucepan or pot and cover them with water. You don't need a lot of water here, just enough to cover the eggs. Place your pot on a burner and heat on medium-high. Let the water boil for one minute. After the minute is over, turn off the heat and let the eggs sit (and cook) for another ten minutes, then transfer them to a bowl of ice cold water using a slotted spoon. They should sit in the cold water for just a minute or two and should be good to go from there. The eggs can be refrigerated when you're done and can be made days in advance of the ritual.

Decorating eggs is easy too and can be done however the coven wants. I usually just get an Easter egg dyeing kit (they retail for under two dollars) and set everything up on my kitchen table. Make sure to get a kit that comes with a crayon to allow people to write on their eggs. Usually this is a white crayon, but if you're making your own dyes, a regular crayon will work just as well.

Before letting people dye and decorate their eggs, I think it's a good idea to explain exactly what will be done with them. The magick really begins in this rite when the eggs are being dyed and decorated. As people dress their eggs, they should be conscious of what they wish to manifest from those eggs. Thinking about the end goal while decorating the egg will charge it with purpose and intent and will make for stronger magick. After the eggs have been decorated, they can be placed in a bowl or simply transferred back to their original containers and then taken into ritual space.

During the ritual, the decorated eggs will be taken outside and "planted" in the ground to symbolize the things we want to grow this spring. Because the eggs will be put into the ground, I strongly recommend avoiding the use of glitter, which is not a natural substance and can be harmful to plants and wildlife. Digging into the soft March ground is usually pretty easy, and we've found over the years that it typically can be done with a table or space spoon (this is the big spoon in most silverware collections). This will save you from having to come up with a bunch of gardening trowels.

I've been lucky enough to live within eight or nine blocks of a public park the last twenty years of my life, and such places are where we've typically buried our eggs. Backyards also work, of course, and if going outside is impossible, a couple of planters taken indoors will work too. California in March usually means rain, and that's not something we let deter us in ritual, even if it means a lot more prep time before heading outdoors in the middle of the rite.

In addition to eggs, this ritual calls for hot cross buns. These yeasty baked treats have been associated with Easter for hundreds of years. There are even some who claim that their use in the spring dates back to pagan antiquity, but no matter their origin, they are fun to make and will add an extra magickal twist to cakes and ale in this ritual. Recipes for hot cross buns can be found online, and there's also one in my book *The Witch's*

Athame. Hot cross buns take several hours to make, so give yourself a lot of pre-ritual prep time if you use them.

Since most people generally experience at least a little rain in March, this rite includes a little purification using rainwater. Obviously, if the rainwater in your area is discolored, smelly, or otherwise unseemly, you won't want to use it. Alternatively, you could also melt some snow if everything near you is still frozen, gather some water from a nearby creek or stream, or purchase a bottle of spring water.

This ritual is mostly about having fun, getting outside, and connecting with the energy of the season. I've always felt like Ostara is a time for childlike delight, and after watching my coven dye eggs, I've come to the conclusion that they must feel the same way.

Ritual Roles

- High Priestess
- High Priest
- Quarter callers
- Circle caster

Materials Needed

- Regular altar setup
- One hard-boiled, dyed, and decorated egg for each member of the coven
- A tablespoon for most every Witch (though these can be shared too)
- Hot cross buns (for cakes and ale)
- Ale
- Rainwater (or one of the alternatives listed above)

The Ritual: Eggs and the Outdoors

Before beginning the ritual, be sure that everyone's eggs are located inside the ritual space and can be easily and safely accessed. (You don't want to break one during the ritual!) The altar should be set up in the middle of the circle, with the coven standing in a circle around it. The hot cross buns can be placed under the altar or on a side table. As the buns are much larger than the usual "cakes" for cakes and ale, make sure to set aside enough space for them.

Cleansing/Opening

HIGH PRIESTESS: *As the world is renewed by the life-giving spring rains, let us be touched by their energies as well. May this gift of the Lord and Lady cleanse and bless you and prepare you for this rite. So may it be!*

Rainwater is sprinkled around the ritual space and onto the heads of each coven member. As the rainwater touches each covener, the High Priestess may say such things as "Be blessed by the power of the spring!" or "Be renewed by the waters of life!" Once everyone has been prepared, with the High Priest or another coven member sprinkling the rainwater on the High Priestess, the ritual begins in earnest.

HIGH PRIEST: *On this night of Ostara, winter now truly stands behind us, and before us lies the promise of spring. The Maiden walks the land once more, awakening the earth and bringing life to all upon her path. The Horned One lurks in the forest, running with the beasts upon the growing/thawing earth.*[40] *The world around us stands reborn: fresh blossoms, new green grasses, the scent of spring flowers upon the wind. Tonight let us greet the awakening earth and plant the seeds we wish to see bloom this spring. Welcome, Witches all! Blessed be!*

Casting the Circle/Calling the Quarters

Starting in the east, the circle caster creates the magick circle by walking clockwise with an athame, sword, or wand. If the outdoor portion of your ritual is in a backyard, the circle can be cast around the perimeter of the property, eliminating the need to cut people in and out of the circle later.

CIRCLE CASTER: *As the day begins in the east, so too does this circle. In the names of the Lord and the Lady, I cast this circle as a place of love and joy and truth, and as a shield to protect our work from those who would wish us failure or harm. In this place may we find ourselves among the Mighty Ones and between the worlds. The circle is cast. So mote it be!*

Starting in the east, the quarters are called. Candles can be lit at each of the quarters, and invoking pentagrams can be drawn at the end of each invocation if desired.

---

40. Depending on where you are, of course: *growing* if there's green outside your window, *thawing* if there's still snow.

EAST QUARTER CALLER: *I call to the warm winds of the east. Blow away the cold winter and join us in our circle tonight. Blessed be!*

SOUTH QUARTER CALLER: *I call to the bright sun of the south. Melt away the last snows of winter and join us in our circle tonight. Blessed be!*

WEST QUARTER CALLER: *I call to the rushing waters of the west. Bless us with the warm rains of spring and join us in our circle tonight. Blessed be!*

NORTH QUARTER CALLER: *I call to the green growing earth of the north. Free the ground from the icy cold and join us in our circle tonight. Blessed be!*

Calls to the God and the Goddess

HIGH PRIESTESS: *Tonight we call upon the young Horned God. We ask him to grace us with his sense of wonder and delight. May we see the world as he does, as new and beautiful and full of magick and wonderment. His power grows in the sky and his presence stirs the trees, the green of the earth, and our hearts. Great God, be with us tonight. Hail and welcome!*

HIGH PRIEST: *Tonight we call upon the Maiden, the goddess of the dawn and new beginnings. As the earth grows around us, let us bring change and growth into our own lives. Let us manifest your many blessings. You are the jeweled moon in the sky, the breeze that awakens all around us and brings forth new life. Great Goddess, smile down upon us and be a part of our circle this night. Hail and welcome!*

The Working

HIGH PRIESTESS: *We gather tonight to celebrate Ostara, a time of growth, opportunity, and potential. Before we began our ritual tonight, we had everyone in this coven decorate an egg and write upon it what they wish to grow this spring. We might want to grow the love in our lives or our financial opportunities, or give birth to a new project such as a book or a ritual. The possibilities are endless both for ourselves and for this time of year.*

HIGH PRIEST: *The egg has long been seen as a symbol of new beginnings. We know that life arises from eggs and that for many creatures the eating of eggs is essential to living. The symbolism of the egg is so powerful that it was borrowed from us and inserted into the religious traditions of others. In the early spring, the egg is a nearly universal symbol of new beginnings.*

HIGH PRIESTESS: *Tonight we shall take our eggs and bury them in the earth. Like an egg, our world is about potential, and it's also life-giving. Many Witches talk about the natural world as if it's a life-bestowing womb. This is not wrong, for all we are and all we have comes in some way from the gifts of the earth. Each year at this time, new life blooms and arises from the ground, nurtured by the power of the Great Goddess. This night we ask the earth to nurture our dreams and desires and for the Lady and Lord we love so dearly to add their powers to the eggs we will bury in the ground.*

The previously decorated eggs are now handed out. You can either have everyone go forward and look for their egg or simply walk around with the bowl/container holding the decorated eggs and let everyone take the one they created. The passing out of the eggs can be done by anyone in the circle.

HIGH PRIEST: *When your egg comes to you, pick it up and hold it in your hand. Think for a moment about all the potential both within it and within you. Look at what you've written upon your egg and imagine that for just a moment. Picture it coming true, and visualize the steps it will take to reach that place. As Witches, we know that our magick works only when we will it to do so. The eggs we carry are a focal point for our energies and desires.*

HIGH PRIESTESS: *Let us charge our eggs with our desires by chanting together. Repeat after me:*

> *Spring is here,*
> *Our desires near.*
> *What we will,*
> *The earth fulfill.*

You may have to repeat the chant a few times until everybody picks up on it.

HIGH PRIESTESS: *As we chant together, fill up your egg with the energy we raise so that we might manifest what we will!*

The chanting should go on for as long as is deemed necessary by the High Priestess. Generally, the chanting will get louder and more intense as it progresses. When it reaches a crescendo, the High Priestess should indicate that the chanting is done.

HIGH PRIESTESS: *Now we shall prepare to take our eggs outside and put them in the ground, where their energy will radiate out into the world and bring to us all we wish to grow this spring. As you bury your egg in the earth, say this chant:*

"By the power of the moon above and
Gifted by the power of our Lady's love,
As the sun shines high in the sky,
The Horned One shall hear my cry.
By wind, by fire, by land, and by sea,
This desire of mine, so shall it be!"

As you leave the circle, grab a tool to help you dig into the earth. Let your adventures outside be ones of growth and happiness, and may you find just the right space to leave your egg. My friend, (looking at the individual who cast the circle), can you please open our circle?

The circle caster should open the circle in a spot that allows people to leave the ritual space most easily, such as by a door. It doesn't have to be open in any particular spot.

CIRCLE CASTER: *I open a gateway from this circle so that we may journey out into the natural world this Ostara night. So mote it be!*

Everyone leaves the circle with a spoon and their egg. A printed version of the chant to be used while burying the egg (see above) can be handed out as well. If you have candles burning, you should either extinguish them or leave someone inside to watch over them.

What exactly people will do after leaving the circle varies from group to group and person to person. In my coven, we usually walk close to one another, some seriously and some boisterously, to the park across the street from my house. Once there, people separate and find just the right spot to bury their eggs. Often this is near a tree or some bushes, though there's no right or wrong. Some people bury their egg quickly, while others do so slowly. Just don't leave anyone behind outside alone in the dark if possible.

When everyone returns, they can go right back into the circle if the gateway wasn't mended (resealed) on the way out, or the person who was left behind can open and close the circle as needed to let everyone back in. Since we aren't really trying to hold much energy in the circle at this point of the ritual, I just leave the gateway open to make it easier for people to get back in. When everyone is back inside the circle, it should be sealed once more by the circle caster.

CIRCLE CASTER: *As the coven has gathered once more, I close and seal this circle. So mote it be!*

HIGH PRIEST: *That which we will make manifest has been placed in the womb of the earth, where it will grow and come to be! Our magick this Ostara night has been done. Blessed be!*

Cakes and Ale

The High Priestess takes her athame and the High Priest picks up the coven's chalice or cup.

HIGH PRIESTESS: *All stands in balance upon Ostara, night and day, sun and moon.*

HIGH PRIEST: *And that which would be joined together becomes as one.*

HIGH PRIESTESS: *Within and without, I hold the power of creation in my hands.*

HIGH PRIEST: *Within and without, I hold the power of creation in my hands.*

HIGH PRIESTESS: *We perform the Great Rite to remind ourselves of the ultimate mystery and the universal power from which all things are formed.*

HIGH PRIEST: *Knife to chalice,*

HIGH PRIESTESS: *Earth to sky,*

HIGH PRIEST: *Heart to heart,*

HIGH PRIESTESS: *And love to love,*

BOTH: *Worlds are born and the earth is renewed. So mote it be!*

The knife is plunged into the chalice and the cup is passed around to all in the circle. The High Priest then brings up the plate of hot cross buns to be blessed by the High Priestess. As she says the blessing over them, she touches them (or the plate) with her athame.

HIGH PRIESTESS: *In the names of the Lord and the Lady, I bless this bread. May it connect us to this land, our ancestors, and one another. So mote it be!*

The buns should be distributed by the High Priest, who gives one bun to every second person (every other person) in the circle.

HIGH PRIESTESS: *There is a lot of lore associated with the hot cross bun. One of the legends of this particular bun involves the friendships that come from sharing one. So we are going to pass a bun out to every other person in the circle, and those holding a bun should share it with the person on their left. All right? I know some of you can't have bread, so what I'd like you to do instead is to rip the bread and then put it in our libation dish on the altar.*

    The rhyme we will say here is "Half for you and half for me, between us two shall goodwill be!" Let's practice that together before we tear apart and eat our buns: "Half for you and half for me, between us two shall goodwill be!" (Repeated.) *Now all, tear and eat! Blessed be!*

Repeat the rhyme a couple of times with the coven until everyone has the couplet memorized. The easiest way to do this is to simply speak the rhyme and have the coven say it back to you. I usually repeat these four or five times. When you are satisfied that everyone knows the rhyme, you should then instruct the coven to tear and eat. Each pair should tear their hot cross bun in two and eat together, reserving some of the food and drink for the libation bowl.

Goodbyes to the Goddess and God

HIGH PRIEST: *We thank the Maiden for joining us this Ostara night. It is from you that all life springs and to you that all life returns. Walk with us in the days to come and let us feel the joy that radiates from you in the springtime. Bless our magick and our work, and help us to manifest that which we desire to be the best Witches we can be. Until next we meet, hail and farewell!*

HIGH PRIESTESS: *We thank the Horned God tonight for being a part of our rites. Great Lord, you have blessed us with your power and might this night and have helped us to create magick with one another. Allow us to see the world with your eyes and your sense of wonder as we welcome in the spring! Until next we meet, hail and farewell!*

Dismissing the Quarters/Releasing the Circle

EAST QUARTER CALLER: *The warm winds of the east have been a part of our rite and have blessed this circle. Spirits of air, we thank you for joining us this sacred night. Blessed be!*

SOUTH QUARTER CALLER: *The light of the sun has been a part of our rite and has blessed this circle. Spirits of fire, we thank you for joining us this sacred night. Blessed be!*

West Quarter Caller: *The rushing waters of the west have been a part of our rite and have blessed this circle. Spirits of water, we thank you for joining us this sacred night. Blessed be!*

North Quarter Caller: *The green growing earth has been a part of our rite and has blessed this circle. Spirits of earth, we thank you for joining us this sacred night. Blessed be!*

The circle caster picks up their sword or athame and takes down the circle, beginning in the west and moving deosil.

Circle Caster: *As the day ends in the west, so too does this circle. In the names of the Lord and the Lady, I cast this circle as a place of love and joy and truth and as a shield to protect and guard our work against failure and harm. In these tasks, this circle has served us well. We have walked between the worlds and in the steps of the Mighty Ones, and now, with tonight's journey ended, I take down this boundary. With love and light, we walk once more in the waking world. So mote it be!*

High Priestess: *Together we have celebrated the start of spring and planted that which we wish to grow in the coming months. Until next we meet, I say unto you, merry meet, and merry part, and merry meet again!*

FIN

CHAPTER 19

OSTARA SOLITARY RITUAL

Seeds in the Earth

A common feature of many sabbat rituals is the planting of seeds. This is a popular activity at spring rituals, especially because it mimics what's happening outside our bedroom windows. The only real downside to using seeds in ritual is that the seeds selected for use are often hard to cultivate or aren't all that useful. This rite calls for the ritual planting of three herbs that are all easy to grow from seed and have a variety of magickal uses.

Not every Witch has a green thumb, but most every Witch I know generally likes the *idea* of gardening. I realize that in this day and age, gardening can be difficult. It requires time, patience, and often money. (Have you ever heard the story of the sixty-four-dollar tomato?) It also generally requires space, but the plants used in this ritual are easy to grow indoors and don't require that much room. All that's really necessary is a window that gets at least a few hours of sunlight a day.

If you've never grown plants from seed before, it can be a bit more complicated than you think. Instead of using regular old potting soil, you'll generally want to start your seedlings in a soil mix designed especially for seedlings. The dirt in your backyard or the average bag of topsoil at a gardening store is often way too dense for seedlings to sprout in. Potting soil designed specifically for seedlings will increase your chances of success with this rite.

In this ritual, I've chosen to plant basil, mint, and thyme. I've selected these three herbs for several reasons. The first is that they grow easily from seed and are rather hardy. Even someone with a black thumb should be able to cultivate these plants. I've also chosen them because they have readily identifiable magickal properties and can be used in cooking. All three can be grown year round indoors too!

In addition to seeds and seedling soil, you'll need some small containers that drain reasonably well to hold your seeds. Once the seeds sprout, you'll most likely want to move them to a larger container and put them into regular potting soil. If you want to move the basil and thyme outdoors after Beltane, they should do well there. Just don't move the mint outside, as it's quite invasive and will take over your garden, your yard, and the yards of all your neighbors!

I've also combined the quarter calls and circle casting into one rite. For this you'll need four items to represent the elements, or you can simply light four candles and place them around the perimeter of your circle. I like flameless items best because there's less to worry about. When I create sacred space this way, I tend to use leaves for air (they blow in the wind), chili peppers for fire (hot!), a seashell for water, and a small bowl of rice for earth. Anything will work though, as long as the correspondence makes sense to you.

Materials Needed

- Regular altar setup
- Seed packets of basil, mint, and thyme
- Soil for seedlings, with containers
- An extra cup of water (to pour into your containers)
- A candle (if you don't normally have one on your altar)
- Four items to represent the elements (earth, air, fire, water)
- Lavender incense
- Cakes and ale

The Ritual: Seeds in the Earth

Start by lighting your lavender incense. Lavender is great for purification, so breathe in its smoke. As you smell the lavender and the smoke enters your body, imagine it cleansing you from the inside out. Allow it to work its magick and remove the stresses of the day, along with anything else inside your mind that might be keeping you from focusing on your rites. Let the incense smoke drift around your ritual space, and as you do so, visualize the smoke removing any negative energy there.

When you feel cleansed and focused, announce the start of your ritual.

I celebrate Ostara this night, the Spring Equinox. I honor the equal day and night and the potential to be found this time of year. Lord and Lady, stand with me in my rites as I honor you and the earth. Blessed be!

Casting the Circle/Calling the Quarters

Begin in the east and set your object representing air down upon the ground and welcome in the air.

I create this sacred space with air. May the winds of spring be a part of my rite and my magick. Hail the spirits of the east!

Move around the circle deosil, placing your remaining items at each of the cardinal points and then greeting each elemental power in turn. As you move around the circle, imagine the four elemental energies linking up to create your circle and sacred space.

I create this sacred space with fire. May the increasing warmth of spring be a part of my rite and my magick. Hail the spirits of the south!

I create this sacred space with water. May the power of the spring rains be a part of my rite and my magick. Hail the spirits of the west!

I create this sacred space with earth. May the power of the reawakening spring be a part of my rite and my magick. Hail the spirits of the north!

After calling to the north, return once more to the east and draw an invoking pentagram and declare your circle complete.

With air, fire, water, and earth, I have cast this circle! I am between the worlds. So mote it be!

Calling the Goddess and the God

I call to the Goddess of the Spring, the Maiden who walks the world anew at this turn of the wheel. Bless my rite and my work with your life-giving powers. Help me to manifest my dreams and desires and to grow closer to you and your mysteries. Hail and welcome!

I call to the God of the Wild Hunt, the lord of the wild spaces who roams the night. Be with me as I work my magick and my will. Lend me your power and energy and help me to realize my place on the wheel this Spring Equinox. Hail and welcome!

Planting Your Seeds

Start by looking at the small pots of soil upon your altar. Pick one up and lightly touch the dirt inside of it. As you touch the soil, think of all that the earth gives us. Remind yourself of its life-giving properties and how at this moment, at Ostara, it is slowly waking up, ready to create new life once more. I often think of the earth as a churning force in the early spring, gearing up to release all of its power in the coming weeks and months.

Set the pot of soil down and pick up your basil seeds. Not only is basil great on pizza, but it has all sorts of magickal uses too. One of its primary associations is with love and relationships.[41] As you hold your seeds, think of the things you care about and the love you have for those things growing in the coming months. Think about your connection to the earth, and how you feel (or don't feel) each turn of the wheel. Focus on your love of the earth for a moment, and see yourself in your mind's eye reacting to the change of the seasons and doing things that help the environment and actively put you outside. Place the basil seeds into the soil, and as you do so, push some of your energy into the soil as well.

I plant this basil for my love of the earth. May it draw me closer to those things I care about and keep those things that would do me harm far away. So mote it be!

Next pick up your mint seeds and imagine yourself healthy and strong over the coming months. Visualize yourself doing all the things you wish to do in this lifetime, and doing them successfully. Mint is useful for healing spells and is a practical remedy for an upset stomach and other ailments. It's also effective in travel and money spells, so don't hesitate to picture yourself outside and away from home.

---

41. All herbal correspondences in this ritual are taken from *Cunningham's Encyclopedia of Magical Herbs*, published by Llewellyn. My copy is the twenty-third printing from 1997.

I plant this mint for my love of self. May I be healthy, successful, and able to do all that I desire as long as it harms none. As my mint grows, may my ability to work my will grow along with it. So mote it be! (As you say "So mote it be!" the seeds should be in the earth.)

Finally, pick up the thyme seeds and hold them in your dominant hand. Thyme, like mint, is associated with health and healing but was traditionally burned in Greek temples to cleanse them magickally. It can also allow us to see the fair folk when kept on the body and help develop psychic powers. All of these characteristics are useful when making magick.

Plant your seeds as you say these words:

I plant this thyme for my love of the Craft. May it purify my altar, my tools, and this ritual space so that I might grow closer to the Lord and Lady. As my thyme grows, I vow that my abilities as a Witch will grow along with it. So mote it be!

Take your athame and stick the point of it into each of the three pots of soils. As you do so, push some of your own energy into the earth and the seeds you've planted. If you don't have an athame, you can use a wand or even your finger. As your plants grow, the energy you've placed in them and the soil will grow too, and anytime you use them magickally (or even just when cooking dinner), you'll tap into that energy.

Nothing occurs in a vacuum, and that's even more true when it comes to the creation of new life. To grow a plant, you need seed, soil, warmth, sunlight, water, and a safe environment. In this section of the rite, your seed and soil will be blessed by each of the elements (air/incense, water/water, light/fire, and earth/the warmth of your hand). Take each of your small planters and run them through your incense, hold them up to the candlelight, pour a bit of water into them, and then pick them up one last time, infusing them with the warmth of your hand. When you're done, recite this blessing upon them:

> *Seeds and magick grow,*
> *My true will shall flow.*
> *This Ostara night,*
> *I chant by candlelight.*
> *Seed and soil, light and rain,*
> *So may it be ardane!* [42]

---

42. *Ardane* is a word found in some Witchcraft traditions that basically means "may it be so."

At the conclusion of your ritual, place your potted plants in a sunny spot, and occasionally infuse them with energy if you feel the need. Because you grew, planted, and infused them with your energy, they should work even more powerfully for you when using them in magickal work.

Cakes and Ale

Take your chalice and raise it up toward the Goddess, thanking her for the drink you are about to consume.

> *Gracious Goddess, it is your abundance that is poured out upon the earth. At Ostara, I feel your rising power and thank you for your gifts. Blessed be!*

Take a deep drink from the cup and set it upon your altar. Pick up a cake (or whatever it is that you're eating) and hold it aloft for the God.

> *Giving God, it is your sacrifice that turns the wheel and sustains us in winter. Reborn, we thank you for your emerging gifts once again. Blessed be!*

Be sure to put some of your food and drink in your libation bowl to give to the Goddess and God at the conclusion of your ritual. As you eat and drink, reflect for a moment on the balance of Ostara and the magick that's created when two things come together. Seed and soil, Goddess and God, night and day, spring and fall, cakes and ale … there are always at least two sides of everything worth exploring.

Thanks to the Goddess and God

> *Lord and Lady, you have blessed my rites and touched me with your magick. I thank you for joining me upon this Ostara night. May I feel your presence in the longer, warmer days ahead. Watch over my seedlings, and as they grow, may I be reminded of your blessings. Blessed be!*

Releasing the Circle / Thanking the Elements

Starting in the east and walking widdershins, pick up each of the four items you originally placed on the ground. As you pick up each one, visualize that section of the circle drifting out and away. If you like, you can thank each element as you pick up their symbol, but no words are truly necessary. Walk the entire perimeter of the circle, returning to the east. Once there, announce the release of your circle and the end of your rite.

With air, fire, water, and earth, I cast this circle, and now I release that energy out from whence it came. In this space I have celebrated the Spring Equinox and joined with my Lord and Lady. Spring lies ahead and winter behind. May the gods ever preserve the Craft!

FIN

CHAPTER 20

BELTANE
Spring's Delight

Name of Sabbat: Beltane (also spelled Bealtaine, Beltain, Beltene, Beltin, and Belltaine;
also known as May Eve, Walpurgis Night, and May Day)

Date: May 1 or April 30

Pronunciation: "BELL-tane"

Beltane was originally an Irish-Celtic holiday that later spread throughout the British
Isles. There are several different spellings of Beltane, but the most familiar one (and the
one I use in this book) comes from Sir James Frazer and his book *The Golden Bough*. The
origin of the word *Beltane* most likely lies with the Celtic root word *bel*, which translates
as "bright" or "fortunate." Many erroneously link Beltane to particular deities, most notably the Austrian Belenus or the Canaanite Baal (later turned into a Jewish/Christian
demon), but there's no evidence in Ireland (or anywhere else) for this.[43]

Beltane first shows up in the historical record in the year 900 CE, where it's referenced in the *Sanus Chormaic* (or *Cormac's Glossary)*, a glossary of Irish words most likely
written by someone connected to the Catholic Church. The author of *Cormac's Glossary*
doesn't mention Witches in their work, but they do mention Druids:

> BELLTAINE 'May-day' i.e. *bil-tene* i.e. lucky fire, i.e. two fires which Druids used to
> make with great incantations, and they used to bring the cattle [as a safeguard]

---

43. Hutton, *Stations of the Sun*, 218–219.

against the diseases of each year to those fires [*in marg.*] they used to drive the cattle between them. [44]

The Beltane (or *Belltaine*) outlined in *Cormac's Glossary* doesn't have much in common with most modern Beltane celebrations. For many centuries (if not millennia), Beltane was primarily a fire festival.

Even after the British Isles had mostly converted to Christianity, fire continued to play a large role in Beltane celebrations (which in some places were celebrated on May 2). Fire was used to protect people, villages, and especially cattle right up until the early twentieth century. In modern-day Edinburgh, Scotland, Beltane is still celebrated as a fire festival, though its reestablishment as a fire festival is relatively recent, having started in 1988.[45]

The Irish weren't alone in celebrating late April / early May as a fire festival. A similar thing was happening in Germany on Walpurgis Night (April 30). Named after the Christian Saint Walpurga (710–778), who helped Christianize Germany, Walpurgis Night was thought to be an especially active night for Witches in some parts of Germany. So great was the presence of Witches on that particular evening that the night was also known as *Hexennacht*, or "Witches' Night." Scared Christians built bonfires to keep the Witches away and invoked Saint Walpurga to protect them. Due to the distance between Germany and Ireland, it's unlikely that Beltane and Walpurgis Night are directly related, but it's interesting that the energies on that particular night inspired similar practices.

Beltane, as we know it today as Witches, comes in large part from the English celebration of May Day. May Day itself might possibly be connected to the Germanic paganisms that were practiced in England during the medieval period or somehow linked to Beltane as it was practiced in Ireland and later Scotland. Celebrations near the first of May can be found throughout Europe (not just Great Britain) and are generally festive, which is in direct contrast to the Irish-Celtic Beltane.

It's from the English celebrations of May Day that we get the maypole, Jack in the-Green, May Queens, and a Beltane that is more celebratory than ominous. By the end of the nineteenth century, many of the traditions that were a part of the English May Day were being associated with ancient pagan practices and, by extension, Beltane. Things

---

44. O'Donovan, *Cormac's Glossary*, 19.

45. "About Beltane Fire Festival," Beltane Fire Society, https://beltane.org/about/about-beltane/.

like the maypole and May Queens (some of which we'll look at more extensively shortly) might very well be survivals from the pagan past, but they weren't originally associated with the Irish-Celtic Beltane.

The first reference to the English celebration of May Day dates to 1240 and was written by a bishop demeaning his priests for "games which they call the bringing-in of May." [46] From 1240 right up until the present day, reflections on the English May Day have revolved around joy, games, frivolity, and dalliances. It was a time to decorate with what was in season, namely flowers and other blooming foliage. The decorations we most associate with Beltane today come from the "less heavy" celebration of May Day and the start of the English summer.

What I think many people miss when it comes to the sabbats is that how we celebrate them should be directly tied to the ideas and themes that resonate most within us. Many people see spring as a celebratory time of year, and because of that, Beltane has become a sabbat focused on things that are joyous: the green earth, fertility, frolicking, and fun. The sabbats are a cause for celebration and Beltane is the biggest celebration of them all. There were no Druids doing maypole dances in the year 100 CE, but that's inconsequential.

Ways to Celebrate Beltane

My earliest Beltane rituals generally revolved around the idea of the Maiden Goddess consummating her relationship with the young Horned God. My friends and I often did rituals featuring our young Horned God (the Goat Boy) chasing the Maiden before finally wooing her and going back to her bedchamber. In recent years I have decided such rituals are problematic because they don't do a very good job of portraying consent and they limit expressions of human sexuality to the female-male dynamic. I still think the idea of beginning a sexual relationship can be a welcome one at a Beltane ritual, as long as it's done in a way that explicitly conveys consent and is open to many interpretations of sexuality.

In recent years I've seen female representatives of the young Goddess joining together to celebrate the earth's fertility at Beltane, and pairs of male ones too. Witchcraft is a path that deals with adult issues in a responsible way, and ignoring the desire many of us have for sex and companionship seems just as limiting as devoting our rites only to

---

46. Hutton, *Stations of the Sun*, 226.

female-male sexual union. Our circles should be inclusive spaces, so whatever we do for a Beltane ritual should resonate with everyone we celebrate with. And private explorations of love and desire are most certainly a tradition for many at Beltane. It was such a part of my early life as a Witch that my friends and I used to call the sounds of desire we'd hear on May Eve "Beltaining."

Though it generally takes place away from most Witch circles, the custom of Morris dancing on Beltane morning can be found all over the English-speaking world and beyond. The exact origins of Morris dancing will probably always be in dispute (is it an ancient pagan practice or a more modern one?), but it's been a part of Beltane traditions for hundreds of years. Luckily for us, many Morris sides (a *side* is a name for a troop of Morris dancers) contain a couple of Pagan folk, and if you know just the right person, you might be able to work some Morris dancing into your Beltane ritual.

The maypole is seen by many as the primary symbol of Beltane, and it's a good one, but it doesn't have to be the focus of every Beltane ritual. A good maypole dance before or after your primary Beltane rite can be a joyous end or beginning to a full day of festivities. Traditionally, kings and queens were selected at many May Day and Beltane celebrations, and rituals proclaiming everyone in attendance the Queen or King of the May can be a lot of fun. Alternatively, simply picking two people as May Day royalty and giving them certain responsibilities both during and after ritual is a great way to make the most of this old custom.

The first Beltane celebrations were fire festivals, and kindling a Beltane fire can help us get in touch with our ancient ancestors. Though we don't associate Beltane with protective magick very often today, Beltane fires were lit primarily for that purpose. They were thought to keep maleficent fairy folk away at a crucial time of the year—planting season. Cattle were also made to jump over small fires to safeguard their health in the summer and to make sure their milk didn't sour.[47] In some parts of Scotland, the ashes from Beltane fires were used as a form of protection and scattered around the village or inside one's home.

For many people, Beltane is the height of spring and their first real chance to spend some quality time outdoors. When I lived in Michigan, Beltane was a celebration of high spring. There were (finally) trees with leaves on them, and the scent of flowers. When you've been cooped up inside for the first half of the year, that stuff means a great deal.

---

47. Hutton, *Stations of the Sun*, 219.

Celebrating those events also connects us to the Wheel of the Year in a very real and tangible way.

The tradition of Jack in the Green has been linked to the start of spring by many Witches over the years. Originally a promotion for chimney sweeps, the colorful figure known as Jack in the Green evolved out of a custom featuring dancing milkmaids with their heads and milk pails adorned with flowers and May greenery. Eventually this evolved into a decorated wooden pyramid on top of their heads, which was later picked up by English rag pickers and eventually chimney sweeps.[48]

I've always seen Jack in the Green as a Green Man–like figure celebrating the joys of spring. This makes him a very Pagan and, by extension, Witch-like figure in my book, and bringing him into our May Day rites seems more than appropriate. Beltane is a time for joy and is one of the most beloved sabbats on the Witch's Wheel of the Year.

---

48. Ibid., 242.

CHAPTER 21
BELTANE CIRCLE RITUAL
Hail the Maypole!

When it comes to large Beltane gatherings, the maypole is a must! Luckily, maypoles aren't all that difficult to build, and the dances that revolve around them are fun and easy to coordinate. Most maypole dances are about nothing more than celebrating the spring, community, and the beauty of the now green earth, and I think that's great! Sabbats don't have to be about anything more than having fun, but I'm of the opinion that if a group of Witches is going to go through all the trouble of casting a circle and raising energy, then that energy should be put to good use.

When trying to think of a magickal activity to include with a maypole, my mind kept coming back to what a maypole dance with ribbons most resembles: a binding spell. This particular ritual is about tying up the past and moving forward with life, just as the earth does in the spring and early summer. What's great about the magick being woven in this ritual is that it doesn't take away from the joy of a maypole dance and puts all the energy raised during it to work!

While maypoles are thought of as phallic symbols by many people today, that association is a rather recent one, and is only about 150 years old. When the maypole first shows up in the historical record (in about 1300), it's simply as a place for people to congregate after the long winter.[49] Eventually people began to dance around it and decorate it with greenery and flags. In the nineteenth century, people began to tie ribbons to the top of it,

---

49. Hutton, *Stations of the Sun*, 233–234.

and the dances that revolved around it began to resemble the ones most familiar to us today. Maypoles are not meant to be penises, and maypole dances are for everyone.

Maypoles are rather easy to make and can be constructed from PVC pipe (especially useful if you plan to reuse your maypole from year to year), metal pipe, or a wooden pole. At the top of your maypole you'll want to place a "crown," or hoop, that has your ribbons attached to it. I generally attach the hoop to the pole by inserting (or securing) a large screw with an eyelet into the top of my pole and attaching the hoop to that. I think thicker, wide ribbon works best for a maypole, and the length of each ribbon should be double that of your maypole. (So if your maypole is ten feet high, each ribbon attached to the hoop should be twenty feet long.) Securing your maypole in the ground almost always requires a bit of substantial digging, but it's worth the effort.

Before the ritual starts, you'll want to have each participant write what they wish to bind on the maypole. If you plan on reusing your maypole from year to year and your maypole is made of PVC pipe, erasable markers can be used. If your pole is made of wood or metal and you want to reuse it, simply take some sort of durable tape (like masking tape) and wrap it around one or two feet of the maypole, enough so that everyone participating has enough room to write on the pole. (When reusing your maypole the following year, simply remove the tape, and voilà!)

Maypole dances always require at least a little bit of music. If you have access to drummers or simply people who can keep a steady beat while clapping their hands, that works really well. Recorded music also works and is probably easiest if you don't know a lot of drummers. I'm a fan of Celtic jigs and reels for my maypole activities, though preferences vary, of course, and you should use whatever works for your group.

The most common maypole dance is one that weaves the ribbons onto the pole and, in the case of this ritual, binds what everyone has written on the pole. When starting the dance, have every participant grab a ribbon and then count off: 1, 2, 1, 2, etc. Be sure there's an equal amount of 1s and 2s. Once everyone has counted off and has hold of a ribbon, have everyone face inward toward the maypole. The 1s should be instructed to all turn to their left and the 2s to their right. When the dance starts, the 1s will raise their ribbons over the heads of the 2s, walking clockwise, and the 2s will duck under the ribbons of the 1s, moving counterclockwise. This is followed by the 2s going over the 1s with their ribbons: 1 over 2, 2 over 1, 1 over 2, 2 over 1, repeated over and over again.

Instead of trying to chant something complicated when everyone is engaged in the maypole dance, my groups over the years have simply chanted "one, two, one, two" over and over, with one being an indication that the 1s should go over the 2s and two being an indication that the 2s should now be going over the 1s. In large groups, maypole dances can get quite chaotic, and there's no harm if someone messes up at some point during the dance. When a dancer runs out of ribbon, they are out of the dance and should retreat to the outside of the circle and cheer on the remaining participants. (The instructions for the ritual provide a specific chant at the end of the dance.)

There's nothing particularly different or complicated about this ritual, minus the maypole. Since Beltane is generally celebrated as a fun sabbat these days, and most large rites are done during the daytime, there's no reason for an overly protective circle or to call more defensive energies such as the watchtowers. The method of circle casting used in this ritual, "hand to hand we cast this circle," is one of my favorites for the spring and summer sabbats, especially at public rites.

Materials Needed

- Standard working altar
- Maypole (with ribbons)
- Markers (and possibly tape, depending on what your maypole is made of)
- Cakes and ale
- Music player (optional)
- Floral (naturally) scented essential oil (Be sure to inform everyone what you're using before the ritual starts in case of allergies.)
- Incense sticks (something earthy)

Ritual Roles

- High Priestess
- High Priest
- Four quarter callers
- Drummers (if possible)

The Ritual: Hail the Maypole!

The maypole should be set up in the middle of the circle. The working altar should either be one that can be easily moved (to get it out of the way for the maypole dance/working) or be situated a fair distance away from the maypole. My Beltane rituals often start in a *U* shape, with the altar placed near the edge of the circle and no one behind it except for those conducting the rite.

Before the ritual begins, everyone in attendance should be instructed to write "that which they wish to forget about or be rid of" on the maypole in whatever fashion works best for your group. This can be done during the ritual but often results in a rather chaotic scene, so it's easiest to do it before everything officially starts.

Statement of Intent/Cleansing

High Priestess: *Today we celebrate Beltane. In many ways Beltane is the most joyous of all the sabbats. It's the celebration of high spring and the start of summer. It's a day designed so that we can be free of care and worry, and it's an opportunity to set aside the things that have been troubling us. Our rite is about happiness, community, the beauty of the now green earth, and looking forward so that we might embrace the summer with joy in our hearts. Hail Beltane!*

The High Priest places a bowl of water upon the altar's pentacle and places a few drops of essential oil in it.

High Priest: *Lord and Lady, lead us into the magick and wonder of summer. May this scented water cleanse and refresh us so that we might truly be ready to celebrate with you. So mote it be!*

The High Priestess places a candle upon the altar's pentacle and lights it, then lights a few sticks of incense with the candle flame. If outdoors, I suggest using a jar candle or other type of candle that won't be blown out by the spring breeze.

High Priestess: *Lord and Lady, blaze a trail and lead us toward the high spring. May this incense smoke bless and consecrate not just us but also this space as we prepare for our Beltane revels. So mote it be!*

The High Priestess and High Priest walk around with the scented water and incense, purifying the participants and the space. In the case of a very large group, this should be done quickly. In other words, unless you want the ritual to last for three hours, you can't realistically spend three minutes cleansing every participant.

Casting the Circle/Calling the Quarters

The method of circle casting being used in this ritual is called "hand to hand we cast this circle," which means everyone in the rite is casting the circle together. The High Priestess should start with the High Priest on her left and say, "Hand to hand we cast this circle," while placing her left hand into the right hand of the High Priest. He then repeats this phrase and action, with the person after him repeating it until everyone is holding hands. The idea here is that everyone is sharing energy and creating a magick circle. This sounds far more complicated than it really is, and everyone who has ever participated in a circle casting this way has figured it out pretty quickly.

HIGH PRIESTESS: *And now together we shall all raise the magick circle.* Looking at the High Priest: *Hand to hand we cast this circle.*

HIGH PRIEST: *Hand to hand we cast this circle.* And so on until returning to the High Priestess.

HIGH PRIESTESS: *As one, we have cast this circle and created sacred space. So be it done!*

Starting in the east, call the quarters. Candles can be lit at each of the four quarters if you wish, but this can be cumbersome with the maypole dance yet to come.

EAST QUARTER CALLER: *I call to the spirits of the east to attend this circle and harken to our call. Powers of air, be present in our ritual and bless us with your gifts of creativity and inspiration this Beltane rite. Hail and welcome!*

SOUTH QUARTER CALLER: *I call to the spirits of the south to attend this circle and harken to our call. Powers of fire, be present in our ritual and bless us with your gifts of energy and passion this Beltane rite. Hail and welcome!*

WEST QUARTER CALLER: *I call to the spirits of the west to attend this circle and harken to our call. Powers of water, be present in our ritual and bless us with your gifts of emotion and compassion this Beltane rite. Hail and welcome!*

NORTH QUARTER CALLER: *I call to the spirits of the north to attend this circle and harken to our call. Powers of earth, be present in our ritual and bless us with your gifts of stability and understanding this Beltane rite. Hail and welcome!*

Calls to the Goddess and God

HIGH PRIEST: *We call to the Great Lady to join us in our Beltane rite. Gracious Goddess, bring us your gifts of love and joy as we conjure the summer in. In the spring you walk the world anew, bringing forth life and abundance with every step. In the sky, you are the Mistress of the Moon, bringing us all magick and mystery! You are the beauty of the green earth from which all things grow. Touch our circle as you do our lives. Hail and welcome!*

HIGH PRIESTESS: *We call to the Great God to join us in our Beltane rite. Shining One, bring us your power and energy as we welcome the summer in and celebrate spring in all its glory and abundance. Come to us as the Horned One who runs wild and free upon the land, bringing joy and merriment to all the folk. Shine down upon us as the Lord of the Sun, awakening the earth and all the green growing things. Hail and welcome!*

Maypole Working

HIGH PRIEST: *Beltane is a time for looking forward. Ahead of us are long days full of sunshine and abundance, crops to harvest, and magick to manifest in our lives. With the last vestiges of winter now far behind us, we use this opportunity to set aside and forget the things that are not useful to us. Upon this maypole we have all written down things we would rid from our lives, and from this moment on, those things are in the past. With this pole and our community and the love we share for the earth and one another, we will bind them and remove them from our lives. Let us forget that which troubles us and embrace the wonder of this season. So mote it be!*

Getting everyone lined up and ready to start a maypole dance is no mean feat. Whoever is best at managing organized chaos should take the lead here. Instructions are given for organizing a maypole dance in the write-up that proceeds this ritual. Whatever you do, be patient and kind, and be prepared to go over the how-tos needed here slowly. Even the most experienced groups often have trouble getting a maypole dance started. When everyone is clear about how to proceed, the High Priestess should continue.

HIGH PRIESTESS: *Today we look forward and not backward. We celebrate Beltane and put behind us those things we would get rid of. Focus not on worries this day but on the joy of this holiday. And now let the dance begin!*

Whatever form of music you're using should start now with the dancing. Many people like to chant while the dance is going on, but that can be a bit distracting. Eventually a group of forty dancers will turn into one of six or eight. When the numbers begin to decline to that extent, you'll want everyone who is out of the dance to start clapping, chanting, and raising energy. The chant I like to use here is "Look ahead!" since it fits the intent of the rite.

Everyone should continue to chant "Look ahead!" until everyone dancing has run out of ribbon. When that happens, the High Priestess should direct all the energy that's been raised up and out of the circle, taking everyone's worries away with it. We usually do this by indicating something like "three more times," letting everyone know that the chant is almost over and that we will end together after three more refrains. Usually everyone's energy ratchets up when this happens. After the energy has been released, have everyone take a deep breath before beginning cakes and ale.

HIGH PRIESTESS: *And with that, all that no longer serves us has been taken away. Let all be free to start the May with happiness and joy. So mote it be!*

The Great Rite/Cakes and Ale

The High Priest holds the ritual cup while the High Priestess picks up her athame or wand. At the conclusion of the Great Rite, the athame is plunged into the chalice. If you need to reset the altar, as in move it back toward the center of the circle, do so before starting this part of the ritual.

HIGH PRIEST: *Life is more than a gift; it is a promise. All that dies in the autumn and winter shall be reborn to us in the spring.*

HIGH PRIESTESS: *As the sky joins with the earth, we too shall celebrate the joys of union.*

HIGH PRIEST: *As the cup is to the earth,*

HIGH PRIESTESS: *The athame is to the sky.*

Both: *United in life and abundance. Blessed be!*

The cakes and ale are brought forward by the quarter callers, blessed by the High Priestess and High Priest, and then distributed to everyone at the ritual.

High Priest: *In the names of the Lord and the Lady, we bless this drink.*

High Priestess: *In the names of the Lord and the Lady, we bless this bread.*

As each item (drink and food) is blessed, it (or the serving platter it might be on) is touched by an athame or wand. When I do this rite, I just have the High Priestess bless everything, since she already has her athame in her hand.

Goodbyes to the Lady and the Lord

High Priest: *We thank the Great Lady for being with us in these rites. Gracious Goddess of earth, sea, and sky, continue to watch over us and those we love in the days ahead. May we ever continue to see your beauty in the world around us. Hail and farewell!*

High Priestess: *We thank the Great God for being with us in these rites. O Horned One, continue to walk with us and be a part of our journey through this life. May we ever feel your power in the world around us. Hail and farewell!*

Dismissing the Quarters/Releasing the Circle

Starting in the north, dismiss the quarters, moving widdershins. Be sure to blow out any candles (if used) as each quarter is dismissed.

North Quarter Caller: *Spirits of the north, you have attended our circle and blessed us with your gifts. Powers of earth, we thank you for being present in our rites. Hail and farewell!*

West Quarter Caller: *Spirits of the west, you have attended our circle and blessed us with your gifts. Powers of water, we thank you for being present in our rites. Hail and farewell!*

South Quarter Caller: *Spirits of the south, you have attended our circle and blessed us with your gifts. Powers of fire, we thank you for being present in our rites. Hail and farewell!*

East Quarter Caller: *Spirits of the east, you have attended our circle and blessed us with your gifts. Powers of air, we thank you for being present in our rites. Hail and farewell!*

To release the circle, indicate that everyone should once again hold hands. This can be done silently (everyone usually picks up on it pretty quickly) or with an announcement. Once everyone is holding hands, the High Priestess should address all of those gathered and then release her hand from the one she is holding on her right. In this way, the circle is taken down counterclockwise. Unlike the casting of the circle, no words need to be said by the ritual's participants.

HIGH PRIESTESS: *Hand to hand we did cast this circle, and now we release that energy, which has served us so well.*

Once the circle releasing has gone around and reached the High Priestess, she should indicate once more that the circle has been released.

HIGH PRIESTESS: *Our circle is now open, but our fellowship will never be broken. So mote it be! And now with our Beltane rites having ended, I wish you the joy of the May and the summer season! May the sun ever be at your back and the road ahead be free of obstacles. Until next we gather, I say to you, merry meet, and merry part, and merry meet again!*

FIN

CHAPTER 22
BELTANE COVEN RITUAL
A Joyous Beltane to You

Beltane might be the most celebratory of all the sabbats. Spring is in full-bloom in most places by May 1, with summer right around the corner, and it's hard not to get swept up in that kind of energy. It's also traditionally a time for lovers and rendezvous in the now green grass under the moonlight. When I was younger, many of the rituals I conducted focused on the more amorous aspects of Beltane, but as I've grown older, I've moved away from that model because I don't think it's representative of the more inclusive Witchcraft I practice today. (Not everyone is looking for such things on Beltane.)

Today the rites of my coven during Beltane focus on harnessing the growing energy of the earth and building community. At the end of the working, all that energy is then gathered up and sent to where it's needed most. There are no goddesses or gods drawn down in this ritual, and there is only one small magickal working. The focus is mostly on the joy of the season. In order to link this rite with the Beltane of the ancient past, it does include a ceremonial jump over a candle.

For this ritual you'll also need some sort of music player and ideally a musical version of the 1906 Rudyard Kipling poem "A Tree Song," which was set to music in 1970 by Peter Bellamy and renamed "Oak, Ash and Thorn." The song has been covered numerous times since then, often by Pagan artists. (My favorite version is by the band Coyote Run.) It's been a part of Witch circles for nearly as long, and can be heard playing in the rites of many Witch covens at Beltane (despite its references to Midsummer).

This rite can be done indoors or out, and while many public groups prefer to hold their Beltane rituals during daylight hours, I think coven rites are always better at night. Instead of the usual incense and salted water, this rite utilizes a besom (broom) and a bowl of water for the cleansing. I like to use rainwater here when I can, but if that's unavailable in your area, any other sort of water will work just as well.

Ritual Roles

- High Priestess
- High Priest
- Circle caster
- Four quarter callers

Materials Needed

- Usual altar setup
- Music player with the song "Oak, Ash and Thorn" (unless you just want to recite the poem as a group)
- Candle in a solid, stable candleholder; alternatively, two candles for people to walk between
- Besom
- Bowl of rainwater (or any type of water available to you)

The Ritual: A Joyous Beltane to You

The altar should be placed in the center of the circle, with everyone in the coven gathered in a circle around it. When everyone is attentive and focused, the High Priestess should begin the ritual.

Statement of Intent/Purifying

HIGH PRIESTESS: *Tonight we celebrate Beltane, the ancient fire festival of the Celts. For the Celts, Beltane was the start of summer and offered a brief respite after planting the grain. It was a time of spellcraft, when magick was used to protect what was planted in the spring and ensure a bountiful harvest in the fall. Tonight we celebrate the fire of Beltane, and we do so with love in our hearts and joy in our souls. So mote it be!*

HIGH PRIEST: *I now ask all of you to put your hands together and dust off from them all that does not serve you. Brush away any worries or mundane problems so that we might cast them out of this circle.*

After everyone has brushed off any negativity upon them, the High Priest begins sweeping around the circle clockwise, collecting all of the negative energy. It should then be swept out of the circle in either the north or the west (or, if indoors, through whatever door is available). The High Priest may need to make a few circuits around the circle to sweep out all that is undesired. When he's done, the High Priestess should pick up the bowl of rainwater.

HIGH PRIESTESS: *As the rain falls from the sky and refreshes the earth, let it now refresh those of us gathered in this place. May this gift renew and cleanse you as it does the earth.*

Walking clockwise, the High Priestess sprinkles water upon the ritual space and all gathered within it. (We usually lightly sprinkle it over the heads of those we're circling with.) When the High Priestess is done, the High Priest or another member of the coven can sprinkle the water upon the High Priestess.

Circle Casting / Quarter Callers

Beginning in the east and walking clockwise, the circle caster takes up the coven's sword (or their own athame) and casts the Beltane circle.

CIRCLE CASTER: *With love and joy I cast this circle. May it serve to safeguard our Beltane rite and bring us ever closer to one another and our Lord and Lady. This circle shall be a bridge between the worlds and an entryway into the realm of spirit. All in this space will be of love, and love is what creates this circle. The circle is cast. So mote it be!*

The quarters are called, beginning in the east and proceeding clockwise. Candles can be lit at each of the quarters if desired, and invoking pentagrams may be drawn at the end of each call.

EAST QUARTER CALLER: *I call to the spirits of the east, spirits of air, knowledge, and freedom. Be with us in our rites and lend your warm breezes to the magick we raise together this night. Hail and be welcome!*

SOUTH QUARTER CALLER: *I call to the spirits of the south, spirits of fire, enthusiasm, and passion. Be with us in our rites and lend your heat and vitality to the magick we raise together this night. Hail and be welcome!*

WEST QUARTER CALLER: *I call to the spirits of the west, spirits of water, initiation, and emotion. Be with us in our rites and lend your life-creating power to the magick we raise together this night. Hail and be welcome!*

NORTH QUARTER CALLER: *I call to the spirits of the north, spirits of earth, stone, and field. Be with us in our rites and lend your steadfastness and energy to the magick we raise together this night. Hail and be welcome!*

Calls to the Lord and Lady

Candles can be lit for the Lord and Lady by the coven during these invocations, if so desired.

HIGH PRIEST: *Tonight I call to the Great God in his many forms. I call to him as the waxing sun still growing into his power in the Beltane sky. I call to him as the keeper of the wild places, the god who dwells in the deep forests and resides in the mountains and hills. I call to him as the lord of the green growing places whose fertility renews the earth and turns the Wheel of the Year. Great Lord of the Witches, join us tonight in our rites. Grace our Beltane gathering with your joy, passion, laughter, and love. Hail and be welcome!*

HIGH PRIESTESS: *I call to the Great Goddess in her many forms. I call to her as the lady of the moon whose energy resonates both within and without us. I call to her as the beauty of the green earth, the fertile mother from which all is born and comes to be. I call to her as the queen of love and earthly delight who inflames our passions and resides within our hearts. She is the protectress, the huntress, and the warrior who guards her folk. Great Lady of the Witches, join us tonight in our rites. Let us feel your love for us and this earth. Touch our rites with your energy and magick. Hail and be welcome!*

Oak, Ash, and Thorn (Dance)/Fire Blessing/Energy Release

HIGH PRIEST: *Beltane is a night for dance, joy, and love and to celebrate what it means to be a Witch! To the Celts, Beltane was the start of summer, and so tonight we dance the summer in together as a coven! Tonight we welcome in the warmer days with Oak, Ash, and Thorn!*

High Priestess: *Together, hand in hand, dancing in this circle, we will all sing the chorus of this very witchy song. For those of you who may have forgotten the words, they are as follows:*

"Sing Oak and Ash and Thorn, good sirs
(All of a Midsummer morn!)
Surely we sing no little thing,
In Oak and Ash and Thorn!"

And now to the dance!

As the music begins, everyone in the coven should hold hands and begin dancing clockwise around the circle. The dance should be joyous and most of all fun! If the High Priestess desires, she can make the dance even more fun by yelling "jump!" periodically while everyone is moving around the circle. (The jumping represents plants coming up and out of the earth.) From experience I can tell you that six or seven minutes of dancing is usually enough for most covens. Those who can't dance should sing or clap along, or make their way to the center of the circle to call out the periodic jumps.

When the dance ends, everyone should be given a few minutes to catch their breath before moving to the next part of the ritual. For the fire blessing, a candle should be set up in the middle of the circle, with enough room for people to jump over it easily and safely. If there are people with mobility issues in the coven, they can choose instead to walk between two candles instead of jumping over the one. We usually have to move our altar a little bit to clear enough room in the center of the circle for this rite.

High Priest: *In Beltane celebrations of old, cattle would be prodded to jump over a small fire or run in between two larger ones to protect them from disease and starvation. Since we have no cattle ourselves, we shall jump over our Beltane fire instead!*

The High Priestess lights the candle for the rite and sets it in the middle of the circle.

High Priestess: *Behold the Beltane flame! The fire of Beltane cleanses and protects and contains within it the power of our Lord and Lady! As you jump over the flame, shout out to the Lord and Lady what you would be shielded from this summer. Now let all jump the Beltane flame and receive the protection of the Lord and Lady for the days ahead!*

Everyone should jump (or step) over the candle while stating what they wish to be protected from in the coming months. They might say "let me have safe travels" if they're going on a long trip, or "no bad grades!" if they're still in school. There's no right or wrong, and the gods are almost always aware of our true intentions. People can jump over the flame more than once if they desire. In my coven we all usually jump at least three times.

If someone extinguishes the candle while jumping over it, the High Priestess can choose to "punish" them if she desires. "Punishments" should obviously not be severe, and the punishment can be something silly, like making the guilty party answer a "truth or dare" question/challenge. People should be encouraged to cheer and yell with those doing the jumping and should shout "So mote it be!" after each covener jumps the candle. When the fire rite comes to an end, the High Priestess should pick up the candle and return it to the altar.

HIGH PRIESTESS: *These things we've asked for in the names of the Lord and the Lady, may they come to pass! And may the light and fire of Beltane keep us all healthy and successful over the long summer days ahead! So mote it be!*

Between the previous dancing and all the jumping, there should be a lot of energy in the circle. Instead of just letting that energy drift out into the world, it should be put to good use. That energy can be given to a sick friend or people who need protection. Here I've chosen to give it to the earth to help repair some of the damage our species had done to her over the past few centuries.

Everyone in the coven should be instructed to hold hands once more and turn inward toward the circle's altar. The High Priestess should lead a chant of "To the earth! To the earth!" and while doing so, she should slowly raise her arms up, with everyone in the coven following suit. As arms are raised, the intensity of the chant should increase until it reaches a climax when everyone's hands are raised over their heads. At this point, the High Priestess should shout "Now!" with everyone then releasing all the energy in the circle and dropping hands.

HIGH PRIESTESS: *And what was raised here has been given back to the earth on this merry celebration of the May! Hail Beltane!*

Allow a few moments for all the energy to dissipate and everyone to catch their breath before moving on to cakes and ale.

Cakes and Ale/The Great Rite

HIGH PRIEST: *At Beltane we celebrate the quickening of the earth, when earth joins with sky and all is brought back to life. It is the original source of magick, the power that gives birth to universes, galaxies, planets, and those of us here in this circle.*

HIGH PRIESTESS: *When two forces come together, there is life, love, and renewal. Through the power of the Lord and Lady, worlds are born!*

The High Priest picks up the wine-filled chalice and the High Priestess her athame.

HIGH PRIESTESS: *Through the power of the Lord and Lady, all that lies between,*

HIGH PRIEST: *We celebrate the world's renewal this Beltane!*

The High Priestess places her athame in the chalice.

BOTH: *So mote it be!*

HIGH PRIESTESS: *As the Lord and Lady have shared the bounty of this world with us, we shall now share it with one another. Drink from this cup and know the mysteries of our Lord and Lady, and may you never thirst!*

The cup is passed around the circle, with everyone in the coven drinking from it. As the cup moves around the circle, the High Priest picks up the cakes and presents them to the High Priestess, who blesses them with her athame.

HIGH PRIESTESS: *We thank the Lord and Lady for this gift and are grateful for the power and magick that went into their creation. May you never hunger!*

Cakes are passed around the circle. A portion of the cakes and ale should be placed in a libation bowl and set aside for the gods and the fey. If the ritual is being conducted outside, this can be done now or at the end of the ritual.

Farewell to the Gods

HIGH PRIESTESS: *Gracious Goddess, Great Lady of the Witches, we thank you for being with us in our circle this night. Continue to walk with us as we take the blessings of Beltane forward into our lives. Hail and farewell!*

HIGH PRIEST: *Giving God, Great Lord of the Witches, we thank you for being in our circle this night. Shine down upon us from the sky as we make our way through your world in this time of growth. Hail and farewell!*

Any candles lit for the Goddess and God are blown out at this time.

Dismissing the Watchtowers / Releasing the Circle

Beginning in the east, dismiss the quarters in the order they were called. If any candles were lit in their honor, they can be blown out at the conclusion of each dismissal. A banishing pentagram can also be drawn at that time as well.

EAST QUARTER CALLER: *Spirits of the east, spirits of air, knowledge, and freedom, we thank you for joining us in these our rites and infusing our magick with your gifts. Until we meet again in the circle, hail and farewell!*

SOUTH QUARTER CALLER: *Spirits of the south, spirits of fire, enthusiasm, and passion, we thank you for joining us in these our rites and infusing our magick with your gifts. Until we meet again in the circle, hail and farewell!*

WEST QUARTER CALLER: *Spirits of the west, spirits of water, initiation, and emotion, we thank you for joining us in these our rites and infusing our magick with your gifts. Until we meet again in the circle, hail and farewell!*

NORTH QUARTER CALLER: *Spirits of the north, spirits of earth, stone, and field, we thank you for joining us in these our rites and infusing our magick with your gifts. Until we meet again in the circle, hail and farewell!*

Starting in the east and moving deosil, the circle caster should release the circle using the coven sword or their athame.

CIRCLE CASTER: *I cast this circle to be a place of love and joy to safeguard our Beltane rites. It has served us well in that purpose and has brought us ever closer to one another and our Lord and*

Lady. We have walked between the worlds and looked into the world of spirit. What was created with love has now been released with love. May the emotions felt while in this circle ever reside in your hearts. The circle is now open. So mote it be!

HIGH PRIESTESS: *Together we have celebrated this joyous Beltane. The summer stands before us and the Lord and Lady stand ever with us. Until next we meet, merry meet, merry part, and merry meet again!*

FIN

CHAPTER 23

BELTANE SOLITARY RITUAL
The Magick of Joining

In my coven's version of the Great Rite, we often use the words "the magick of joining." For many decades, "joining" in the context of Witchcraft (and especially Wiccan-Witch-craft) revolved around ideas limited to male-female energies. This sort of narrow thinking has never worked for me because nature and the greater universe have never embraced such absolutes.

The universe was created at the big bang when matter and force collided, resulting in gas and dust hurtling through space and forming galaxies, suns, and planets. Closer to home, wonders like the Grand Canyon arose due to the erosion of rock by water and wind. The life in my backyard garden came to be because I put seeds in the ground, where they were nourished with dirt and water and then eventually came up from the ground and embraced the life-giving power of the sun. Nothing exists in a vacuum, and we are all influenced and prodded along by the people and circumstances around us.

Even "solitary practice" is a bit of a misnomer, because if we are practicing the Craft properly, we aren't alone while we do it. In the circle, we are surrounded by the forces of earth, air, fire, and water. For many of us, there are also goddesses and gods lending their power and their presence in our rites. Magick may not have a consciousness of its own, but it's most certainly something we can feel during ritual and when performing spellwork.

When we practice magick, we are fusing energy with our intent to achieve a desired outcome. We are applying our wants and needs to a natural force that would otherwise not have an agenda. Magick by its very nature is an act of joining. Intent alone is not enough, and simply lighting a candle and walking away is not enough either.

At Beltane, I probably feel the magick of joining more acutely than at other times of the year. Some of this is because of the holiday's associations with sex and dalliances, but a lot of it is because many things outside have all joined together quite recently. The green grass in my front yard is a reminder of how the earth and sky have come together to produce something truly wondrous, and signs of new life are everywhere in early May. There are bugs buzzing around in the air and bird songs on the breeze. It's all so magickal and all the result of different forces coming together to create something new.

This ritual utilizes the magick of joining in a twofold way. The working begins with a personal affirmation, followed by an invitation for deity to settle down right alongside of us. Many of us typically call our deities into ritual, but rarely do we ask them to be right up next to us. This ritual does that to remind us that we are never truly alone while performing a solitary rite. If you want to adapt this into a ritual for more than one person, the affirmation can be turned into a drawing down the moon experience, which takes the idea of joining to an entirely different level!

For this part of the rite, you'll need some sort of essential oil. Because of the season, I suggest choosing something floral to help connect with the natural world. If you're using a pure essential oil, make sure to add a base oil (such as olive) so it doesn't burn or hurt your skin.

The second part of the working utilizes the chalice and athame and is a magickal version of the symbolic Great Rite. There are many Witches who see the athame and chalice in such situations as representative of a penis and a vagina, but an athame is not a penis nor is a cup a vagina. Both tools are simply representative of natural forces, and how we interpret them is really up to us. In this rite, the chalice is representative of the things we wish to bring into our lives, while the athame is representative of our will or intent.

If you don't have an official working athame and chalice, any old cup will do, as will a kitchen knife, a wand, or even your finger! Witchcraft doesn't require a bunch of tools, despite what books like this one might suggest. This ritual can be done indoors or out, and at any time of day.

Materials Needed

- Standard altar setup
- Essential oil
- Charcoal tablet for incense (If indoors, be sure to buy a type of charcoal designed for indoor use, which is easily picked up at any metaphysical/New Age store.)
- Chalice (containing wine or other liquid)
- Cakes (or whatever food you wish)
- Athame/knife
- Powdered or natural incense

The Ritual: The Magick of Joining

Start by taking a deep centering breath and look over your altar to make sure everything you need for the ritual is there. When you feel ready to start the ritual, begin by stating the ritual's intent:

I come here this night (or day) to celebrate the festival of Beltane. Tonight I shall weave my will and walk in step with the natural world and the Goddess and God who dwell within it. I shall make magick and celebrate my connection with those deities I walk with. Blessed be!

Place a bowl of water on your altar's pentacle and then place three measures of salt into it using your fingers or athame. Sprinkle or place the salt in the water, then mix the two elements together with your blade. Then say:

Earth and water have joined together so that I might purify myself and this place as I prepare for these my rites. By the power of the Lord and Lady, all negativity shall be banished so that I might celebrate the mysteries of May. So mote it be!

Sprinkle the water about your ritual space and yourself. I'll generally place a few drops on my head and my heart and, while doing so, picture the mundane concerns that get in the way of my magickal self melting away. If you're doing the ritual inside, be sure to sprinkle your water in any corners or entryways. Once the water has been sprinkled, take your charcoal tablet and light it. Once it's lit, place it in a dish or holder where it can burn safely, then place that on your altar's pentacle and sprinkle your incense over it while saying:

> *Fire and air have joined together so that I might charge myself and this space as I prepare for these my rites. By the power of the Lord and Lady, I assert that I and all within this working space are prepared for magick so that I might celebrate the mysteries of May! So mote it be!*

Walk around your ritual area with the incense, feeling its energy and heat charge your space. When this is done, make sure to waft some of the incense smoke upon yourself. As you truly smell the smoke, imagine it charging you, awakening all the magick and energy inside of you. When this is done, prepare to cast the circle using your athame (or preferred tool).

Casting the Circle/Calling the Quarters

Begin casting the circle in the east, walking around your ritual space clockwise. Use your athame, sword, wand, or finger to cast the circle.

> *By my will and the power of the Lord and the Lady, I cast this circle! May all within it assist me in my magick, and may all negative energies and those that would wish me harm stay beyond its boundaries. This circle is a protection and a doorway between the worlds! By my will, it is done. The circle is cast. So mote it be!*

Call the quarters starting in the east, moving clockwise from there. If you're using candles, you can light them at the conclusion of each quarter call.

> *Spirits of the east, spirits of air and wind, join me tonight in this place! May I feel your power and energy upon the breeze as I celebrate this Beltane night. Hail and welcome!*

> *Spirits of the south, spirits of fire and sun, join me tonight in this place! May I feel your warmth and see your light as I celebrate this Beltane night. Hail and welcome!*

Spirits of the west, spirits of water and sea, join me tonight in this place! May I feel the life-giving energy you bring to all things as I celebrate this Beltane night. Hail and welcome!

Spirits of the north, spirits of earth and mountain, join me tonight in this place. May I feel your powers with every step I take as I celebrate this Beltane night. Hail and welcome!

Calls to the Goddess and God

Now call to the Lord and Lady (or any specific deity you choose). If you have candles to light in their honor, do so after each invocation.

Lovely Lady, Great Goddess, Mistress of the Heavens, Earth Mother, join me tonight in my rites! Allow me to feel your presence and power in all that I do. Draw me closer to the wonder of this world and the magick and mystery of high spring. Let me feel your energies as I celebrate this Beltane rite. Hail and welcome!

Horned One, Great God, Lord of the Sun, Jack in the Green, join me tonight in my rites! Bless this Beltane ritual with your powers of growth and rejuvenation. May I feel your presence and power as I work my magick and will. Be with me both within and without the circle. Hail and welcome!

The Working

Take your anointing oil and hold it in your dominant hand for a few moments. As you hold it, think about yourself in a positive manner. Know that you are a worthy child and a devotee of the Lord and Lady and a powerful Witch. Take society's expectations for appearance, dress, and decorum and throw them out of your mind. You are a beautiful creature worthy of love and acceptance, and you have both of those things within the Craft. Infuse your oil with these ideas; let this true image of yourself move through your body, through your arm, into your hand, and then into your oil. When the oil is warm and charged in your hand, reach out to the deity you are closest to:

Great Lady, Goddess of the Witches, on this sacred night of joining, I ask that I truly feel your presence in this ritual space. May I feel your love for me fill up this circle. Draw me ever closer to your mysteries. So mote it be!

Now anoint yourself with the oil, starting at the feet.

Blessed be my feet, which have brought me to thee.

Using the finger of your dominant hand, lightly dab each foot with your oil before moving to your knees.

Blessed be my knees, which kneel upon your green earth.

Dab each knee before moving to your heart.

Blessed be my heart, which loves and feels love.

Dab the oil between your breasts before moving to your lips. For your "lips," you'll probably want to dab the oil on your upper lip (right below your nose) or on your chin.

Blessed be my lips, which have allowed me to call thee.

Finally, dab some oil on your forehead, representative of your spirit.

Blessed be my spirit that seeks thee.

Then say:

I am a Witch and worthy of the love of my Goddess! It is she who walks with me upon the path of the wise. Dear One, be with me in my circle, for I am your child and my love for thee is pure and true!

Let all go still for a second and reach out with your senses for a sign from her (or him). Deities do not always communicate like we humans do. Be alert for an odd breeze or a patch of warm energy next to you. I often feel the Lord and Lady as if they are standing right behind me, with one of their hands upon my left shoulder. As you wait for a sign, concentrate on them, think of them, and reach out to whoever it is you wish to be in your circle. They will come. Once you've felt them, thank them for reaching out to you before moving on with the rest of the ritual.

With your dominant hand, pick up the chalice of wine on your altar and look into it. Let your eyes unfocus and sink into the wine in the chalice. The chalice is representative of the earth and all of the potential it holds. As you look into the cup, imagine all of the possibilities in your life and see them within the wine. When one of those possibilities that you're especially attracted to swirls in front of your eyes (or in your imagination), hold onto it for a second and try to visualize it more clearly.

It could be something like you having a new (happier) job, or you engaging in a hobby or pasttime you've been putting off for a while. Whatever it is, focus on it. If it's something you truly want, hold the image. If it's not, let it go and repeat the steps above to see what else comes up.

When you finally come across a possibility that appeals to you and is one you truly and absolutely want, pick up your athame. Let all of the want and need for this possibility go racing through your body and direct it toward the hand holding your athame. This is your true will, and the athame was designed to wield such energies. Slowly insert the athame into the cup, joining the possibilities, energies, and potential of the earth with your own will as wielded by the athame. As the athame enters the wine, say:

By my will, this thing shall be! Possibilities and potential reached this Beltane night!

When the athame enters the wine, your will shall fuse the idea you're trying to manifest with the energy in the cup, creating a magickal elixir. If you've put enough energy into the wine, it might even feel a bit electric to the touch or when you drink it. Take the cup to your lips, drink, and say:

In Beltane's cauldron, all is possible! May it be so!

Drink deeply from the cup, remembering to set aside a little bit for the gods. (Alternatively, you can pour some upon the ground now if you're outdoors.) Let the energized wine flow through you, and open yourself up to its energies. Let that energy fill every cell of your body, and know that you will be using that energy over the next few months to achieve your goal.

Set the cup down and pick up a cake (or whatever food you wish) with your non-dominant hand. Place your athame back into the chalice, then touch the tip of your blade to the cake, saying:

By the powers of the Lord and Lady, I bless this cake. I thank them for their gifts. Blessed be!

Eat the cake, saving some for the gods as an offering. Enjoy the energy of your Beltane rite for just a few moments more, then move on to thanking the gods and dismissing the energies you have gathered.

Farewells to the Lord and Lady

Great Goddess, you have stood beside me tonight in my ritual, and for your presence I am truly grateful! Remind me in the days ahead of my worthiness as a Witch and that I am loved by you. I thank you for being a part of my rite and my life.

Great God, thank you too for lending your energy and exuberance to my rite. Thank you for all of your gifts and standing beside me. I am a Witch. I am a child of the gods. Blessed be!

Dismissing the Quarters/Taking Down the Circle

Starting in the north, dismiss the quarters, moving widdershins and extinguishing any candles for the quarters (if lit).

Spirits of the north, spirits of earth and mountain, I thank you for joining me in this space and watching over my rite. May I feel your power in the summer days ahead! Hail and farewell!

Spirits of the west, spirits of water and sea, I thank you for joining me in this space and watching over my rite. May I observe and delight in your gift of life in the summer days ahead! Hail and farewell!

Spirits of the south, spirits of fire and sun, I thank you for joining me in this space and watching over my rite. May I feel your warmth upon my face as we journey toward the summer! Hail and farewell!

Spirits of the east, spirits of air and wine, I thank you for joining me in this space and watching over my rite. May your warm breezes bring us the gift of rain this summer season. Hail and farewell!

Using your athame, wand, or finger, release the circle, starting in the east and moving widdershins.

By my will and the power of the Lord and Lady, I did cast this circle. I now release it and all of the energies I have raised within. May my magick leave this space and hold true, bringing to me that which I desire. The doorway between the worlds is now closed, but what was done here I shall carry with me, and the love of the Lady and Lord will be forever with me. The circle is open. So mote it be!

Before leaving, thank the Lord and Lady for your Beltane rite and take any libations outside in honor of the deities who stood with you this night. Hail the May!

FIN

Part Four
Summer (Midsummer & Lammas)

The days are now long,
The grain growing in the field.
Harvest soon to come.

CHAPTER 24

MIDSUMMER
The Summer Solstice

Name of Sabbat: Midsummer (also known as Litha, the Summer Solstice, Saint John's
   Eve, and Saint John's Night)

Date: On the day of the summer solstice (which occurs on or about June 21 in the Northern Hemisphere)

Pronunciation: "LITH-uh"

I had a friend ask me once why the Summer Solstice is often referred to as *Midsummer*. It
does seem like kind of a misnomer, as the solstice is the start of summer after all. But if
we look to the greater sabbats as the start dates of the four seasons, then Midsummer is
comfortably right in the middle of things. In addition, several early calendars (including
Icelandic and Germanic ones) acknowledged only two seasons, winter and summer, with
seasons starting and ending on or near the equinoxes. When one looks at the Wheel of
the Year in such a way, Midsummer truly is midsummer!

   Litha has only been used as a name for the Summer Solstice since 1974 and comes to
us from Aidan Kelly (see chapter 3) via the English historian Bede. Bede listed Litha as
the name of a "double month" roughly equivalent to our June and July. Because the Anglo-Saxon calendar that Bede was writing about was lunar, it needed an extra month
added periodically to balance things out, and what better time to add an extra month than
in summer? Unlike Ostara, Litha does not refer to a goddess. According to Bede, Litha

means "gentle" or "navigable," because in both these months (June and July), "the calm breezes are gentle, and they [the Anglo-Saxons] were wont to sail upon the smooth sea." [50]

Pagan sabbats with a direct descendent in Christian practice are often the easiest to trace historically, and luckily for us, Midsummer has one of those: Saint John's Eve (also sometimes called Saint John's Night). Saint John's Day (June 24) is the celebration of the birth of Saint John the Baptist, which allegedly occurred six months before the birth of Jesus. The major festivities associated with John the Baptist occurred on the night before his feast day, June 23. The term *Midsummer* also serves as another name for Saint John's Eve among Christians, and the two are used interchangeably in many places without much fuss.

Though there are few truly *ancient* accounts of Midsummer as a pagan holiday, they do show up in the historical record about when one would expect them to: in the early twelfth and thirteenth centuries, when people started keeping more detailed records. The use of bonfires to celebrate Saint John's Eve was first recorded in Paris in the twelfth century, and has been recorded in most every European country since then, along with a few countries in North Africa too. In many parts of Northern Europe, the holiday was seen as the *most important* festival of the year. [51] (And in the world of New Orleans Voodoo, Saint John's Eve has this distinction as well.)

Even today, Saint John's Eve is marked with the building of large bonfires to celebrate the holiday. The fires are lit not just in tribute to the sun near the height of its power and influence but because of fire's magickal properties. Fire was prized for its ability to protect people from supernatural forces, including the fey and, apparently in at least one English village, dragons. [52] Even with Christianity dominant during the early modern period (1400–1700), belief in the fair folk and other supernatural entities was widespread, and people were genuinely scared of them.

Bonfires and the resulting smoke served another purpose: to protect crops and livestock. The most direct way to use a bonfire for this purpose was to build a fire (or fires) near where one's crops were growing. It was believed that the smoke would help protect them against disease and any maleficent magick that might be directed at them. The tradition of fire and smoke being used to protect growing agricultural goods can be found

---

50. Wallis, *Bede: The Reckoning of Time*, 53–54.

51. Hutton, *Stations of the Sun*, 312.

52. Ibid., 313.

in the works of the Roman writer Pliny (23–79 CE), and most certainly predates his work.[53]

Fire as a form of protection on Saint John's Eve was portable too. It could be transferred to a torch, with the torch then taken to harder-to-reach areas such as livestock pens. Torches could also be run between rows of grain, the smoke cleansing and purifying the crop.[54] If this seems like overkill, it's important to remember just how important a good harvest was a thousand or even just two hundred years ago. A bad harvest could mean hunger, starvation, and even death. Nearly *everything* depended on a successful harvest.

Midsummer fires also served recreational purposes. They provided a place for people to congregate, feast, and drink. In other words, they were fun! Midsummer provided an excuse for a festival with all the attendant merrymaking one would expect on such an occasion. Musicians played to village streets full of people with flowers around their necks, most likely wearing whatever finery they possessed.

Midsummer bonfires weren't made only of wood. In some parts of England, they included animal bones. A fourteenth-century English monk wrote that the Midsummer fires were done in triplicate, with one fire of only bone, one of only wood, and one of both materials. The stench from the burning bones was thought to have extra protective power.[55] How a Modern Witch might go about incorporating animal bones in their Midsummer fires is lost on me, but the idea of three fires is at least interesting.

Ways to Celebrate the Summer Solstice

Midsummer might be most famous today for its association with the fey. This association is the result of people being fearful of the fey on celestially auspicious occasions such as the Summer Solstice (and Beltane, Samhain, and Yule) and because of the enduring popularity of William Shakespeare's *A Midsummer Night's Dream* (1595/96). This play did more than just forever wed the fey to Midsummer; it changed how they were viewed in popular culture.

Before *Dream*, the fey were generally seen as troublesome at best, and usually as evil. (Considering how well we take care of our world, can we really blame them?) But this

---

53. Ibid., 320.

54. Ibid., 319.

55. Ibid., 312–313.

play transformed the fairy folk into kindly creatures. As one scholar put it, Shakespeare's fairies "were 'benevolent' and 'completely identified with buds and blossoms, dew-drops and butterflies.'"[56] This was a far cry from how they were seen in the centuries leading up to Shakespeare's play.

In my own practice, I have embraced Midsummer's association with the fey. I use it as an opportunity to honor them, bribe them, and generally make sure our relationship remains a positive one. The Midsummer coven ritual in this book includes an invitation for the fey to be a part of ritual and asks for their blessings both before and after the ritual. Even if you don't choose to work with the fey on Midsummer, it's probably a good idea to at least acknowledge them on the night most associated with them.

The story of the Oak King and Holly King is also popular at Midsummer. In fact, I think I see it far more often in June than I ever do in December. Much of that is probably because December is just such a busy month when it comes to magickal associations, while June is a little less so (though as this book points out, that might not actually be the case!). One of my favorite Midsummer rituals ever had the Goddess of Summer deliver the killing blow to the Oak King in order to keep the earth fertile. It was a new twist on the sacrificial god story, and the first time I'd ever witnessed such a telling of the tale.

Rites involving fire have been popular at Midsummer for hundreds if not thousands of years. Bonfires, or even just a small fire in a charcoal grill, are a great way to connect to our ancestors who celebrated long ago on Saint John's Eve. Fire is a powerful magickal tool, and simply throwing things (and ideas) that we want out of our lives into a fire can make for effective spellwork. The smoke from Midsummer fires can be used to protect a home or covenstead from negative influences.

Rituals involving the power of the sun are especially popular at the Summer Solstice. Rituals can be built around specific solar deities or around the idea of the sun's power giving life to the grains, fruits, and vegetables we eat. I also think there's something extra special about the magick that happens at sunset when the longest day meets up with the shortest night.

One of the oldest traditions associated with Midsummer is that of a burning wheel. Though seldom practiced today, people have been rolling flaming wheels down hills for thousands of years. The first recorded instance of this practice dates back to the fourth

---

56. Farah Karim-Cooper, "Fairies Re-fashioned in *A Midsummer Night's Dream*," British Library, March 15, 2016, https://www.bl.uk/shakespeare/articles/fairies-re-fashioned-in-a-midsummer-nights-dream.

century CE, and the first reference to the practice happening specifically on Midsummer dates from the sixteenth century.[57]

What's most interesting about the solar wheel is that it's clearly a symbol of the sun, which is perfect for Midsummer. Solar wheels can be found on the solar chariots driven by gods such as Apollo and Helios and on lots of other more mundane items. Solar wheels have appeared on ancient pottery, jewelry, and coinage, and have been used by humans to represent the sun for over five thousand years. (The first recorded instance we've been able to find dates back to the third millennium BCE, which means they might be even older.[58])

Divination has been a part of this holiday most likely from the beginning. Writing in the twelfth century, a rather un-fun Christian monk wrote of Midsummer: "He who at the feast of St. John the Baptist does any work of sorcery to seek out the future shall do penance for fifteen days." [59] This tradition has lasted until the present day in many places, with many divination spells centered around romantic pairings and potential spouses.

Midsummer offers a little bit of something for everyone. It's a time for doing magick, celebrating the sun, and getting a sneak peek into the future. It also features traditions that have been a part of the human experience for thousands of years. Hail the Midsummer fires! Hail the sun!

---

57. Hutton, *Stations of the Sun*, 311.

58. West, *Indo-European Poetry and Myth*, 201 and 210.

59. Hutton, *Stations of the Sun*, 312.

CHAPTER 25

MIDSUMMER CIRCLE RITUAL

Summer's Cauldron

At the urging of my local Witch shop, I began teaching Wiccan-Witchcraft publicly in 2017. At the end of our first session of classes, my students and I presented a Summer Solstice ritual for a local open circle. Because many of the participants did not want a speaking part, this particular ritual doesn't contain a whole lot in terms of speaking roles. When I initially presented it, I ended up in the High Priest role, while one of my coven sisters was the High Priestess. The four quarter callers are active throughout the ritual, with more lines and responsibilities than usual. This ritual is designed to be done outside, preferably while the sun is still in the sky.

In this ritual, everyone in attendance receives four "summer gifts," each coming from one of the four elements (air, fire, water, and earth). These items are then charged and placed in a fire, the fire activating the magick put into them. (If you're in a spot where you can build a bonfire, even cooler, and a charcoal grill will work well for this too!) If you don't have access to fire, that's okay. The four gifts can be placed in any old container and either burned later or simply placed outside in a secluded spot as an offering.

I added a few twists to this particular ritual, my favorite one being the use of petals to cast the circle. Instead of using an athame or sword, each of the quarter callers sprinkles flower petals while the circle casting is read. If the ritual is done outside, there's no need to even pick up the petals, as they'll just eventually blow away. Visually, it's a fun way to cast the circle too.

The only large prop beyond the usual is a fire pit or cauldron. For our ritual we used a portable fire pit, allowing us to burn our offerings during the course of the ritual. Alternatively, a fire-free cauldron or large bucket will work just as well. We put our fire pit in the center of the circle, but what's most important is to place it in a safe spot. If you have a permanent fire pit in your backyard, you can build this ritual around that. There's a small symbolic fire lighting in this rite that can easily be dropped if you're in a spot where fire is not allowed.

This ritual mentions California's ongoing drought. That idea can be dropped if it's not applicable in your neck of the woods, but the factors causing the drought out here are wreaking havoc in other ways around the country and the world. Part of being a Witch is fighting for beneficial change, and that includes protecting our earth and her environment.

The end of the working features music. As is my modus operandi, we used recorded music, mostly Celtic jigs and reels, because they always put me in a summer frame of mind. Pop songs with a summer vibe are also fun at Midsummer, and live drumming is always welcome!

Ritual Roles

- High Priestess
- High Priest
- Four quarter callers/elemental powers

Materials Needed

- Standard altar setup
- Three chalices
- Cauldron/fire pit/large bucket or bowl
- Music (recorded or drummers)
- Four different colors of flower petals, ideally yellow, red, blue, and green
- Sage (representing east/air)
- Rose petals (representing fire/south)
- Dried seaweed (representing water/west)

- Acorns (representing earth/north)
- Champagne (sparkling wine or sparkling grape juice)
- Fruit juice (something seasonal, such as orange, strawberry, watermelon, raspberry, blackberry, etc.)
- Fresh fruit (or cake)

The Ritual: Summer's Cauldron

The ritual begins with the quarter callers and the High Priestess and High Priest standing in the middle of the circle. Four altars to the individual elements are set up at the perimeter of the circle at each of the cardinal points of the compass. On the top of each altar is the "gift" that will be distributed by the person representing that direction, along with the flower petals corresponding to that element. Candles are also appropriate, though it's often hard to keep candles lit outdoors, and they aren't really needed if the ritual is done during the day.

Opening, Cleansing, Statement of Intent

HIGH PRIESTESS: *We gather to celebrate the longest day and shortest night. We honor the sun that shines down from on high at the Summer Solstice, bestowing upon us the many gifts of the earth. United with the land and the rain, the sun's power ripens the grain and brings forth life from the soil. Tonight we honor those blessings while reveling in the mysteries of summer's cauldron and reaffirming our commitment to this world we live in. Hail Midsummer!*

The High Priest picks up a pair of Tibetan cymbals or a bell to help cleanse those gathered.

HIGH PRIEST: *With this instrument I do cleanse and consecrate this space and all those gathered here. As the pure sound of the cymbals (or bell) washes over you, let it take away any negative energy upon you. May its vibration center you and prepare you for tonight's rite. So mote it be!*

The cymbals or bells are rung once at each of the cardinal points of the circle. Let the sound carry outward from the circle and fade away before moving on to the next spot and ringing the chimes a second/third/fourth time. All should be quiet as the tone purifies and cleanses.

Casting the Circle

As the circle casting is being read, the quarter callers should all begin walking around the entire perimeter of the circle scattering their flower petals. As they scatter their petals, they should be consciously casting the circle and visualizing its construction. The High Priestess reading the circle casting is not casting the circle; she is just verbalizing intentions.

HIGH PRIESTESS: *On this the longest day of the year, we create our magick circle, a place of love and joy and truth. With flower petals of red, we create a place where mortals may tread. With flower petals of blue, we open the entryway into the realm of spirit. With flower petals of yellow, we open the doorway to the realm of the Mighty Ones. With flower petals of green, we welcome those unseen who come to us in good faith. In the names of the sun and sky and the earth and moon, we bless and consecrate this space. The circle is cast. So mote it be!*

Calling the Elements

EAST QUARTER CALLER: *I call to the spirits of the east, spirits of air. Bring to us your powers of wisdom and knowledge this night as we conjure the summer in. Hail and welcome!*

SOUTH QUARTER CALLER: *I call to the spirits of the south, spirits of fire. Bring to us your powers of light and desire this night as we conjure the summer in. Hail and welcome!*

WEST QUARTER CALLER: *I call to the spirits of the west, spirits of water. Bring to us your powers of mystery and initiation as we conjure the summer in. Hail and welcome!*

NORTH QUARTER CALLER: *I call to the spirits of the north, spirits of earth. Bring to us your powers of place and abundance as we conjure the summer in. Hail and welcome!*

Candles may be lit at each of the quarters if desired.

Calling to Deity

HIGH PRIESTESS: *We call to the Great God this night of the longest day. Join us as the sun, fiery Lord of the Heavens, blesses our land with the sunshine that makes our world grow! Join us as the Creator joins with the Great Mother to bring forth new life! May your purifying light and fire bless us this night as we celebrate your mysteries and what we can give back to your world. Be a part of our rites as you are a part of our lives! Hail and welcome!*

HIGH PRIEST: *We call to the Great Goddess this day of the shortest night. Join us as the moon, cool orb of the nighttime sky, lights our way and adds to our magicks! Join us as the Great Mother brings forth new life from the eternal womb! It's your touch that makes the blossoms bloom and the crops ripen with grain! May that same touch reach us this night to inspire us in our rites and in our lives! Be a part of our ritual as we celebrate your gifts of love and the joys of the summer! Hail and welcome!*

The Working: Summer's Cauldron

HIGH PRIESTESS: *The Lord and Lady and all that lies between weave their spell together in summer's cauldron. With athame and wand, they mix the elements of earth, air, fire, water with the power of the sun, binding them all together to produce the joys of summer. Within the cauldron, days are long and warm, fruit ripens, magick happens, love grows, and leisure finds a place to dwell. We are given so much by the gods and the earth at this time of year, but can we give them something in return?*

HIGH PRIEST: *We are not apart from the earth but a part of the earth. The earth is a gift, and a gift that often feels more joyous at Midsummer, but we also have a responsibility to the earth. The Witches of old were the healers, the wise folk, the ones who helped turn the seasons and bring about the fertility of the earth. Today our charge is similar, we must be wise Witches and work to ensure the well-being of the land we walk upon.*

HIGH PRIESTESS: *Tonight we add our own ingredients to summer's cauldron. We add powers and promises to what the Lord and Lady have given us this summer night. What shall be the first ingredient we add to our cauldron?*

EAST QUARTER CALLER: *I come from the east bearing the gift of sage. Sage is an herb of healing and cleansing, and tonight we add it to our cauldron as a reminder of our duty to keep the land beneath our feet healthy and happy.*

Everyone is given a small piece of sage. The High Priest should continue to speak while the sage is being shared.

HIGH PRIEST: *Place the sage you are about to receive in your dominant hand and take a moment to notice how it feels. Bring it up to your nose and breathe in its scent. As you smell the sage, visualize what it can do. Imagine the smoke of the sage going out from our cauldron and cleansing the world around us.*

Now stop and think about the air that we breathe and what you can do to make it better. Picture yourself doing just one small thing that might make the air around us sweeter. Now take that idea and place it into your sage. Charge the sage in your hand with the picture in your mind, and when you are done, let out a mighty "So mote it be!" and place the sage in your non-dominant hand.

SOUTH QUARTER CALLER: *I come from the south, and I too have a gift for our cauldron this night. I bring this gathering the petals of the rose, red like fire and containing the scents of love and desire. Tonight we will add these rose petals to our cauldron as a reminder of our love for the earth.*

The rose petals are handed out while the High Priestess speaks.

HIGH PRIESTESS: *Hold your rose petals in your dominant hand and think about what it means to be a Pagan and to love the earth. Is that love a piece of lip service or is it something that you are passionate about? What do you love most about the earth? What draws you closer to her?*

Think of the things that you love in the natural world and what you can do to make sure they are available for future generations. Charge those petals, adding your energy to the love contained within them. Picture the places that you love and see them being here in 100, 200, 500 years and push that love and energy into your rose petals, and when you are finished, let out a big "So mote it be!"

WEST QUARTER CALLER: *From the west I come with another present for our cauldron. This one comes from the sea and is one of the most important threads in the web of life. To all of you I pass out seaweed, one of the waters' great gifts. It is a symbol not just of the sea but of all the waters—rain, river, and ocean.*

The High Priest speaks while the seaweed is handed out.

HIGH PRIEST: *Much of the world is green at Midsummer, though the rains that blessed us this spring and winter are long gone, but their power lives on. We can see it in the trees around us and in the bounty that appears on our kitchen tables.*

Though the earth is recently abundant, we know that there are things wrong with it that make the life-giving waters from the sky more and more rare, especially here where we live. With no water, there is no life, so we must always be vigilant and respectful of how we use this precious resource. Think of what you can do in your own life to preserve the waters that sus-

tain us. Charge your seaweed and place your promise within it, and we will make it a gift for the cauldron and the earth. When done, of course, say, "So mote it be!"

NORTH QUARTER CALLER: *Lastly I come from the north with a gift to place in our cauldron. The acorn is a symbol of the wild earth, and from it forests and wilderness are born. Though small, it gives birth to the mighty oak that towers above us, with its roots deep in the earth. The acorn symbolizes that from the tiniest of seeds the largest of promises can grow.*

I'm guessing you know how this works by now.

HIGH PRIESTESS: *And lastly, tonight we ask that you make a promise here in this sacred space. It's not a promise that must be spoken aloud, just one that is felt within your heart and goes out to the earth and the goddesses and gods that you serve and honor. Here in this place, near summer's cauldron at this time of great abundance, make a promise to be the best Witch you can be, the most honorable Pagan, or the most reverent of stewards. Make a promise detailing how you will serve the earth in the coming months and years ahead.*

When you have thought of your promise, take your acorn up to your lips and whisper or blow that promise into your acorn. So mote it be!

Pause for a second here and make sure everyone has ample time to think of their promise and put it into their acorn.

HIGH PRIEST: *And now the time has come for us to add our ingredients to summer's cauldron. Feel the powers of earth, air, fire, and water in your hand. Feel the promises and energies you've put into those tokens and add even more energy to them as we dance and chant. When you feel your power at its height, come forward and place your ingredients in our cauldron. After you're done, return to the circle and we will all end our dance together with a mighty "Blessed be for our earth and for those of us here tonight!"*

Because everyone has stuff in their hands, certain types of circle dances are not very practical here. When we did this ritual, we had everyone dance around the circle a few times, with the High Priestess or High Priest shouting instructions and intentions: "Think about what you can do for the earth! Charge the items in your hands! Work your magick!" etc. When the energy started to peak, the High Priestess began leading people inward toward the cauldron and then back out to the perimeter of the circle.

If you're lucky enough to have live drummers, this is a great place for chanting. Chants to prerecorded music can be done, but they can be far more difficult. As for chants, you'll want something simple that expresses the intention of the ritual:

> *Solstice bright, solstice light,*
> *Lord and Lady, bless our rite!*

The one above is so simple that we even use it with recorded music.

If people say "Blessed be!" or "So mote it be!" as they throw their gifts in the fire/ cauldron, it's likely that everyone in the circle will begin repeating those phrases. Encourage that, since people love having their intentions affirmed by their friends. Once everyone has thrown their gifts in the fire, lead everyone in one "BLESSED BE!" to finish the rite.

Cakes and Ale

The High Priestess and High Priest each pick up a chalice. One chalice contains fruit juice and the other champagne or some other sparkling liquid. A third, larger chalice either sits on the altar or is held between the High Priestess and High Priest by an assistant.

HIGH PRIEST: *The gifts of the gods are best when shared. And of all the gifts given to us, it is the magick of joining that might be most sacred. For whenever two forces combine, something greater is created.*

HIGH PRIESTESS: *To our chalice I add this gift of earth and water. From soil tended with loving care and with the blessings of the rain, this gift of fresh (insert the name of the type of fruit juice you're using, such as orange, strawberry, etc.) juice has come to us.*

HIGH PRIEST: *To our chalice I add this gift of air and fire. From sun-soaked vines and now carried to us on joyous bubbles of air, this gift of effervescent champagne has come to us.*

HIGH PRIESTESS: *And now united, air, water, fire, and earth create the joy and blessings of summer!*

HIGH PRIEST: *Blessed be!*

Both drink from the chalice. The High Priest then picks up a platter of fresh fruit (or cake) and holds it out toward the High Priestess. She picks up her athame and lightly touches the plate with her blade and says:

HIGH PRIESTESS: *We thank the sun in the sky and the ground beneath our feet for these gifts. Long may the world be abundant! Long may we feel the love of our Lady and Lord!*

HIGH PRIEST: *Blessed be!*

The High Priestess and High Priest each take a piece of fruit (or cake) and eat it. The quarter callers then all step forward and pass out the cakes and ale. As is the case with most large rituals, my suggestion is to have everything pre-measured and ready to go on a few trays that can be easily carried around by the quarter callers.

Goodbyes to the Gods

HIGH PRIESTESS: *We thank the Great Goddess for being with us for our Midsummer rite. You are the Mother of us all, and as your children, we honor you on this the shortest of nights with promises that we shall keep. May the blessings we have received tonight be a continual reminder of your love, care, and concern for all of us. Our solstice celebration is near its end, but you walk with us both within and without the circle. Hail the Lady! Hail the moon! Hail the summer! Blessed be!*

HIGH PRIEST: *We thank the Great God for being with us this night. As you sink now beneath the trees and hills, we thank you for your presence in our lives. Your presence in the sky will be a daily reminder of our promises and love for the earth. Our solstice celebration is near its end, but you walk with us both within and without the circle. Hail the God! Hail the sun! Hail the summer! Blessed be!*

Dismissing the Quarters

NORTH QUARTER CALLER: *Spirits of the north, spirits of earth, thank you for your presence in our ritual tonight. We give thanks for your many gifts this time of year. Blessed be!*

WEST QUARTER CALLER: *Spirits of the west, spirits of water, thank you for your presence in our ritual tonight. We give thanks for your many gifts this time of year. Blessed be!*

SOUTH QUARTER CALLER: *Spirits of the south, spirits of fire, thank you for your presence in our ritual tonight. We give thanks for your many gifts this time of year. Blessed be!*

EAST QUARTER CALLER: *Spirits of the east, spirits of air, thank you for your presence in our ritual tonight. We give thanks for your many gifts this time of year. Blessed be!*

Candles are blown out at each of the quarters if necessary.

Taking Down the Circle

HIGH PRIEST: *This circle has served as a meeting place for those with love and joy in their hearts and as a place to celebrate the sun and the summer. We now pick up a green flower petal and say goodbye to those unseen who have visited us in good faith. We now pick up this flower petal of yellow and thereby close the doorway to the realms of the Mighty Ones. By picking up a petal of blue, we seal the entryway from spirit. Finally, we pick up a petal of red to bring us back from between the realms. All will now be as it once was, and what was once here has been dismissed in the names of the Lord and the Lady. So mote it be!*

The High Priest releases the circle by picking up at least one of every color of flower petal dropped earlier. As he picks up the petals, he is consciously undoing the circle. The quarter callers who originally cast the circle should each pick up one of the flower petals they originally dropped and also consciously release the energy of the circle.

Closing

HIGH PRIESTESS: *With gifts given and blessings received, I proclaim this rite to be at an end. Blessed be the summer, blessed be the gods, and merry meet, merry part, and merry meet again!*

Extra Optional Piece

This extra bit is designed to be used when a real fire can be kindled, and can be inserted in several different places. It can be done after the calling of the quarters or immediately after the calls to the Goddess and the God. Sometimes doing it early is helpful so there are no large flames during the working.

Lighting Summer's Fire

The High Priest stands before the fire pit, which has been previously prepared. Ideally some sort of accelerant has been added so the fire will start quickly.

HIGH PRIEST: *Tonight we call to the power of the sun to be with us in our ritual. Help power our cauldron so that we might share our gifts with you and this world. Let us feel your power on this your longest day! Goddesses and gods of the sun, bless our rites and share with us your light! (Lights the fire.) The sun is above and below and summer's cauldron has come to this place! Blessed be!*

FIN

CHAPTER 26
MIDSUMMER COVEN RITUAL
Hail to the Fey and the Solar Wheel

There's an old folk tale that says if a person walks around a fairy mound three times on Midsummer night and then knocks three times upon it, they will be transported to the world of the fey. Bravely (or foolishly), I've tried this a few times myself. The fact that you're reading this means I wasn't successful. However, just because I've never been whisked away to the land of the fair folk doesn't mean I doubt their existence. I believe wholeheartedly that there are magickal creatures and races out there, just beyond our mortal sight.

I wish I could offer you a Midsummer rite that promises a glimpse of the fey, but they only appear to people as they will. They can't be commanded or forced to do anything. And before you even think of engaging with them, some sort of relationship should be established first. So instead of promising an encounter with the fair folk, this ritual is about establishing a relationship with them.

The fair folk can most often be found outdoors, and this ritual requires finding a spot where you feel as if they gather. If you don't have a backyard or much green space, not to worry; relationships can be established with the fey at a local park or nearly any spot that has at least a little bit of green once or twice a year. In my coven (and yard), we honor the fey by our lemon tree. As the biggest tree in our backyard, it just feels like the spot where they are most likely to congregate, and it has an energy that one can feel when they are nearby. All of the coven's libations are poured here, and we often leave gifts to the fey there too. If you can't figure out where the fey might be in your yard or neighborhood based on energy, simply pick a secluded shady spot near a tree, bush, or body of water. If you leave them gifts, they are bound to show up!

This ritual calls for the gifts to the fey to be taken to "their spot" in your yard if you can. If your ritual is being done indoors, simply do this part after the ritual proper is done, either with the coven or alone. In addition, if you feel as if there are some fey in your home, you can reserve some of the honey and glass beads as an offering for those already in your house. Just be sure to put whatever you leave for them in a spot where they won't be bothered by children or pets.

The quarter calls for this rite are all to the fey and are written in the form they are because all four of them are haikus! I've also opted to place them before the circle casting, breaking up the usual order of ritual in this book. As noted earlier, there's no right or wrong when it comes to the order of those procedures, but since the fey are sentient beings, I wanted them to know that they are welcome before casting a barrier designed to keep a lot of energies out of the circle. In honor of Shakespeare, the circle casting in this ritual is also a sonnet.

This ritual also includes a solar wheel. If you're like me, your partner probably won't let you race a flaming wheel down a hill. Instead, you'll want to make a simple circle shape that will burn easily. I suggest using grapevine, since it bends pretty easily while dry and is available at most craft stores. After you've fashioned the grapevine into a circle (figure 6), finish your wheel by adding spokes to it to form a Celtic cross. To do this, you can use a few strands of grapevine or even a couple of sticks, and tuck them into your wreath so they run across the middle of it. You'll be tying little pieces of ribbon onto the grapevine, so have some shortish pieces of ribbon or yarn cut up and ready for the ritual. Also, many craft stores sell grapevine wreaths for just a few dollars fully assembled!

This ritual calls for the grapevine wheel to be burned during the ritual, so you'll need a fire pit or barbeque grill. If the ritual is being done indoors, the burning of the wheel can be done after the ritual. If fire is a no-no both before or after ritual, the wheel can simply be buried in the ground or left in a secluded area to decompose naturally. Since you'll be putting things you want to get rid of into the wheel, don't leave it for the fey!

Figure 6. Solar Wheel Made of Grapevine

Many years ago I was given a large rock with a house painted on it. For many years I was unsure what to do with it, and then I read an article suggesting that many of Iceland's fair folk lived inside rocks.[60] Thinking it would make a fine gift for the fey, I dedicated it to them at one of my coven's Midsummer rites, and that's included in this particular ritual. Alternatively, one could build an entire fairy house for the fey, but a painted rock is probably a lot easier to put together for most of us.

Since cleansing with smoke is pretty traditional at this time of year, the cleansing in this ritual calls for it. I suggest white sage,[61] which is readily available in most Witch stores, but whatever appeals to the coven is fine.

---

60. Nickolaus Hines, "4 Times Iceland Made Major Decisions Based on Elves," All That's Interesting, April 26, 2016, http://allthatsinteresting.com/iceland-elves.

61. There is a lot of incorrect information circulating in many Witch spaces about white sage. At this time, it is not endangered.

Ritual Roles

- High Priestess
- High Priest
- Quarter callers (The fey are not "quarters," but using this term seemed easiest.)
- Circle caster

Materials Needed

- Regular altar setup
- Grapevine (for the solar wheel)
- Small pieces of ribbon or yarn
- Glass beads or shiny pebbles or stones in a bowl (The fey like sparklies!)
- A bowl half-full of spring or rainwater
- Honey with a honey dipper or spoon
- An empty bowl to collect the honey
- One large rock, preferably with a house painted on it
- Cakes and ale
- Fire pit
- White sage

The Ritual: Hail to the Fey and the Solar Wheel

The coven should assemble in a circle around the altar and/or fire pit. If it's possible to do this near the area where you will be leaving gifts for the fey, all the better. I also like to cast my circle large enough to include the area where the gifts will be left. The fire pit should all be set up and ready to go, as the ritual opens with its lighting.

Opening, Cleansing, Statement of Intent

High Priestess: *We light this fire in honor of the sun! May its light, heat, and smoke convey to us the same blessings the sun does to the earth below it. (Lights fire.) Hail the sun!*

High Priest: *We celebrate the longest day and shortest night, and we do so by honoring the sun above and those seen and unseen who dwell in this world alongside us. As the sun begins to* wane, we shall use its power to remove what is negative in our lives. But before we begin, all must be cleansed and prepared for our rite.

The High Priestess grabs an herb bundle of white sage from the altar and lights it using the fire that was just started.

HIGH PRIESTESS: *I light this sage from our sacred fire. May its smoke clear from you any un-wanted or negative energy. So mote it be!*

The High Priestess walks around the circle and cleanses all the participants. If there are a lot of folks, the High Priest can light his own bundle and cleanse half the circle too.

HIGH PRIEST: *And now that all are blessed, we begin this rite! Hail Midsummer!*

Calling the Fey/Quarters

If desired, candles can be lit at each of the four quarters.

HIGH PRIESTESS: *We now call to those seen and unseen, the fey who would willingly join us in our rite.*

EAST QUARTER CALLER: *Fair folk of the east,*
   Keepers of breeze, wind, and air,
   You are welcome here!

SOUTH QUARTER CALLER: *Fair folk of the south,*
   Keepers of flame and passion,
   You are welcome here!

WEST QUARTER CALLER: *Fair folk of the west,*
   Keepers of rain and ocean,
   You are welcome here!

NORTH QUARTER CALLER: *Fair folk of the north,*
   Keepers of mountains and plain,
   You are welcome here!

Circle Casting

The circle caster picks up a sword or athame and, beginning in the east, casts the circle, walking around it three times.

CIRCLE CASTER: *Three passes with my magick sword I make.*

> *First that we all might meet in sacred space,*
> *In a land where Goddess and God lie awake,*
> *Where the Mighty Ones bless all with their grace.*
> *Second to keep out those that wish us harm,*
> *Those without perfect love and perfect trust.*
> *Third I cast with magick glamour and charm,*
> *To hold our energy this circle must.*
> *In the names of the Lady and the Lord,*
> *I have cast this circle with will and sword!*
> *So mote it be!*

Calling the Goddess and God

HIGH PRIEST: *We call to the Great God this night of longest day. Join us as the sun, fiery Lord of the Heavens, blesses our land with the sunshine that makes our world grow! Join us as the Horned God runs wild and free in the summertime woods. May your purifying light and fire bless us this night and drive away all that is negative in our lives. Be a part of our rites as you are a part of our lives. Hail and welcome!*

HIGH PRIESTESS: *We call to the Great Goddess this day of shortest night. Join us as the moon, cool orb of the nighttime sky, lights our way and adds to our magicks! Join us as the Great Mother brings forth new life from the eternal womb! It's your touch that makes the blossoms bloom and the crops ripen with grain. May that same touch reach us this night to drive away any sorrow and sadness that doesn't contribute to our lives. Be a part of our rites this night as we celebrate your gifts of love and summertime. Hail and welcome!*

The Working

HIGH PRIEST: *The sun has long been revered among Pagans and Witches. The sun was seen not just as one of the forces that gave life to the world but as a source of truth and justice. One of the most common depictions of the sun was as a solar wheel. The wheel represented the con-*

stant presence of the sun in our lives and how no one could escape its eye or that of its driver, the goddesses and gods of the sun. Long after the new religion pushed aside the beliefs of the folk, people continued to celebrate Midsummer with the solar wheel!

HIGH PRIESTESS: *In many places, solar wheels were created and then lit on fire and hurled down mountains and hills. If the wheel made it safely to the end of its journey without falling over, all would be well with the coming harvest. The wheel falling over, however, was a bad omen, but thanks to the power of the gods, this rarely happened. Tonight we will not be sending wheels down a hillside, but we will be honoring the solar wheel and harnessing the power of the sun.*

HIGH PRIEST: *While the days are long and summer's power is all around us, today also begins the waning of the sun. We can use that energy to make changes in our own lives. We'll use the sun's waning energies and the Midsummer fire to burn away those energies that no longer serve us. One by one, I want you all to come up to the altar and take a piece of ribbon. Pour some of your own personal energy into your ribbon and envision yourself leaving that which you wish to be rid of behind you.*

Everyone can go up to the altar and take a piece of ribbon, or the ribbon can simply be passed around while the High Priest is talking.

HIGH PRIESTESS: *Into our solar wheel we place our troubles and cares. We cannot roll them away, but we can cast them into our fire and be done with them. We now pass our solar wheel around the circle. Tie your ribbon onto its vines. As you tie your ribbon, say with one word that which you wish to be rid of.*

The solar wheel is passed around, with people tying their ribbons/pieces of yarn onto it. After each ribbon is tied to the wheel and an exclamation is made, follow with "So mote it be!" as a group. Words have power and can add a great deal to the spell. The High Priest should be the last person to receive the wheel.

HIGH PRIEST: *We have shared and we have passed along all that we wish to get rid of this night. May that which we wish to be rid of leave us this night, cleansed by the sun and the Midsummer fire! Chant with me simply, "Away! Away! Away!"*

The coven chants and the intensity builds.

I now cast this solar wheel into the flames! Take these burdens from us! So mote it be!

COVEN: *So mote it be!*

HIGH PRIESTESS: *As Midsummer is one of the most sacred times of year for the fey, we honor them so that we might know them better. Fair folk, those who exist just beyond our line of sight, we call to you this night. We call to you not to ask a favor or a boon but to offer you gifts. We realize that our stewardship of this world is often lacking, but we wish to live with you, not to drive you away.*

HIGH PRIEST: *We offer you several gifts this night. First we offer you shiny baubles and cool spring water.*

A bowl is passed around with stones, pebbles, beads, etc., and each coven member takes one.

HIGH PRIEST: *Within these baubles we place just a little bit of our energy so you might know us and who we are.*

HIGH PRIESTESS: *Grasp your stone (or pebble, bead, etc.) with your dominant hand and place a little bit of yourself inside of it. Feel your energy going down through your body and into the stone.*

The High Priest picks up a bowl with spring or rainwater in it from the altar and carries it around the circle, allowing each coven member to place their stone in the water.

HIGH PRIEST: *As you place your stone in the water, verbalize your intention and say who it is meant for. To the fey, we offer these things in love and friendship.*

Everyone should say "for you" or "to the fey" as they place their stone in the water. Once the bowl has been around the circle and everyone has added their stone, the High Priest should take the bowl to where the offering will be given (or place it upon the altar). As the High Priest pours the contents of the bowl onto the ground, the High Priestess asks that the fey accept the gifts of the coven.

HIGH PRIESTESS: *Fair folks, hidden friends, accept these gifts! Blessed be!*

After the bowl is emptied or set down and the High Priest returns to the circle, the High Priestess picks up a bowl of honey along with the honey dipper/spoon.

HIGH PRIESTESS: *We realize that relations between mortals and the fey have not always been good. Our kind often tramples upon your special places, with no regard for your needs or that of this earth. We, though, are the Wise Ones, those who practice the Old Religion and want you to know that we are different. We do hear you, and we do care about you and this world. In order to know us better, we'd like to introduce ourselves to you.*

The High Priest picks up the empty bowl for the honey and stands next to the High Priestess. She puts some honey on the honey dipper and places it in the bowl held by the High Priest. While doing this, she introduces herself to the fey.

HIGH PRIESTESS: *I am (Name) and I wish you no harm and offer this honey in love and friendship. Blessed be!*

The honey is passed around, with everyone repeating the actions of the High Priestess. The High Priest follows the honey around the circle carrying his bowl, collecting the offerings of honey for the fey (and preventing a huge mess!). Finally, the honey should come back around the circle to the High Priestess, who takes the bowl being held by the High Priest and gives him the honey and honey dipper, allowing him to introduce himself to the fey. The High Priest then walks the gift of honey over to the spot set aside for the fey as the High Priestess asks them to accept the coven's offering.

HIGH PRIESTESS: *Fair folk, we of this coven introduce ourselves to you and give you this gift of honey. May our interactions ever be sweet! Blessed be!*

The honey is poured out upon the earth by the High Priest or placed on the altar to be shared later. Once the High Priest has returned to the circle, the High Priestess picks up the large rock with a house painted on it.

HIGH PRIESTESS: *And finally tonight we offer you this small representation of a house to let you know that all who come to us with good intentions are welcome. To those who would happily dwell among us in this place, we say welcome!*

The rock house is passed around, with each coven member saying something about the fey being welcome in this place. I like to intentionally add that this welcome goes only for those who would do us no harm. You don't want a member of the fair folk who hates humans living next to you!

After everyone has handled the rock house and spoken to the fey, the High Priestess places it in the area set aside for the fairy folk to receive their gifts. As she places the rock house in their area, the High Priest asks the fey to accept the coven's gift.

HIGH PRIEST: *We place this house here for your use. Know that those who come here in good faith are wanted and welcome. Blessed be!*

Alternatively, the fairy rock can be put on the altar and moved outside later.

Cakes and Ale

HIGH PRIEST: *On this the shortest night, I call to the powers of the moon to be with us and bless our food and drink.*

HIGH PRIESTESS: *On this the longest day, I call to the powers of the sun to be with us and bless our food and drink.*

The High Priestess picks up her athame and the High Priest the cup full of wine, beer, or whatever it is you're using for cakes and ale. She places the athame in the cup while saying:

HIGH PRIESTESS: *As the sun is to the day,*

HIGH PRIEST: *And the moon is to the night,*

HIGH PRIESTESS: *May their blessings ever pour down upon us.*

BOTH: *So mote it be!*

The High Priest presents the High Priestess with the cup, and she drinks deeply from it before handing it back to him. After drinking, he then passes it around the circle The High Priestess now takes her athame and touches each cake with it (all the better if the athame still has a bit of wine on it), blessing them before offering the plate to the High Priest, who then eats one before passing them back to her. The cakes are then distributed to the rest of the coven, making sure to add some cake—along with some wine—to the libation bowl.

Goodbyes to the Gods

HIGH PRIEST: *We thank the Great God for being with us this night. As you sink now beneath the trees and hills, we thank you for your presence in our lives. As you set in the sky upon this enchanted night, take away those things we burned in the sacred Midsummer fire. Our solstice celebration is near its end, but you walk with us both within and without the circle. Hail the God! Hail the sun! Hail the summer! Blessed be!*

HIGH PRIESTESS: *We thank the Great Goddess for being with us for our Midsummer rite. You are the Mother of us all, human and fey, and as your children, we honor you on this the shortest of nights. May the relationships we've begun tonight prove beneficial for all involved. Our solstice celebration is near its end, but you walk with us both within and without the circle. Hail the Lady! Hail the moon! Hail the summer! Blessed be!*

Taking Down the Circle

The circle caster picks up their sword or athame and, beginning in the east, walks around the circle widdershins three times, releasing the circle.

CIRCLE CASTER: *Three passes with my magick sword I made.*
First that we all might meet in sacred space,
In a land where all would stand unafraid,
Where the Mighty Ones did show us their face.
Second to keep out those that wish us harm,
In this task our circle has served us well.
That I cast with magick, glamour, and charm,
And we return to where we mortals dwell.
In the names of the Lady and the Lord,
All is now released by my will and sword!
So mote it be!

Goodbyes to the Fey/Quarters

EAST QUARTER CALLER: *From the east you came,*
Fey of air, breeze and whisper,
Thanks for your blessings.

SOUTH QUARTER CALLER: *From the south you came,*
  Fey of fire, stirrers of souls,
  Thanks for your blessings.

WEST QUARTER CALLER: *From the west you came,*
  Fey of water, sea and spring,
  Thanks for your blessings.

NORTH QUARTER CALLER: *From the north you came,*
  Fey of earth, soil and mountain,
  Thanks for your blessings.

HIGH PRIESTESS: *The time of waning is now at hand. The days grow shorter, but the summer is just beginning. With the blessings of the Lord and Lady and those seen and unseen, we leave this place with joy and full hearts. Merry meet, merry part, and merry meet again! And may the gods preserve the Craft!*

FIN

CHAPTER 27

MIDSUMMER SOLITARY RITUAL

High Noon

This ritual is designed to be done at (or near) noon on the Summer Solstice. Since for many of us that might mean "while at work," this is a stealth ritual requiring only a secluded park bench or perhaps just a shady spot under a tree. (It's perfect for doing over a lunch break!) It also lacks a ritual script, and instead internalizes everything that goes on in the rite. If there are words you want to say aloud, by all means add them, but they aren't specifically included here.

The amount of stuff needed for this ritual is also minimal. Cakes and ale are optional here, and if you do sneak off to do this on a work break, you can use your lunch as cakes and ale! Alternatively, I suggest using something seasonal, such as fresh fruit, perhaps with an iced tea.

Materials Needed

- Glass of water
- Essential oil (that reminds you of summer; diluted)
- Pinch of salt
- Cakes and ale (if desired)

The Ritual: High Noon

Find a secluded spot and set out all the items needed for this ritual. Close your eyes and take a deep centering breath, then release it and focus on the world around you. Feel the breeze, even if it's slight, and imagine it cleansing your body, carrying away any negative thoughts or energies. If the breeze is mostly absent, this may take a little while, but be patient, the wind will eventually come.

Instead of casting a circle, survey your surroundings. Notice the grass. Is it green or is it dry and brown? Are there trees? The scent of flowers on the breeze? Perhaps you hear people laughing nearby. That's all good too. Imagine everything around you as an interconnected web, with you in the middle of it all. In this place and at this time, you are one with your environment and your surroundings.

Take your essential oil and dab just a tiny bit of it on a finger of your non-dominant hand. Hold that finger up to your nose and breathe in the scent (I use jasmine here). Let the scent take you back to childhood memories of summer. The scent should diffuse into the air a little bit and should be something you notice throughout this solstice rite.

As it's June, the air around you is most likely warm. Feel that warmth on your skin, even if it's only through your clothes. Notice your body's own heat and then travel inward toward your will. Your will is ruled by fire and is the essence of everything you are. Feel it burning within you, fueling your magick and intent.

Pick up your cup of water and have a drink. Taste it on your tongue, then feel it as it slides down your throat and into your stomach. If it's cold, you might be able to feel the water travel all the way into your stomach. Think of how much of your body is made up of water and how important it is to us on a daily basis.

Finally, put a bit of salt on your finger and taste it. Feel how your body reacts to the salt on your tongue. As an element of earth, salt always has a very grounding effect on me. Being grounded is often a good thing too. It keeps us aware of what's going on around us and gives us the clarity to understand and interpret our experiences.

If there are any goddesses and gods you're close to, call out to them now, perhaps whispering verbally, or reach out to them with your intention. Many of the deities I'm closest to seem to follow me around and are always nearby. Often all I have to do is simply say their names. If there are no particular deities you want to invite, call to the Lord of the Sun and Mother Earth. Picture them in your mind's eye however it is that you view them.

Is the Lord of the Sun fiery and red? Perhaps he rides in a chariot, or maybe he's the sun itself. Mother Earth can be blue or green, large or small. I often see her as a tree with feminine features: her branches are her many arms reaching upward and her legs are her roots digging into the ground.

The natural world is often at the height of its power in the summer. The sun sits high overhead, providing the warmth and light needed to ripen the grain and ensure a good harvest. The earth is the cradle where all life emerges. When the two forces come together, we are presented with endless possibilities.

Hold your head up toward the sky, close your eyes, and feel the power of the sun upon your body. Feel the sunlight soaking into your skin, and notice the orange-red of the sun's power on your eyelids. Imagine you are a solar cell for just a moment, the sun's rays charging your body with energy, its light warming you. Even on a particularly hot day, sunlight still feels good on the skin, so soak it all up for just a few moments.

Now wiggle your toes and be aware of your feet. Send your essence outward and down into the ground below you. Feel the cool of the earth, the dampness of the soil (and it's there, eventually, no matter where you are), the life-giving properties inherent in the earth. If there's concrete below your feet, power through it. The natural world is still under there somewhere.

As you push your senses deeper into the ground, feel the heat begin to surround you. This is the heartbeat of the natural world, the furnace of Gaia. Draw some of that energy into yourself and picture the joys of summertime, the harvest, fruits, grains, and vegetables. Imagine the warm days and long nights.

Focus on the sunlight again and follow it down through your body to where it meets with the energy of the earth. This is the crucible from which all things are possible. In that space where those two energies mix, you are feeling the height of summer and the magick that occurs when two forces intermingle and become one. As you feel the earth and sun energy, think of the various deities and forces that make up that power. There are both sun goddesses and sun gods, and earth gods and earth goddesses. Both powers are full of endless possibilities.

As the energies course through you, become aware of your surroundings again and drift back into the mundane world. Open your eyes and notice the green around you, the lives (human, animal, and plant) nearby, and the powers of all four elements manifest in nature. Take some of your sun/earth energy and put it away somewhere deep inside of yourself, to draw upon during a bad moment or when you feel disconnected from the earth.

If you've brought something for cakes and ale, eat it now. You can consume your food and drink quickly as a form of grounding or simply take a leisurely lunch. Your feet may still be pulsing from the power of the earth, and your skin will probably still feel the sun's energy. Revel in these feelings; let them and the food you eat connect you to the world. You are still the center of your web.

Pour some of your water or drink upon the ground, thanking the spirits of place and the deities close to you for being a part of your rite. If you're in a place where you can make a physical offering, do so, sharing a cake, a bit of fruit, or perhaps a piece of your sandwich. If you can't really do that, find a bush or secluded spot on your way out to leave your libation.

When you're done, thank the sun and the earth for their many gifts. If you called upon any specific deities, thank them as well and indicate to them that the rite is over. You can do this verbally or simply by sending out your intention.

Take your salt and put a bit of it on your tongue. This will help to ground you and get your head out of ritual space. Rub your fingers together, shaking any salt off them and onto the ground. Thank the element of earth for being at your ritual as you do this.

Drink a bit of water and pour whatever remains upon the earth, thanking the spirits of water for being at your ritual. Your skin will most likely be warm now after all this time spent in the sun. Notice that feeling for a second, then let it go, releasing the spirits of fire who have joined you. And finally take one last deep breath and release it. Feel the air move through you and back out into the world.

Envision yourself at the center of your web and slowly begin cutting the threads around you, disconnecting from the trees, the ground, and everything else. This part can be done while sitting or while you're leaving your ritual spot. Finally, see yourself whole and in the mundane world, still a part of everything but once again in the natural world. The rite is done. Hail the summer!

FIN

CHAPTER 28

LAMMAS
The First Harvest

Sabbat Name: Lammas or Lughnasadh (also spelled Lughnassa, Lughnassadh, and Lugh-
   nasa; also called First Fruits and First Harvest)

Date: July 31, August 1, August 2

Pronunciation: Lammas = "LAH-muss," Lughnasadh = "Loo-NAH-sah"

Lammas (or Lughnasadh) is probably the most curious of all the sabbats, given its many
names and various celebration dates. *Lughnasadh* is an ancient Irish-Celtic holiday, just like
Imbolc, Beltane, and Samhain. It was originally celebrated beginning at sundown on July
31 with festivities carrying on into the following day. Because most of us don't start our
days at sunset, the majority of Witches celebrate the holiday on August 1.

   Lammas is the name of an Anglo-Saxon holiday also celebrated at the start of August.
It could be a borrowing of the Irish-Celtic *Lughnasadh*, or it might have arisen indepen-
dently. Lammas later became the name of a holiday in the Catholic Church, where it was
also known by the name *loaf mass*, and was a celebration of the grain harvest and the
bread that went along with it.[62] Lammas was generally celebrated on August 1, though
some Witches use the date of August 2, which comes from *The White Goddess* (1948) by
Robert Graves. Some Witches, such as author Silver RavenWolf, differentiate between

---

62. Hutton, *Stations of the Sun,* 330.

the two sabbats, with Silver giving the date of Lammas as August 2 and Lughnasadh as August 7.[63]

No matter what it's called or when it's celebrated, Lammas is undoubtedly a harvest festival. In Ireland and Scotland, it marks the beginning of the cereal grain harvest, which has always been a cause for celebration. Most Modern Witches celebrate it in this fashion too, regardless of where they live. Though I've never lived in an area where the majority of grain is gathered in early August, many of the Lammas rituals I've participated in over the years have involved bread.

Irish mythology doesn't have much to say about Lughnasadh as a harvest festival, but a clue to that part of its history can be found in an alternative name once used to describe the holiday. In medieval times, Lammas was also called the *Gule of August*, with many people believing that this meant that Lammas was the "Yule" of August. A more likely explanation is that this alternative name comes from *gwyl aust*, the Welsh name for August 1. The Welsh word *gwyl* translates as "feast," meaning Lammas and Lughnasadh celebrations were "feasts of August."[64]

Lughnasadh is often connected to the god Lugh. They share a name after all, and for many Witches he is a central figure in their holiday celebrations. (There's more about Lugh in chapter 30 in the coven ritual dedicated to him for this sabbat.) Lugh is seen by many as a solar deity, but the Irish-Celtic Lughnasadh was never a fire festival in the way that Beltane and Samhain were. This again makes it a bit odd when compared to the other greater sabbats.

In the medieval period, the celebration of Lammas coincided with the payment of rent, local elections, fairs, and the opening of public lands.[65] Echoes of this practice can still be seen throughout North America and the British Isles in the tradition of August state and county fairs. Nearly every city I've ever lived in has had some sort of August fair, and many of them revolve around agriculture (and those carnival rides that always go around in circles and usually make me ill).

For many Witches, the heat of August and the various vacations that many of us take with our friends and loved ones make Lammas a challenging sabbat to celebrate. If my coven is going to miss a sabbat, it's generally Lammas, and that's a shame. It's an impor-

---

63. RavenWolf, *To Ride a Silver Broomstick*, 36.

64. Hutton, *Stations of the Sun*, 330.

65. Ibid., 331.

tant spoke on the Wheel of the Year, and while it doesn't mark the start of autumn for many of us in the Northern Hemisphere, it does signify that seasonal change is coming.

Ways to Celebrate Lammas

Lammas was originally a celebration of the harvest and bread, and both things offer a lot to build a ritual around. Many Witches I know make corn dollies for Lammas. Corn dollies are generally seen as being representative of the Goddess in her role as the Earth Mother. One of my favorite Lammas rituals ever wasn't really a ritual, it was just a bunch of us in the middle of a friend's family cornfield making corn dollies as the sun set.

In my personal practice today, I often honor the harvest that's going on around me instead of grain harvests hundreds and thousands of miles away. In California, early August is the end of blueberry season and the start of apple season, and I like to decorate my altars with both fruits (and eat them too of course). It's also a time for fresh green beans and tomatoes, and sometimes the first ears of sweet corn (though that gets better later in the season). Nearly every area has something that's harvested in early August, and no matter what it is, it's worth celebrating.

Metaphorical harvests are another idea to build rituals around. Perhaps the work put in at Ostara and Beltane is ready to be reaped and gathered up at Lammas. Dried wheat (available at most craft stores) can be used to symbolize the things we are bringing into our lives at this time of year. With school starting for many people in August these days, and the accompanying back-to-school sales, transitional rituals about this change are appropriate for many families and covens with college-age members.

One of my coven members often bakes bread during ritual in her Lammas rites. Bannock bread is extremely easy to produce, and baking it during ritual makes for a memorable rite. If you are celebrating outdoors, it's easy to do this with a charcoal grill or small fire. It's a little trickier if you are celebrating with a group indoors, unless you have access to a fireplace or can gather round the oven for ritual.

Lammas is the first of three holidays often associated with the idea of the sacrificial god. There are many deities that can be used for such rituals. Adonis, Tammuz, and Osiris immediately come to mind, but the most popular is not a traditional deity, but John Barleycorn, a figure from English folk songs. The story of John Barleycorn is the story of the barley getting cut down and turned into beer, though the musical versions sound far more violent than the reality of the process.

Beyond the sacrificial god, solar deities are popular at Lammas. Though the sun has begun to wane, August is often the hottest month of the year. Sun deities aren't limited to male deities either. Goddesses such as Hathor (Egyptian), Bast (Egyptian), Saule (Lithuanian), Olwen (Welsh), and Sunna (Norse) are welcome reminders that our ancient ancestors saw the sun in a variety of different ways.

Because Lammas is not about the grain harvest in many locations, it's a great opportunity to stretch one's ritual wings. I've always felt that just about any sort of ritual is acceptable at Lammas because people have generally low expectations for this sabbat. I had a friend whose public Lammas ritual was built around *The Wizard of Oz*, complete with a tin man, scarecrow, wizard, and cowardly lion. Everyone in the ritual got to be "Dorothy" experiencing "Oz" for the first time.

Unconventional Lammas rituals extend beyond book and movie adaptations. The ritual itself could be held in an unconventional spot. How about a ritual in a pool on a hot August day? Or a coven trip to the local county fair? Rituals and Witch activities don't necessarily have to be done inside the standard magick circle. With some of the public groups I've been a part of over the years, I've often used Lammas as an opportunity to expose people to Druid-style rites, along with those of other Pagan groups outside the world of Witchcraft.

The sabbats are a gift, not a requirement. Celebrate in a way that works best for you and those you share your ritual space with. Lammas may be sort of an outlier, but it's our outlier and still has a lot to offer.

CHAPTER 29

LAMMAS CIRCLE RITUAL

The Earth Mother and the Harvest Lord

I'll admit to Lammas not being one of my favorite sabbats. I like the ideas behind it, but I've never lived in an area of the United States where the bulk of the grain harvesting was done in early August. From a seasonal perspective, it doesn't resonate with me as much as the Autumn Equinox does (which was when grain was harvested when I lived in the American Midwest). While Lammas is often thought of as the start of autumn, to me it's always been high summer.

But when I've asked my friends about what they expect in a Lammas ritual, the ideas of the harvest and to a lesser extent the god Lugh generally come up. One of the most frequently requested motifs linked to the harvest is that of John Barleycorn, a stand-in for the god whose sacrifice takes place at the harvest so that the crops might ripen. When I think of his sacrifice, I imagine his transformational energy being put to use in ways other than just ripening crops. What if it's his sacrifice that acts as the catalyst for change? Grain is good and all, but it can't become bread unless it's mixed with other ingredients and baked. Maybe his magick is also in the baking (and the brewing and the fermenting).

So this ritual is about just that. It's about the gifts of Mother Earth (the grain), the elemental powers that help turn that grain into bread (salt, baking powder, water, and spices, the last one being especially important if you want some really tasty bread!), and the transformational power of the sacrificial god whose power turns those five substances into bread. Over the course of the ritual, each participant gets a chance to help make the "bread," with everyone adding ingredients such as salt and grain to the cauldron of the Harvest Lord, who then transforms.

Each element/ingredient in this rite has a specific correspondence: salt is used for protection, baking soda for inspiration, water for health and healing, and spice for adventure. What people add to the bread represents what they want to add to their own lives. Then the magick happens when people eat the bread, since their energies, along with their wants and needs, have been put into it.

This rite doesn't require a lot of extra tools, though it does call for a large cauldron. It makes far more sense to put the ingredients we use to make bread into an oven or large bowl, but cauldrons are just so closely associated with Witchcraft! Obviously, any substitute you want to use for the cauldron is fine. The rite also requires four bowls for all the ingredients, though you can get extra creative if you want and add more ingredients if you so desire.

The working part of the rite ends with the "reveal" of the finished bread that has been (metaphorically) created using the four or more ingredients outlined above. I like to keep this finished bread on an extra table or altar and covered by a tablecloth to keep the bread hidden and safe from bugs. A second tablecloth is also used to place over the cauldron itself to symbolize the change that happens when the ingredients that make up bread are combined and baked.

I've tried to keep all of the rituals in this book on the simpler side, but if you want to take this experience up another level, you can literally bake the bread during ritual. All that's really required is a regular little fire or even a charcoal grill. Mix the ingredients into dough, place the dough in a cast-iron skillet over a fire, flip once after five to ten minutes, cook for another ten minutes or so, and voilà! Bread. Alternatively, you could have everyone around you put their dough on a stick and "roast" the bread like one generally roasts a marshmallow.

In order to make the ritual more participatory, instead of using the quarter callers to hold the elemental powers found in the salt, baking soda, water, and spices, you could take volunteers from the audience. There are all sorts of ways to tweak this rite to suit the needs of your group or large circle.

There's nothing particularly out of the ordinary in this ritual. I did start the circle casting and the quarter calling in the north simply for variety and because I know several Witch traditions that do so. This ritual honors the Earth Mother and the Harvest Lord, but you could also have a Harvest Lady and an Earth Father, or an Earth Mother and a Harvest Lady. The ritual roles can be switched around depending on who you have to help you with the rite.

Ritual Roles

- High Priestess/Earth Mother
- High Priest/Harvest Lord
- Circle caster
- Four quarter callers

Materials Needed

- Regular altar setup
- An additional altar for the finished bread
- Cauldron (or large bowl—something to put the bread ingredients into)
- Grain (Flour is messy and I don't recommend it. Actual grains can be used, or failing that, oatmeal, which is of course also a grain and doesn't end up all over your clothes.)
- Salt in a bowl (You can use salt already on the altar.)
- Water in a bowl or cup (You can use salted water already on the altar, or a fresh bowl of water, preferably spring water.)
- Baking soda in a bowl (or yeast—what you use to make the bread rise is symbolic of air)
- Spices in a bowl (I suggest cinnamon or rosemary. You could also use raisins, which are dried by the sun. This is where you can be really creative!)
- Two tablecloths (one to put over the finished bread and one for the transformation part of the rite)
- Finished bread, at least enough for everyone to have a decent-size piece
- Wine and/or grape juice (if celebrating the grape)
- Circlet for the High Priestess

• Circlet or horns for the High Priest

• Incense sticks

THE RITUAL: THE EARTH MOTHER AND THE HARVEST LORD

The altar stands in the center of the circle, and a cauldron or large bowl, along with a second altar or table, are located in the circle's south (figure 7). The cauldron will receive the ingredients used to make bread, while the covered altar will hold the finished bread to be revealed near the close of the ritual.

The ritual begins with all in attendance gathered in a circle. The High Priestess and High Priest stand in the center of the circle behind the altar. Inside the circle but toward the edges stand the four quarter callers and whoever is casting the circle. The rite begins with a cleansing and the High Priestess sharing the ritual's intent.

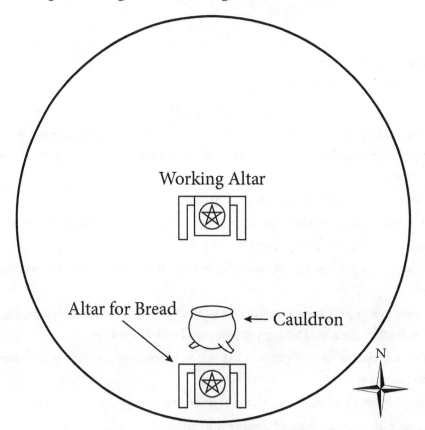

Figure 7. Lammas Circle Ritual Setup

Statement of Intent/Cleansing

HIGH PRIESTESS: *We come here today to celebrate Lammas, the first harvest. Today we honor the Earth Mother and the Harvest Lord. Through her all grows, and through his sacrifice all is transformed. We revel in the first fruits of the harvest and give thanks for it. Hail the harvest!*

The High Priestess places her athame in the bowl of salt upon the altar and blesses it.

HIGH PRIESTESS: *In the names of the Lord and the Lady, I bless and sanctify this salt. May it serve to cleanse this space and those within it. So mote it be!*

The High Priestess then takes her athame and places it in the bowl of water upon the altar.

HIGH PRIESTESS: *In the names of the Lord and the Lady, I bless and sanctify this water. May its gifts touch all within this space. So mote it be!*

The High Priestess then takes three measures of salt using the blade of her athame and places them into the water.

HIGH PRIESTESS: *Once for those who are here, once for those who will be here, and once for those who are missed. So mote it be!*

The High Priestess mixes the salt and water with her athame and then sets the bowl of salted water aside. Using a lighter or a match, the High Priest lights the candle representing fire upon the altar and blesses it.

HIGH PRIEST: *In the names of the Lord and Lady, we welcome the power of fire. May it cleanse all here and ignite their will. So mote it be!*

The High Priest now takes several sticks of incense and lights them with the candle.

HIGH PRIEST: *In the names of the Lord and the Lady, I bless and sanctify this creature of air. May it charge this space and those within it. So mote it be!*

After blessing and lighting the incense stick, he hands them to the south quarter caller. The north quarter caller then comes forward and takes the salted water. Both then proceed around the circle censing and asperging those in attendance. While walking around, they might say things such as "I bless and charge you with air and fire" (incense) and "With salt and water I do cleanse you." If the circle is especially big, you can light several sticks of incense and have the south and east quarter callers each do half the circle. The same applies to the north and west quarter callers, though you'd have to bless and cleanse another bowl of salted water. (This can be done before the ritual if that makes it less awkward.)

Care should be taken to bless and cleanse not just the participants but also the ritual space. This means paying extra attention to windows (if you are indoors of course), shadows, and anything else that might be hiding some sort of unwanted energy.

Casting the Circle/Calling the Quarters

Using an athame, sword, or wand, the circle caster casts the circle starting in the north. They may make three journeys around the circle if necessary. An invoking pentagram can be drawn at the end of the circle casting when the circle caster returns to the north.

CIRCLE CASTER: *I cast this circle so we might stand between the worlds and dwell in a place beyond time where we may look into the face of the Goddess and God and all that lies in between. May the spirits of nature, the Old Ones, the power of the elements, and those who are of the wise folk be welcome in this space. The circle is cast. We are between the worlds. So mote it be!*

Starting in the north, call the quarters. An invoking pentagram can be drawn as each quarter is summoned or immediately afterward. Quarter candles can be used as well, though if you are doing this ritual outdoors, be sure to use tiki torches or hurricane candles (something that will stay lit). Light each quarter candle at the beginning, during, or at the end of each quarter call.

NORTH QUARTER CALLER: *I summon, stir, and call you up, watchtower of the north, spirits of harvest and grain. Be welcome in our circle and guard and witness this our rite. So mote it be!*

EAST QUARTER CALLER: *I summon, stir, and call you up, watchtower of the east, spirits of seed and leaf. Be welcome in our circle and guard and witness this our rite. So mote it be!*

SOUTH QUARTER CALLER: *I summon, stir, and call you up, watchtower of the south, spirts of sun and plow. Be welcome in our circle and guard and witness this our rite. So mote it be!*

WEST QUARTER CALLER: *I summon, stir, and call you up, watchtower of the west, spirits of rain and stream. Be welcome in our circle and guard and witness this our rite. So mote it be!*

Calls to the Lord and Lady

HIGH PRIESTESS: *We call tonight to the Earth Mother, she who is the beauty of the green growing places and the source of all life. It is from you that our first harvest comes, for upon your world and in your nourishing soil, life grows. Yours is the magick that gives rise to the grain and ripens the fields. The gifts of the reaping are yours to bestow, and we accept them gladly. Be with us in our circle tonight. Lend us your might, majesty, and magick as we celebrate the magick of the harvest and praise your gifts. Hail and welcome!*

HIGH PRIEST: *We call tonight to the Lord of the Harvest, the sacrificial god who stands tall in the fields, only to be cut down in his prime so that our lives may continue on this earth. Your sacrifice is the crucible from which new beginnings and possibilities arise. You are the change that allows us to create new life from the ashes of the old. At the first harvest, we celebrate your greatest gift, and the one that will be a part of our harvest rites until you return to us reborn. Lord of the Harvest, join us tonight as we celebrate your gifts and love for us. Hail and welcome!*

The Working

HIGH PRIESTESS: *It takes many hands to bring in the first harvest. There are those who tilled the soil, planted the seed, watered the crops, weeded the fields, watched the Wheel of the Year, and built the plow. Beyond that are those who provided comfort and sustenance to those who toiled among the crops. It is the work of the many that allows us to be well fed and live in relative security and comfort.*

HIGH PRIEST: *Just like the crops that we harvest at Lammas-time, the bread we make this time of year is made from many ingredients. There's the flour from the wheat, barley, oats, and maize in the fields, but that's not all that's required. There's the life-giving water that gives shape to our lives and is a part of most everything we eat or drink. Bread made from just flour and water is not very good though. It also requires a pinch of salt for flavor, and baking soda or yeast so that it may rise. And often the best bread is touched with just a hint of spice.*

The High Priest walks over to the altar and grabs a circlet, then stands next to the High Priestess.

HIGH PRIEST: *What we need now is a Priestess to personify our Earth Mother. My lady* (looks at High Priestess), *will you accept this task?*

HIGH PRIESTESS: *I shall.*

HIGH PRIEST: *Then I shall ask she who is the harvest and she who is the grain to stand side by side with you. Great Lady, walk with this your servant and share with her your voice and mystery. Harvest Goddess, Earth Mother, share your blessings with us this night through she who is your Priestess. Blessed be!*

The High Priest should bow before the High Priestess and then place upon her head a circlet signifying her representation of the Earth Mother.

HIGH PRIESTESS: *The grain in our bread comes to us from the grace of the Mother. It grows upon her back and under her care. From her, and now me, we receive it this Lammas-tide. But as has been said, it is not grain alone that makes the bread. Many hands and many gifts are needed. The Lady turns the wheel, but the elements give it seasoning and character.*

> *I have need of four who will represent the elements: one for the salt of the earth, one for the life-giving waters, one for the magick that makes the bread rise, and one for the spice that makes life such a wonderful adventure. Who will hold these powers for me?*

It's probably best to just have your four quarter callers represent the elements here, but if you want to see who else will participate, you can open it up to anyone in the audience. If you go that route and have many people volunteer, you could make them play a quick game or solve a riddle to determine who holds which element. (Games are most likely an ancient Lammas custom.) Whatever you do, do it quickly, so as not to lose the attention of your audience.

After the four representatives of the elements are chosen, each is given a bowl containing their element.

HIGH PRIESTESS: *Tonight as a group we shall all together make bread with my gifts and those of the elements. Listen closely and take what you need to add to our bread so that it might benefit you.*

> *For the element of earth, salt! This salt is a source of protection for all who would eat of it! May it keep away sickness, those who are unwanted, and all negativity from our lives. So mote it be!*

> *For the element of water, fresh spring water! It's water that keeps us well, and without which we would not be! Drink of the water and add it to your bread so that it may bring love and healing to those who need it. So mote it be!*

For the element of air, baking soda! For bread and many other things are always better when they have risen! The air is the gift of breath in our lungs, and the breeze the inspiration that drives our imagination and creativity. Add this to our creation tonight if you so need it! So mote it be!

And lastly, for the element of fire, spice! Spice is what makes every life unique. Some of us require a lot, some very little, but we should all have just what we need to get by. Add this ingredient if you have lost your lust for life or just need or crave excitement! So mote it be!

But there is one last ingredient we truly need to make our bread, and that is the element of change. This is sometimes the hardest of all things to grasp. At Lammas, the change comes with the sacrifice of the Harvest Lord. His death is his most powerful gift. It's what allows the grain to ripen and gives us the power to strike down the sheaths of grain in the field. In order to fully grasp his power, we must have one stand for him.

The High Priestess walks over to the High Priest (or again, you could seek a volunteer) and looks him in the eye. If you do get a volunteer, you'll probably want to have something prepared for them to read off.

HIGH PRIESTESS: *My Lord, will you accept this duty?*

HIGH PRIEST: *Yes, my Lady.* (Since she is representing the Goddess here, he should bow.)

HIGH PRIESTESS: *Lord of the Harvest, God of the Grain, we ask that you would stand beside your servant here. Lend him your energy so that all we touch may be transformed! You are the crucible of the early autumn that changes my gifts into those that can be enjoyed by all the folk! Harvest Lord, be with us now! Blessed be!*

The High Priestess crowns the High Priest with a circlet, crown, or pair of horns (something representing his connection to the God).

HIGH PRIEST: *At the harvest I am the sacrificial god. I give my life so that which you eat and drink may be reborn in a new form. I am the heat that bakes the bread, the yeast that ferments the grape, the fire that distills the whisky, the coals that brew the beer. I am the change as summer gives way to autumn.*

As my Lady has said, tonight we bake our bread together. Gather whatever ingredients you need for this time of year and bring them here into my cauldron. As you gather your ingredients, fill them with your intent. What is it you wish to transform in your life during the months ahead? Select the items needed for that transformation and then infuse them with your will. When they have been charged, drop them here in my cauldron.

HIGH PRIESTESS: *All journeys begin with the grace of the Mother and end with he who stokes the fires. Take from me a bit of grain, or from those representing the elements, salt, water, baking soda, and spice! Come let us make bread together and celebrate the first harvest!*

The High Priestess picks up the bowl containing the grain as everyone is invited to move around the circle and grab whatever ingredients they want to add to the cauldron. Everyone who is holding ingredients should say something to those who take an ingredient. The High Priestess might say, "Take of the gifts of the field," or just "Blessed be!" What is said is not of the utmost importance, but you want everyone to feel acknowledged and like they are participating. Drumming or music makes for good background noise during this part of the ritual. (One of those songs might be "John Barleycorn," for instance.)

Once the ritual winds down, everyone should be instructed to return to their spot in the circle. Two of the quarter callers should go and stand near the High Priest and be ready to move the altar with the bread on it when ready.

HIGH PRIEST: *Into this cauldron you have placed what you need to make our bread, along with what you yourself would reap from this year's harvest. To this cauldron I add one more ingredient: my sacrifice. Through my power, I now change what has been received by me here. I forfeit my life so that my folk might have an abundant harvest and see their kin once more at Samhain. I am the Lord of Life and the Dread Lord of Shadows, I am the Lord of the Harvest! I now add my power to this cauldron!*

With a dramatic flair, the High Priest should remove his circlet/head gear/necklace and place it into the cauldron. He should then drape a tablecloth over the lid of the cauldron and grab the sides of the vessel with both hands. He should then will the energy of the transformation and change wielded by the Harvest God at Lammas into the cauldron and feel it mix with the ingredients within. Once they have all been mixed, he should slowly turn and will all of those energies into the bread on the altar behind him. When done, he should indicate this with a hearty "So mote it be!" to the quarter callers, who will then move the altar in front of the cauldron. He should then go around and carefully remove the tablecloth from the altar, revealing the bread.

HIGH PRIEST: *With my power, what has been reaped and blended together has been made whole. Eat of my Lady's gifts, but as you eat, take in the energies you willed into this bread! Let that power spread through you, and may your will be done at this time of the first harvest! Blessed be!*

Cakes and Ale

The quarter callers who moved the altar out in front of the cauldron now distribute the bread to all in attendance.

HIGH PRIEST: *The bread we now share has been touched by the Lady and the Lord and all that lies between them. It has been nourished by the flame of the sun, the water of the rains, the soil of the earth, and the breath of air that pollinates all growing things. It was then gathered, transformed, and brought to us today so that we might share in it. Blessed be!*

HIGH PRIESTESS: *In the late summer, we celebrate the gift of the vine. From earth, wind, rain, and sun, this drink has come to us to take away our troubles and give us cause to celebrate. As it takes many hands to gather this harvest, today we shall use many hands to bless our wine. For within us, about us, and beyond us lies the power of the Harvest Lord and the Earth Mother and all that exists betwixt and between them. Extend your arms toward the center of our circle and push your blessings and good intentions into the wine we share here today.*

All extend their hands and bless the wine in the center of the circle, the High Priestess humming or toning a little bit to direct the energy.

HIGH PRIESTESS: *And now let all eat and all drink and all be welcome in this our circle and harvest rite! Blessed be!*

Wine and any leftover bread are passed around the circle. The quarter callers who are not distributing the bread should share the wine—and something nonalcoholic, such as grape juice—with all those gathered. When all have eaten and drank of the wine, the rite resumes.

Goodbyes to the Lord and Lady

HIGH PRIEST: *You have worked hard tonight, my Lady. It is time to relieve you of your burden.*

The High Priestess takes off her circlet and places it on the altar.

HIGH PRIESTESS: *Earth Mother, we thank you for being a part of our rite. We thank you once more for your gift of the grain and all that you have given us in this lifetime. Walk with us in the waning days of summer and be with us in the autumn soon to come! Blessed be!*

HIGH PRIEST: *Harvest Lord, we thank you for joining us in our rite. May we honor your sacrifice in the months ahead as that which we have reaped tonight comes to fruition in our lives. Be with us in the bread and the other miracles of harvest time! Blessed be!*

Dismissing the Quarters/Releasing the Circle

Starting in the west, dismiss the quarters, moving deosil. If desired, a banishing pentagram can be drawn during or at the end of each dismissal. If you've lit quarter candles, blow them out after each quarter is dismissed.

WEST QUARTER CALLER: *Watchtower of the west, spirits of rain and stream, we thank you for witnessing and guarding these our rites. Blessed be!*

SOUTH QUARTER CALLER: *Watchtower of the south, spirits of sun and plow, we thank you for witnessing and guarding these our rites. Blessed be!*

EAST QUARTER CALLER: *Watchtower of the east, spirits of seed and leaf, we thank you for witnessing and guarding these our rites. Blessed be!*

NORTH QUARTER CALLER: *Watchtower of the north, spirits of harvest and grain, we thank you for witnessing and guarding these our rites. Blessed be!*

Starting in the north and using an athame, sword, or wand, the circle caster moves deosil around the circle, undoing the energies used in creating the magick circle. If they cast the circle thrice, they should release it thrice. After returning to the north, they draw a banishing pentagram.

CIRCLE CASTER: *We have stood between the worlds and have dwelled in a place beyond time and space. Once there, we looked into the faces of the Goddess and God and all that lies between them. But now the time comes to return to our waking world. All will be as it once was, though we shall keep the magick raised here forever in our hearts. The circle is open, but our bonds are unbroken! So mote it be!*

Final Thoughts

HIGH PRIESTESS: *As we leave this place, we take the love of the Earth Mother and the Harvest Lord with us. When we look upon the harvest this autumn, may we see their faces reflected in the gifts and the bounty we might receive. Until then, we say merry meet, and merry part, and merry meet again!*

FIN

CHAPTER 30

LAMMAS COVEN RITUAL
A Meeting with Lugh

Lughnasadh (Lammas) is the only traditional sabbat name that might possibly reference a specific deity, in this case, the god Lugh.[66] History doesn't tell us very much about Lugh. We know he was a member of the Tuatha de Danann (the "children of Danu"), a group of gods who were said to have invaded and ruled Ireland over four thousand years ago. In the Welsh *Mabinogi* (better known to Americans as *The Mabinogian*), there's a character with a similar name, Lleu Llaw Gyffes, but the two figures are very different in their respective mythologies, although they do share the same epithet, "skillful hand," which makes their connection at least a little more likely.[67]

The most common translation of *Lugh* is "shining" or "bright," which makes a lot of sense when attached to a sabbat that's celebrated in the summer. Over the last couple of centuries, the god Lugh has been linked to the continental Celtic god Lugas (who was worshiped in present-day Spain and France by the Celts who lived there two thousand years ago). Place names thought to be connected to Lugas have a variety of meanings, including a "dark place" a "raven," or an "oath or vow." This suggests that Lugh's name might have other associations outside of "shining" or "bright."[68] Because of the possible link to "bright" and "shining," Lugh has often been worshiped by modern Pagans and

---

66. Remember, Ostara might be named after a goddess, but there's no evidence of a holiday named Ostara in the historical record.

67. Hutton, *Pagan Britain*, 366.

68. Ibid., 365.

Witches as a solar deity, but I've always been far more attracted to him in his other guise, the god of the skillful hand and the "patron of all human skills." [69]

Most human endeavors require a wide range of skills, and agriculture is no exception. When we think about what's necessary to produce an abundant harvest of grain (and the life-giving food that is made from it), all sorts of different skills come to mind. There's the saving of the seed from the previous year, storing that seed safely, planting that seed in the spring at just the right moment, keeping the growing grain alive once it's been planted, harvesting the grain, turning the grain into flour, and then finally baking with that flour. Lugh as a god of many skills certainly comes in handy at Lammas! Whether or not the sabbat was truly named after the god Lugh is immaterial. What's most important is that a god with a wide range of skills is truly needed at harvest time.

Instead of focusing on the harvest or grain (as in most Lammas rituals), this rite is all about having an experience with Lugh. Instead of drawing down the moon, the technique used here is called the *Witches' Mill*. The Witches' Mill was first articulated by English Witch Robert Cochrane (birth name Roy Bowers, 1931–1966) and can be used for a variety of purposes. The most common is as a magickal technique for raising energy, but the mill can also be used to produce an altered state of consciousness in order to interact with deity (which is how I use it here).

Cochrane is most associated today with the practice of Traditional Witchcraft (a name that's recently been given to a wide variety of magickal practices with roots in English cunning-craft), and I've adapted that practice in this ritual. (The solitary Samhain ritual in chapter 39 also utilizes it.) I feel like I should stress the word *adaptation* here, since this ritual utilizes the ideas of Cochrane but is still probably pretty different from what he would have done fifty years ago.

Most of the tools found in Traditional Witchcraft are also present in other forms of the Craft, with the exception of the stang. Because this is a harvest ritual, I've chosen to utilize the stang in its form as a pitchfork (which is also easily acquired). The pitchfork-stang is often decorated by tying various colors of ribbon or flowers onto its tines for each sabbat, but that's not necessary.

In many Traditional Witchcraft rites, the stang acts as an altar and is the central focus of the ritual. Here it acts as a focus for the turning of the mill and represents the god Lugh. In addition to Lugh, the goddess Danu is also celebrated in this rite. She's repre-

---

69. Hutton, *Stations of the Sun*, 327.

sented by a small cauldron (or a large one if you've got it!) or bowl filled with water during the ritual.

Instead of the more common magick circle, a magickal bridge is built to "cross over" from the realm of the mundane to that of the sacred. This process utilizes a sword and a broom, but you can substitute two brooms if you are lacking a sword. (A third option is to simply use two tree branches.) When the sword and broom are laid down upon the ground, the High Priestess and High Priest of the rite should visualize energy coming up through them and forming a portal. All who walk through that energy into the portal travel to the *Otherworld*, a space between mortals and the divine. In traditional Cochrane-style Craft, three physical circles are often laid out upon the ground before or during ritual. I've skipped that here, but the instructions for it are included in the solitary Samhain ritual.

It probably makes the most sense to perform this ritual outdoors near sunset, but if you are forced to do it indoors, that's fine too. My coven does most of their work indoors, even in summer, because it's the only place where we get enough privacy.

Materials Needed

- Pitchfork-stang
- Sword and broom (or even just two large sticks or branches)
- Cauldron (or bowl)
- Pitcher or bowl of water (for the cauldron or bowl)
- Regular altar setup
- Bowl of ash
- Bowl of salt
- Additional bowl of water
- Bread and drink (for cakes and ale)
- Something representing Lugh
- Small mirror (used during cakes and ale)
- Candle (for use during cakes and ale)

Ritual Roles

- High Priestess
- High Priest
- Quarter callers

THE RITUAL: A MEETING WITH LUGH

Start with the High Priestess and High Priest within the ritual space, and the coven standing just beyond where the ritual will take place. There's no true cleansing of ritual space in this rite, so make sure that's done if necessary before starting the ritual. The altar should be set up in the middle of the ritual space, with the pitchfork-stang nearby though not yet raised upright in the circle.

Fashioning the Bridge/Opening Statement and Blessing

The High Priestess and High Priest move to stand before the entryway into ritual space. Upon reaching it, the High Priestess lays down her sword. Then the High Priest lays his broom on top of the sword, forming an *X*.

HIGH PRIESTESS: *I lay down this my sword.*

HIGH PRIEST: *And I lay down this my broom. Conjoined and bound together, they represent the most ancient of magicks.*

HIGH PRIESTESS: *Once brought together, they form the gate to the Otherworld, where only true Witches may tread.*

Once everyone has stepped across the sword/broom, the High Priest welcomes everyone, lights the candle upon the altar, and shares the statement of intent.

HIGH PRIEST: *All who practice the Craft are welcome in this space. Together we shall celebrate Lammas and experience the god Lugh, he of the clever hand and many skills. So be it done!*

HIGH PRIESTESS: *We give thanks to the Goddess and God for leading us to these ways and this shared magickal space. Through their power we tread the path of the Witch. So be it done!*

HIGH PRIEST: *We dedicate ourselves this night to the service of the Craft and the Goddess and God we honor within it. Hail the Grain God! Hail the Great Mother! So be it done!*

Placement of the Stang and Cauldron (Call to Lugh and Danu)

HIGH PRIESTESS: *In this place I set my stang into the earth, so that we might call upon the God of the Grain, the Lord of the Harvest, the Bright and Shining One, the god of many skills, the god Lugh. Tonight this stang shall be his symbol and the gateway to his mysteries. Here, at the union of stang and earth, great powers shall unite! Lugh, be welcome at our rite!*

The High Priestess plunges the stang into the earth, tines up and handle downward, in the central-north of the circle, near the altar. It's easiest to do some of the digging necessary to secure the stang in the ground before the ritual. If you're doing this ritual indoors, I find that the stang will generally stay upward when placed in a bucket full of rocks and gravel. Using stone also helps with the stang's connection to the natural world.

The High Priest now fills the cauldron for Danu with water from a pitcher or bowl. When the cauldron is full, he calls the goddess to the rite.

HIGH PRIEST: *I fill this cauldron so that we might connect with the power and strength of the mighty Danu, goddess of the earth and the source of all blessings. She lives within the rivers and the land. She is all that is good in the mortal waking world. This cauldron and its waters are a gateway to her mysteries. Here at the union of land and sea, great powers shall unite! Danu, be welcome at our rite!*

Calling the Quarters/The Circle/Blessing and Cleansing

In Cochrane's cosmology, each of the traditional four quarters is ruled by a deity who inhabits their own castle. Each castle is traditionally surrounded by something representative of that element (such as trees for earth). I've taken the deity names out of the quarter calls, along with the terminology "castle," in order to simplify the ritual a bit. For those interested in something a bit more authentic, there are several books in the bibliography that reference versions of Cochrane's ritual system.

Before calling their quarter, each quarter caller should dip their athame (or a shared blade) into the cauldron and shake that water off their blade at the cardinal point they are calling.

EAST QUARTER CALLER: *In the east, we call to the power of fire, spirits of cleansing and the forge. Be here with us!*

SOUTH QUARTER CALLER: *In the south, we call to the power of earth, spirits of harvest and home. Be here with us!*

WEST QUARTER CALLER: *In the west, we call to the power of the sea, spirits of beginnings and life. Be here with us!*

NORTH QUARTER CALLER: *In the north, we call to the power of the sky, spirits of knowledge and inspiration. Be here with us!*

HIGH PRIESTESS: *And now in the presence of Danu and Lugh, surrounded by the powers of the four elements, we begin the final step in our journey to the Otherworld, the land beyond. First we create a circle of salt to represent life and protect us from harm. Second, we create a circle of ash in honor of death and the decline of all things. And third, we create a circle of water that will take us to the shores of the land that hosts both death and renewal.*

As the High Priestess reads the words of the circle casting, the High Priest should sprinkle the salt, ash, and water around the circle. The salt should be outermost from the altar, ash just next to that, and finally water. When the High Priest finishes sprinkling the water, he returns to stand in front of the High Priestess, still holding onto the bowl of water. She then grabs her athame or wand for the water blessing.

HIGH PRIEST: *I call upon Lugh and Danu to bless this water. May it take away any discord, negativity, or feelings of unworthiness within us. May the cleansing waters bring to this coven harmony and union! So be it done!*

HIGH PRIESTESS: *Through the air, I cut with this athame of steel into the waters held up by the earth. With all four elements in union with one another and in the names of Danu and Lugh, I charge this water with the power of the Otherworld that it might cleanse us for the journey to come. So be it done!*

The High Priestess plunges her athame into the water. Moving a little bit away from the High Priest, she then flings the water still upon her blade upon the High Priest, blessing him. She and the High Priest then travel around the circle, with him holding the bowl of water and the Priestess taking water from the bowl onto her blade and directing it at those in the circle, blessing them with the water. While the two walk around the circle, they may say things like "I cleanse you, removing all that would keep you from harmony and union," "All has been washed away," or "You are now ready to face the mysteries/ tread the mill." Saying nothing at all is also acceptable.

Treading the Mill

HIGH PRIEST: *Tonight at Lammas, we celebrate the god Lugh, he of the long arm and many skills. The skills necessary to plant a field, reap the harvest, and win its rewards are many. We ask that Lugh be here with us this night so that we might celebrate those mysteries and connect to the grain through his power.*

HIGH PRIESTESS: *As we tread the Witches' Mill this night, we shall look both inward and outward for the god Lugh. His gifts are many, and without him there would be no harvest.*

EAST QUARTER CALLER: *Lugh is the god of the smith, who makes the plow born in the fire that tills the soil.*

SOUTH QUARTER CALLER: *Lugh is the god of the woodwright, who makes the mortar that grinds the grain.*

WEST QUARTER CALLER: *Lugh is the god of the brewer, who ferments the grain so that we might know happiness.*

NORTH QUARTER CALLER: *Lugh is the god of the historian, who watches the wheel to know when to plant and when to harvest the grain.*

The High Priestess should now stand alone in the center of the circle to oversee the working, with the High Priest going to stand with the other coveners.

HIGH PRIESTESS: *Let us now meet the god Lugh in the Otherworld. We shall tread the mill to change our consciousness and to truly leave the mundane behind. Focus upon the stang and see Lugh there. Deosil we travel upward to the realm of the gods, widdershins we proceed downward to the land of the dead. Tonight we tread deosil!*

Now all turn to your left and place your left hand upon the shoulder of the person in front of you. Extend your right arm toward the center of the circle and point it toward the stang. Now keep your eyes upon the stang. Let it guide you to the footsteps of Lugh!

While we tread the mill, we shall chant the following in honor of Lugh: "Lugh Lugh go leor!" [70] *Now tread the mill and look upon Lugh!*

All should begin turning the mill while focused upon the stang. It takes a while for regular waking consciousness to drift away and be replaced by a state of consciousness that will make it more likely for us to look upon a god. In other words, don't give up on this after just a few minutes. It should be done for a reasonable amount of time: at least ten minutes, though twenty is even better. In the center of the circle, the High Priestess can keep time with a drum or simply lead the chanting as desired. When the energy has climaxed, the High Priestess should indicate that the turning of the mill should stop.

Once the movement and chanting have stopped, the effects of turning the mill may continue for a little while. So even after movement has ceased, coveners should still be aware that they may have a vision of Lugh. When everyone is somewhat settled, they should share whatever they learned while treading the mill. If there's anything of profound importance, it should be written in the coven's journal. When the High Priestess is satisfied that all is done, she should proceed to cakes and ale.

Cakes and Ale

The High Priest picks up the coven's chalice (filled with drink) and a small mirror. The High Priestess should stand beside him with the lit candle.

HIGH PRIESTESS: *I bring you the light of the moon.*

HIGH PRIEST: *For it brings to us the light and love of our lady Danu.*

The light from the candle is now directed onto the mirror, and from there, reflected into the chalice.(If the ritual is taking place outside on a moonlit night, the High Priestess can pick up the moonlight and reflect it directly into the chalice, leaving the candle on the altar.) The High Priestess then sets down the candle and picks up her athame.

HIGH PRIESTESS: *Through the air, I cut with this athame of steel into the waters held up by the earth. As this drink has been blessed by the elements, may it also be blessed by the gods.*

---

70. This translates simply as "Lugh Lugh of the many skills" in Irish-Gaelic and is pronounced "Lugh Lugh skill-lenna go-lore."

The High Priestess plunges the athame into the chalice. She then walks to each of the four quarters and flicks wine (or whatever beverage) from the chalice in the east, south, west, and north. When she returns, she pours a measure of wine upon the ground (or in the libation bowl) for Danu and Lugh.

HIGH PRIESTESS: *For Danu and Lugh we leave this offering. We thank you for the abundance we have been blessed with upon this Lammas!*

The High Priest takes the plate of cakes (preferably bread or seasonal fruits/vegetables) and holds it before the High Priestess, who thanks the gods for the bounty of the earth.

HIGH PRIESTESS: *From the sacred ground where stang and earth meet, where the cauldron cradles the water, we are given these gifts from the gods. Let us ever be mindful of our world and the blessings within it! For Danu and Lugh!* (Cakes or fruits/vegetables are placed upon the earth as an offering or put in the libation bowl.) *Now may all those who are true Witches drink and eat and enjoy this our first harvest!*

Wine and cakes are shared with all in the circle, with the food and drink passed around clockwise of course.

Ending the Rite/Closing the Circle

Instead of reciting words to the Goddess and God (Danu and Lugh in this rite) at this time, their departure is symbolized by the emptying of the cauldron and the pulling of the stang from the ground.

HIGH PRIEST: *From the sky, from the sea, from the earth, from our will, Danu came to be with us. She was here before us, she will be here after us, and she will be with us as long as we keep true to the Craft. So be it done!*

The contents of the cauldron are poured out either upon the earth or back into the pitcher or bowl from whence they came.

HIGH PRIESTESS: *From the sun, from the rivers, from the fields, from our hearts, Lugh came to be with us. He was here before us, he will be here after us, and he will be with us as long as we keep true to the Craft. So be it done!*

The stang is pulled from the ground and laid down next to the altar. Beginning in the east, dismiss the powers of the elements. In many versions of Cochrane's rituals, there is no dismissing of the elements or their powers, but ritual always feels incomplete to me without such things.

EAST QUARTER CALLER: *In the east, we called to the power of fire, spirits of cleansing and the forge. Our time in the Otherworld is now at an end. So be it done!*

SOUTH QUARTER CALLER: *In the south, we called to the power of earth, spirits of harvest and home. Our time in the Otherworld is now at an end. So be it done!*

WEST QUARTER CALLER: *In the west, we called to the power of the sea, spirits of beginnings and life. Our time in the Otherworld is now at an end. So be it done!*

NORTH QUARTER CALLER: *In the north, we called to the power of the sky, spirits of knowledge and inspiration. Our time in the Otherworld is now at an end. So be it done!*

The High Priestess and High Priest walk toward the sword and broom upon the ground at the threshold of the ritual space.

HIGH PRIESTESS: *That which was joined and has now been pulled asunder.*

The High Priestess picks up the sword and the High Priest the broom.

HIGH PRIEST: *The gate to the Otherworld is now closed. Let all Witches who have journeyed into the mysteries be free to depart this place.*

HIGH PRIESTESS: *So be it done!*

FIN

CHAPTER 31

LAMMAS SOLITARY RITUAL

Protect the Home

Because we know so very little about how many of the ancient sabbats were celebrated, I often look for ritual inspiration in Christian sources. This frightens some Witches, but early Christianity in Europe was always far more "Pagan" than it was Christian. It was full of saints (of both genders) who acted much like gods, and what is the Virgin Mary if not a stand-in for the Goddess?

The working in this ritual borrows ideas from the Feast of the Assumption of the Virgin Mary as found in the *Carmina Gadelica*, a compendium of Scottish poems, songs, history, and lore collected by the folklorist Alexander Carmichael (1832–1912) between 1860 and 1909. This small bit in the ritual is based on the poem "The Feast-Day of Mary" in the *Carmina Gadelica* and comes from the island of Barra in Scotland's Outer Hebrides and has been found nowhere else. Today the Feast of the Assumption of the Virgin Mary is celebrated on August 15, but for several centuries (until a calendar adjustment in the 1700s) it lined up nicely with Lammas! There's no way to tell if the ideas behind this ritual date back to the ancient Celts or Saxons or were definitely used in or near Lammas, but it's not impossible.

For this ritual you'll need some dried kernels of corn (or other grain), which will be used to protect your home (and especially your ritual space) in the coming months. The original version of this working (from Scotland) calls for drying out your corn kernels with wood from a rowan tree. If you want to add a little extra energy to this ritual, you can track down something from a rowan tree (either the wood or the tree's berries) and mix that with your drying corn.

After selecting the corn for the ritual (ideally picked from a field, but more likely from a grocery store or a farmers' market), shuck it so the kernels are all visible and then set it outside in the sun for at least an hour. This will begin the drying process but also help the corn absorb some of the sun's protective energy. After it's been in direct sunlight, remove the kernels from the cob and place those on a baking sheet. Set your oven to its lowest possible setting and then bake your kernels for four to six hours until dry. I check on my kernels about every hour and turn them over during that time to prevent one side of the kernels from burning. Once they're dry, allow them to cool and then place them in a bowl suitable for ritual.

During the ritual, the dried kernels will either be scattered or placed (depending on personal preference) around your home, altar, and any place that might need an additional level of protection. When doing this rite at my house, I always place a few kernels in front of my door and either outside my ground floor windows or on the windowsills of my house. Because this ritual requires some walking around, you'll either have to cast a circle large enough to encompass your own house or open up your circle when you distribute the kernels. Because I usually do my solitary rituals when my house is empty, I just cast a super big circle.

One thousand years ago, families in the Hebrides of Scotland would wake up early in the morning, select a few grain ears, and then begin the drying process. When that was completed, the rite would commence. Because of the time necessary to dry the grain, this most likely resulted in the ritual taking place in the late morning or early afternoon. I prefer to do it as the sun sets, but if you find yourself wanting to do it during daylight hours, just dry your corn out the day before the ritual.

In addition to protecting your home, the grain used in this rite can be used to protect family members or pets. If you choose to do that, simply give those you're protecting a few kernels and advise them to store those grains in a safe place. For my cats, I just tape a few kernels of corn under their water bowl. If you want to do a little protection magick for people you don't see regularly, you can tape your corn kernels to a picture and then store them in a safe place.

There's nothing particularly different about this ritual from the majority of the rites in this book. However, I did move the quarter calls up ahead of the circle casting. There was no particular reason to do this other than to illustrate that the order in which things are done is one of personal preference, not any specific Witchcraft rule.

Materials Needed

- Corn kernels (or other grain, dried)
- Regular altar tools
- Bread and drink (for cakes and ale)

The Ritual: Protect the Home

Your pre-ritual preparation will depend on how exactly you want to conduct the rite. If you're going to place your corn kernels in specific spots in your house, you may want to prepare those areas ahead of time. If you're going to place any of the kernels outside, those areas can be prepared ahead of time too. I place a lot of my kernels in the ground near my front and back doors and near (or in the windowpanes of) certain windows. Because the ground is often dry and hard to dig up in early August, I'll prepare it for my kernels before starting my ritual, breaking up the dirt and digging small holes to place my corn in.

If you're going to cast a circle around your entire house, you'll want to cleanse all the areas you'll be ritualizing in. The easiest way to cleanse such a large area is with salted water (blessed and consecrated) and incense. Sprinkle the water wherever your working is likely to take you, paying special attention to windows, doorways, and corners. When that's finished, follow up with some incense or an herb bundle. Think of it as a bit of extra-early fall cleaning. When everything is cleansed, start your rite.

Statement of Intent

Begin the ritual by stating its purpose, with something like this:

I come here tonight to celebrate Lammas, the first harvest. I will use the first gifts of the field to protect my home and prepare it for the months to come. In the names of the Lord and the Lady, so mote it be!

Quarters/Circle

Beginning in the east, call the elements to attend your rite. If you're lighting candles to symbolize the four quarters, do so after the conclusion of each quarter call.

Spirits of the east, element of air and wind, powers of growth and inspiration, I summon you to join me this sacred sabbat night. Guard, protect, and bless this Lammas rite! Hail and welcome!

Spirits of the south, element of fire and sun, powers of fertility and will, I summon you to join me this sacred sabbat night. Guard, protect, and bless this Lammas rite! Hail and welcome!

Spirits of the west, element of water and rain, powers of growth and change, I summon you to join me this sacred sabbat night. Guard, protect, and bless my Lammas rite! Hail and welcome!

Spirits of the north, element of earth and field, powers of harvest and home, I summon you to join me this sacred sabbat night. Guard, protect, and bless my Lammas rite! Hail and welcome!

To cast your circle, begin in the east and move clockwise. If you're casting a circle around your entire house (or even just much of it), be sure to visualize your circle covering all of it. A really big circle casting requires a little more force and may require more than one or even three trips around the room presently inhabited. Because of the size of the circle being cast, you might want to use a sword or an athame for a little extra oomph if that's not something you normally utilize.

Starting in the east, cast your circle while saying:

In the names of the Lord and the Lady, I cast this circle. All within the boundary of my magick circle, I declare to be between the worlds! All within exists outside of mundane time and space! May this circle be filled with the love and power of the gods! So mote it be!

Calling to the Lord and Lady

If you have candles for the Goddess and God, they can be lit after each call.

I call to the Lord of the Grain and God of the Harvest, the Shining Sun who blesses the fields and the fertile Horned One who gives this world the breath of life. Be with me tonight in my circle. Reveal to me the mysteries of the first reaping and bless the fruits of my labor as I honor your toils on my behalf. May your gifts strengthen me for the work ahead. Great God, be welcome here! So mote it be!

I call to the Goddess of the Fields and the Queen of all Bounty, the Silver Moon who guards my gardens and the Earth Mother whose womb is the source of all life. Be with me tonight in my circle! Reveal to me the mysteries of the seasons and the turning of the wheel, and bless the protective working I undertake tonight in your name. Smile upon me as you did your children of old! May your gifts provide strength and sustenance in the days ahead. Great Goddess, be welcome here! So mote it be!

The Working

Start by letting your mind drift back to centuries ago when the failure of the grain harvest meant famine or even death. We are so far removed from where our food comes from today that it often makes being appreciative of it difficult. Think about where the corn kernels you've dried have come from. Is it a nearby field? Or did they come from a faraway place? Take a moment to visualize the fields of grain that are so important to our society and try to feel a real connection to them. Once you feel that connection, pick up your bowl of corn kernels and place some of that energy into them while saying:

On the feast day of Lammas
Goddess of the Grain, Mother of the Earth,
I took a handful of the new corn,
I removed its husk and its threads,
All with my own hands.
I dried it gently in the sun
And then baked it with loving care in my house.
As the gods have shared this with me,
I now share it with all those around me.
I shall scatter it sunwise round my dwelling
In the name of the Great Lady,

Who promised to preserve me,
Who did preserve me,
And who will preserve me,
In peace, in abundance,
In righteousness of heart and purpose.
So mote it be![71]

Once the corn kernels have been blessed, place them wherever you wish inside or outside your house, doing your best to move in a clockwise direction. If your house has more than one story, begin upstairs and then spiral downward. If you wish to spread some of your kernels outside, do that last before returning inside.

Once you've returned to your altar, you can either move on to cakes and ale or do a little extra protection work for loved ones. If you're planning to give some of the corn kernels to friends, place the grain in your dominant hand and picture your friends in your mind's eye. Visualize them healthy, safe, and content. Will some of that energy into the grain and then say something like this:

Preserve my friend with abundance and peace,
May all that they desire only multiply and increase!

The next time you see these friends, give them the grain to carry on their person or put in a safe space. If you find yourself needing a little extra protection away from home, you can also bless a piece of grain for yourself.

If a person you're doing the working for is not one you'll see anytime soon, simply take the kernel you're blessing for them and tape it to the back of their picture (or perhaps to their name neatly written on a piece of a paper) and store in a safe place. When all of your protection magick has been finished, proceed to cakes and ale.

Cakes and Ale

Take a piece of bread and place it upon your altar's pentacle while saying:

---

71. Adapted from the poem "The Feast-day of Mary" in Carmichael's *Carmina Gadelica, Vol. 1*. Here is a link to it from the National Library of Scotland: https://digital.nls.uk/early-gaelic-book-collections/archive/78420434.

By the powers of earth, sea, sky, and wind, this gift made its way to me. Summer rain, soil warm, pollen blown, and sun so bright have all done their work so that I might not know hunger. From the Corn Mother and the God of the Grain, I have received this bounty! May I never hunger!

Eat at least one bite of the bread while recalling all that has gone into its creation. After you're satisfied with your connection to the bread, place your drink (presumably in a cup) upon the pentacle and ask for the gods blessing upon it:

By this gift of the Goddess and God, may I never know thirst! From rain, from vine, from sky, from ground, may I be blessed by all the elements! From the Earth Mother and the Lord of the Sky, I have received this bounty! May all my thirsts be quenched!

Have some sips of your beverage, connecting to where it originated from. That could be a grapevine in far-off France or a spring in another land. It might simply come from a water source near your house or a brewery down the road. Connect to its origins regardless, being thankful for all that we have to drink. Finish eating your bread and drinking your ale, making sure to reserve some and make an offering to the gods post-ritual (or simply place some upon the ground now if you're outside).

Goodbyes to the Lord and Lady

There's no particular order that has to be followed when saying goodbye to the gods. I usually just go in inverse order, meaning I'd say goodbye to the Lady first.

I thank the Great Goddess for being with me tonight in my circle. Goddess of the Grain, Queen of the Harvest, you have shared your bounty with me this night, and for that I am grateful. Continue to walk with me in the waning days of summer, and may your blessings protect me and mine in the days to come. Blessed be!

If you've lit any candles for the Goddess and God, blow them out at the end of each goodbye.

I thank the Great God for being with me tonight in my circle. Lord of the Sun, Horned One of the Fields, you have shared your blessings with me this night, and I am grateful. Continue to walk with me as autumn draws near, and keep me, my loved ones, and this work safe and sacred this turn of the wheel. Blessed be!

Taking Down the Circle/Dismissing the Quarters/Closing Statement

Starting in the east take down your circle widdershins, making sure to visualize all of the energy that you used to create your circle being released. If you cast a circle around your entire house, visualize all of those places returning to our mundane world.

In the names of the Lord and the Lady, I cast this circle wide. All within its boundary were once between the worlds but shall be no longer. All will exist nearly as it once was but now be charged with the protective energy of my Lammas rite. This circle is now open but never broken! So mote it be

Starting in the east, move widdershins around your ritual space, dismissing the elemental energies you have summoned. If you lit candles for the elements, blow them out after each dismissal.

Spirits of the north, element of earth and field, powers of harvest and home, I summoned you to join me this sacred sabbat night. You have guarded my circle well and now I wish you hail and farewell!

Spirits of the west, element of water and rain, powers of growth and change, I summoned you to join me this sacred sabbat night. You have guarded my circle well and now I wish you hail and farewell!

Spirits of the south, element of fire and sun, powers of fertility and will, I summoned you to join me this sacred sabbat night. You have guarded my circle well and now I wish you hail and farewell!

Spirits of the east, element of air and wind, powers of growth and inspiration, I summoned you to join me this sacred sabbat night. You have guarded my circle well and now I wish you hail and farewell!

Finish your ritual with a closing statement.

I have celebrated the first harvest. May the first fruits of this Lammas protect me, this house, and those I love! So mote it be!

FIN

Part Five
AUTUMN
(MABON & SAMHAIN)

The wheel turns to fall,
The Horned One goes to rest.
Hail the blessed dead!

CHAPTER 32

MABON
The Fall Equinox

Name of Sabbat: Mabon (also called the Autumn Equinox and Harvest Home)

Date: On the day of the autumnal equinox (which occurs on or about September 21 in the Northern Hemisphere)

Pronunciation: "MAY-bonn" (sometimes also pronounced "May-BIN" or "Mah-BAHN")

Mabon is both a new holiday and an ancient one. There's no evidence of any specific celebrations of the fall equinox in the ancient record, but there's plenty of evidence for harvest celebrations, and at least one of them occurred in September and has some Pagan and Witch-like attributes as well. While the word *Mabon* as a name for the Autumn Equinox has been in use only since the mid-1970s, there are some genuinely old customs associated with the September harvest.

Most of the sabbats derive their names from genuinely ancient Celtic-Irish holidays (Samhain, Imbolc, Beltane, Lughnasadh) or Germanic/Anglo-Saxon ones (Yule, Lammas). The remaining three were given the names Ostara, Litha, and Mabon by American Witch Aidan Kelly (see chapter 3). Ostara and Litha were inspired by the calendar put forth by the English historian Bede, but Mabon comes from a completely different place. (If Kelly had chosen a name from Bede for the Autumn Equinox, it's likely that we'd be calling it *Halig* or *Haleg* today, his equivalent to September, which translates as "holy month." [72])

---

72. Depending on who is doing the translating, Bede's "holy month" is generally written as *Haligmonað* or *Haleg-monath*.

Welsh mythology tells of a figure named Mabon ap Modron, and he appears in a few of King Arthur's lesser known myths and in the Welsh collection of literature known as *The Mabinogion* (which dates from the twelfth to thirteenth centuries, though the corpus most likely existed long before that as oral lore). In myth, Mabon is most certainly a very minor figure and is not associated with the fall equinox or the harvest in any real way. He generally appears as a young man, and some scholars have connected him to the Celtic *Maponus*, who was a god of youth and was often conflated with the Roman Apollo.[73] All of this lines up quite well with the literal translation of Mabon ap Modron, which means "son of the mother."[74]

Kelly himself admits that when naming the Fall Equinox, he wasn't searching for a historical name associated with the actual event but with a myth that might have been. It was Kelly's belief that throughout Western mythology there was a tale of a young person being saved from certain death near the fall equinox. Mabon just happened to be the name of one of those young deities saved from an early demise, and Kelly chose it as the name for his holiday.[75] How well this all makes sense depends on one's interpretation of mythology, but there's certainly no denying the near instantaneous popularity of Mabon as a name for the Autumn Equinox.

Though there was no Autumn Equinox celebration in the ancient pagan world, the British holiday of *Harvest Home* is nearly equivalent. Harvest Home doesn't line up exactly with the Autumn Equinox. It was celebrated after a community's major grain harvest and could occur in both August and September, but many of its harvest customs feel Pagan (though we don't know for sure when they originated). And customs that were a part of later Harvest Home celebrations can be found in thirteenth-century records, which is just about where one would expect them to be if they were truly ancient.

The most common way of celebrating Harvest Home was with food and drink at the end of a long day of working in the fields. That drink was alcoholic, which might have led to merriment and a party-like atmosphere. Feasting after a successful harvest goes back to at least the Romans in the written record, so this type of tradition is probably to

---

73. Cotterell, *The Encyclopedia of Mythology*, 144.

74. Aidan Kelly, "About Naming, Ostara, Litha, and Mabon," *Including Paganism* (blog), May 2, 2017, https://www.patheos.com/blogs/aidankelly/2017/05/naming-ostara-litha-mabon/.

75. Ibid.

be expected.[76] But Harvest Home was about more than just feasting after a hard day of work. It was truly celebratory.

By the English Renaissance, Harvest Home celebrations had grown in size and scope. In the book *Travels in England During the Reign of Queen Elizabeth*, the German writer Paul Hentzer (1558–1623) mentions a Harvest Home celebration in Windsor:

> We happened to meet some country people celebrating Harvest Home; their last load of corn they crown with flowers, having besides an image richly dressed, by which perhaps would signify Ceres. [77]

An account of Harvest Home from 1710 mentions gifts of ribbons and lace and "rows of pins" for all the children who helped with the work.[78] That same account also mentions tobacco and drink for the adults, and dessert for everyone involved. Gifts, drinks, lots of food, a harvest doll to celebrate the occasion—that sounds like a party to me!

In addition to the general festivities that accompanied the harvest, it was also an opportunity to elect "harvest royalty." Harvest foremen were called Harvest Lords,[79] which not surprisingly led to the election of Harvest Queens as well. This type of August/September royalty has more in common with the "queens" elected at county fairs today than with the Lords of Misrule at Yuletide, but it's still given me fodder for my own Mabon celebrations over the years.

Ways to Celebrate Mabon

For many Witches, Mabon is *the* harvest celebration. Not only are cereal crops harvested in much of the Northern Hemisphere during September, but there are also tomatoes, sunflower seeds, the first pumpkins, and lots of apples to enjoy. Though not included in this book, many of the Mabon rituals I've written over the years have included food. It's pretty easy to build a ritual around all of the great things taken in near the fall equinox.

For many Witches, Mabon is the Witch version of the Canadian and American holiday *Thanksgiving*. Relaxed feasting can be kind of hard to do at Samhain (it's always so

---

76. Hutton, *Stations of the Sun,* 332.

77. Brand, *Brand's Popular Antiquities of Great Britain,* 307.

78. Ibid.

79. This can be found in the Thomas Tusser (1524–1580) poem "The End of the Harvest," as the "lord" led the harvest into the barn with singing and merriment.

busy!), but that's rarely the case in September. When I ran a Pagan college student group, Mabon was our biggest sabbat celebration of the year. We'd always have a giant potluck dinner, and our feasting was just as important to our celebration as any ritual. Victor Anderson (1917–2001), who founded the Feri Tradition of Witchcraft along with his wife, Cora (1944–2008), stated that his first coven back in 1932 (the Harpy Coven) regularly had meals inside their magick circle on the sabbats. Feasting doesn't have to be only before or after a ritual.[80]

Harvest Home celebrations were about more than feasting and drinking. They also included games of skill related to the harvest. In some communities, harvesting that last sheaf of wheat was turned into a contest, with individuals taking turns throwing scythes at it until it fell. While such an activity might be dangerous in a circle, games symbolizing the harvest are often a part of many Mabon celebrations.

In many communities, the last sheaf of grain was gathered up and given both a female form and a name. Often that name was the *Cailleach*, and just how this figure was honored varied throughout the British Isles. In some communities she was sometimes given a place during feasts, and in others she was used to scare children. If her associations in a particular village were positive, she was also sometimes known as the neck, the Old Sow, the Frog, or the Mare. Where she was feared, she was sometimes called the Bitch or the Witch.[81] The Cailleach most likely represented the power of the harvest, along with the coming of winter, and many Modern Witches honor her as the first form of the Crone goddess. The figure identified previously as Ceres by Paul Hentzer (see the quote in the previous section) was most likely a version of the Cailleach.

In addition to the theme of the coming Crone of winter, Mabon celebrations often make use of the theme of the dying and resurrected god. That particular deity isn't just John Barleycorn; his echoes can be found in several other deities. He's in the wine harvest presided over by Dionysus and in the myths of the Egyptian Osiris, who taught people how to cultivate their fields and turn their grain into bread before being killed by his brother Set and becoming the ruler of the land of the dead.

Another deity to work with and build rituals around at Mabon is Persephone, who is seen by many as returning to the Underworld on the Autumn Equinox. Rituals featuring Persephone in the early autumn help prepare us for Samhain and the coming changes to

---

80. Kelly, *A Tapestry of Witches: A History of the Craft in America, Vol. 1,* 29.

81. Hutton, *Stations of the Sun,* 337–338.

the earth. The Irish-Celtic Dagda is another popular deity at Mabon. The Dagda is an agricultural deity and a god of plenty, which is always appropriate at Witchcraft's biggest harvest festival.

Like its March cousin, Mabon is also a time of balance, when light and darkness are represented equally. Magickal workings focused on balance are especially powerful at the Autumn Equinox. Despite not being celebrated thousands of years ago as Mabon, the Autumn Equinox is an intensely magickal and celebratory time of year.

CHAPTER 33

MABON CIRCLE RITUAL
The Three Faces of the Harvest

When we think of harvest celebrations, our minds often picture people outdoors taking in the grain or, more likely, celebrating the fruits of their labor through feasting and celebration. The latter is often what many Mabon rituals are built around, and for good reason. Celebration is fun, and with Samhain often focused on the dead, Mabon has become *the* harvest celebration for many Witches. I know that's how it often is in my own practice, which is why it's personally one of my favorite sabbats.

However, there are other sides to Mabon that we often overlook. Certainly a successful grain harvest is about abundance. For our ancestors, an abundant harvest meant that they would survive the cold days of winter with full bellies and in relative comfort. But Harvest Home was also an exercise in restraint. A portion of the harvest had to be set aside to facilitate the following year's planting and eventual reaping. In addition, what a family harvested was not necessarily just their own. A portion of their crop most likely had to go to friends, family, their extended community, and their gods (or, in the case of many in the Middle Ages and the early modern period, their church).

In many ways, knowing that we can't just celebrate and hoard what we've grown plays into the idea of balance that we often see at the Autumn Equinox. If we simply consume all we've harvested at this turn of the wheel, there will be nothing left for the following year. We all have to keep a little seed in our back pocket to prepare for what's to come.

In addition, our relationships with the earth and the gods are reciprocal. If we don't give back to them, how can we expect them to give back to us? Those of us who garden give back to the land that grows our fruits and vegetables through fertilizer and compost. Without new materials to renew the soil, nothing will grow. If I ask the Goddess to help provide me with a new job and I don't do anything for her after she provides it, where's the incentive for her to help me in the future? We have to give back to the powers and entities we have relationships with. To not do so makes us bad neighbors and bad gardeners (literally and metaphorically).

This ritual features the three very different narratives of Mabon: partaking in food and drink (celebration), thanking the gods and those in our community for the harvest, and preparing for the future. To encompass these various facets, there is a "harvest blessings altar" set up in the circle containing coins, seeds, and aromatic herbs. Those involved in the ritual are encouraged to pick up all of these different things during the course of the rite and distribute them to the appropriate spots.

The coins should be distributed to others at the ritual as a token of friendship, goodwill, and community. The dried herbs are for the gods and/or the earth as an offering for what they have given us. The seeds can either be blessed upon the altar and set aside for a future magickal task, or be sown into the earth representing "winter wheat" and what we might wish to germinate during this dark time of the year. Because Mabon is a time of celebration, cakes and ale are available during the entire ritual to be eaten at the participants' leisure and are symbolic of what people might wish to bring into their own lives in the fall.

In addition to the autumn blessing altar, there are areas for certain activities, the most problematic potentially being an area to burn the offerings to the gods. Small portable fire pits work well here, and if fire is not possible, a bowl filled with water to receive those gifts is more than acceptable. The station to sow the winter wheat doesn't need to be anything more than a pot of dirt, and a table full of the fruit and drink of the harvest is easily put together. (If you use wine or beer, don't let anyone drink too much!)

It goes without saying that the inclusion of fire (unless you have an easily accessible fireplace) suggests that this ritual should take place outdoors. While many of the summer sabbats are celebrated during daylight hours, especially by public groups, my preference for a Mabon rite is at sunset, when night and day come together. I think this maximizes the balancing energies traditionally associated with the equinox. Because this is an outdoor ritual, I left out all references to candle lighting, I just never have much luck with that when I'm outside.

Statues of deities near the offerings station and upon the working altar are welcome and encouraged. If you don't have a Demeter, Ceres, or Dionysus statue, simply making a version of the Cailleach out of corn or wheat will work exceptionally well. Such representations of the goddess do not have to be elaborate; she just needs something that resembles arms, legs, and a head!

Because this ritual's energy is generally festive, I've simplified the quarter calls and circle casting into a combined working. Each element is honored as a symbol of the autumn and sprinkled around the circle. This invokes both the element and casts the circle. This rite also requires four small bowls or dishes of each element to be placed upon the main working altar.

I'm often wary of rituals that encourage people to seek out those they don't know and give them a token. Most local groups contain a "creeper" or two who makes people uncomfortable, so have your ritual crew keep an eye out for anyone who might be behaving inappropriately or violating someone else's boundaries. Despite my reservations, Mabon is meant to be a community celebration, so I've included the sharing of the coin. If you believe that your local group is not in a position to do this part of the ritual, it can easily be dropped.

In addition to keeping an eye on people, you'll want everyone involved in the presentation of the ritual to watch the various stations set up for the ritual. Having someone at the two altars, the fire-offering station, the cakes and ale table, and the pot containing soil will help prevent any problems from arising. This is not the deepest ritual, but I think it captures the excitement and possibilities of autumn, along with the festive atmosphere that must have been a part of Harvest Home celebrations centuries ago.

Materials Needed

- Regular altar setup
- Grain seeds (like corn, wheat, barley, etc.—whatever works for you)
- Pot of earth
- Coins

- Dried aromatic herbs (Common sage, mint, basil, oregano, or even flower petals work too. Try to find something that grows locally.)
- A small portable fire pit, charcoal grill, or contained fire
- Cakes and ale (bread, locally grown produce, wine, grape juice, etc.)
- Small bowl of wine (representing the fire element)
- Small bowl of dried leaves (representing the air element)
- Small bowl of rainwater (representing the water element)
- Small bowl of grain seed or rice (representing the earth element)
- Deity statues (optional)

Ritual Roles

- High Priestess
- High Priest
- Quarter callers

The Ritual: The Three Faces of the Harvest

The various altars and working stations should be set up prior to the ritual beginning (figure 8). Once all the participants have gathered and are focused on the High Priestess, the ritual should begin.

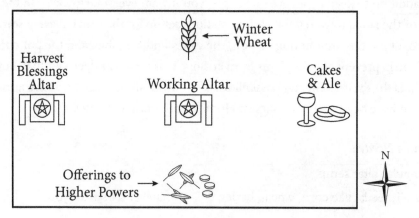

Figure 8. Mabon Circle Ritual Setup

HIGH PRIESTESS: *As day touches night, we gather to celebrate the Autumn Equinox, the harvest, the sabbat of Mabon! Together we shall honor our gods, this community, and what is to come, and partake in the gifts of the season. Blessed be!*

Cleansing

HIGH PRIEST: *The earth and the Lord and Lady are good to us this time of year! Abundance and joy come to us from the land as the energy of the harvest pulses all around us. Set your feet firmly on the ground and reach out with your consciousness, drifting downward into the earth. Feel the Mother there, whose love brings forth new life. Feel the Horned One there, whose sacrifice turns the season. Feel that power, feel that energy, and bring it up through your body. As it courses through you, picture it pushing out all that is unwanted and taking it away from you.*

Feel yourself energized by the powers of the natural world. Feel yourself cleansed by the earth and the energy of the harvest. Take one deep breath, hold it (pause for a moment), and then release your breath, pushing out all that is unwanted inside of you. Know that you are a child of the earth and cleansed by the hands of our Lady and Lord. So mote it be!

Quarters and Circle Casting

One by one, each quarter caller should go up to the altar and pick up the bowl containing what is representative of their element. Each should start and end at their respective cardinal point (east beginning in the east, west in the west, etc., and then ending in the same spot), slowly distributing their element upon the ground and speaking their summoning.

EAST QUARTER CALLER: *By the power of air and fallen leaf, I do charge and consecrate this circle. Spirits of the east, bless our rite and share with us the magick of the harvest. Blessed be!*

SOUTH QUARTER CALLER: *By the power of fire and wine, I do charge and consecrate this circle. Spirits of the south, bless our rite and let us feel the power of sacrifice. Blessed be!*

WEST QUARTER CALLER: *By the power of water and rain, I do charge and consecrate this circle. Spirits of the west, bless our rite and wash away the obstacles between us and all that is magickal. Blessed be!*

NORTH QUARTER CALLER: *By the power of earth and grain, I do charge and consecrate this circle. Spirits of the north, bless our rite and prepare the way forward for us. Blessed be!*

Calls to the Goddess and God

HIGH PRIEST: *I call to the Great Goddess, the Lady of the Harvest, the Earth Mother, to join us in our ritual. Let us honor you this night for your many blessings in our lives. Bring us closer to one another, this earth, and the energy of the season as we celebrate the power of the equinox. Let us celebrate the abundance of the harvest, and may those blessings prepare us for the darker days yet to come. Hail and be welcome!*

HIGH PRIESTESS: *I call to the Horned God, the Harvest Lord, the sacrificial god of the autumn, to join us in our ritual. Bring us closer to your power and energy as we honor the sacrifices that we must make in our own lives and the joy that comes with giving to others. As your golden rays have ripened the grain, may your blessings grow this community and what lies ahead in all of our lives. Hail and be welcome!*

The Working: The Gifts of the Harvest

HIGH PRIEST: *Too often we see the Autumn Equinox as simply being about the harvest and the abundant food and drink it provides us at this time of year and through the winter. But Mabon is about more than that. It's about the choices we make with what we have reaped. We cannot simply consume all that we have. Some of it must be saved to be planted again in the spring or used to begin the winter wheat that germinates in the dark time of the year.*

HIGH PRIESTESS: *Our actions in this life are reciprocal. We would be nothing without the gods and without each other. It takes many to make a circle. It takes many to bring in the harvest and put those crops to use. The grain must be sown, raised, harvested, turned into flour, and then finally baked into bread. No one can do all of these things alone. In days of old, people relied upon their communities to take care of these tasks. They also knew that it was the power of the earth and the Lord and Lady that made the harvest possible. We owe those powers our thanks for what we receive, and use this opportunity of thanks as a way to strengthen our relationships with them and the earth.*

HIGH PRIEST: *Tonight we celebrate, but we thank the powers that have gotten us to this point—divine and mortal—and we prepare for the darker and colder days ahead.*

HIGH PRIESTESS: *Here in this circle are all the facets of the harvest. There is abundance, there are tokens of appreciation and the building blocks of community, and there is that which we sow or take with us to prepare for what is to come.*

EAST QUARTER CALLER: *Here upon this altar in the east lie the joys of the harvest. There is bread, wine, beer, juice, and the fruits of late September. Stop here to appreciate what we have given, or begin your journey here because what you seek this harvest season above all else is a bit of joy and comfort. Toast with those around you and celebrate the harvest through these gifts.*

WEST QUARTER CALLER: *In the west lie the other blessings of the harvest. There are dried herbs grown upon this land and gladly given to our gods. The seeds of this harvest lie here too, to be sown and put to use in the dark days ahead or held tightly until the spring. There are metal coins, whose origins lie deep within the giving earth. Take a coin from this table and give it to someone here in this circle as an acknowledgment that it takes all of us together to build a community. Make sure that your coin is given to someone who has not yet received one, which might take some work, in the same way that growing the grain or building a community takes time and labor.*

SOUTH QUARTER CALLER: *The abundance of this land and the joys we have in this life are gifts of the earth and our Lord and Lady. Our relationships with the gods are reciprocal, and we must give to them as they give to us. Throw an offering of dried herbs into our fire to grow your relationships and show your appreciation. Those who need to become closer to our Lady and Lord may want to come here first.*

NORTH QUARTER CALLER: *In many places the grain is sown in the autumn and the winter wheat germinates in the ground, reminding us that even in times of dark and cold, the earth is still a cauldron of life and possibilities. Cast your grain here to represent that which you will begin manifesting in this dark half of the year.*

HIGH PRIESTESS: *And for those who would take their seed and store it for a future purpose, come up to the altar and seek the blessings of the gods and whatever powers you serve and honor. Charge the seed upon our pentacle, then hold it close to you this winter, using it to prepare the way in the spring.*

HIGH PRIEST: *Take and enjoy the gifts of autumn, all while knowing that which we take we also return. Celebrate, thank, and prepare for the days to come this Mabon night!*

Everyone should be prompted to begin moving around and engaging in the various activities being offered. All directly involved in the presentation of the ritual should make sure that anyone who has given a coin away has also received one from someone else. The High Priestess should stay near the altar to help people charge their grain/seeds as needed.

Each station has its own energy and theme. The table with cakes and ale should be festive, and the east quarter caller should greet all who walk up to it with enthusiasm. In the south, people leaving offerings of dried herbs to the gods should be reminded of the power and solemnity in such an exchange. Due to the sheer number of things that can be taken from the altar in the west, the west quarter caller may find themselves having to explain to people during the ritual exactly what to do with the coins, seeds, and scented herbs. The north quarter caller should watch as the seeds are thrown into the earth, reciting a solemn "So mote it be!" as the grains are cast.

Ending a ritual such as this one can be difficult. When all involved seem to have participated in every activity, you may want to give them a few minutes of warning, stating "Our harvest time has almost ended!" or something along those lines. Music can be played in the background during the ritual, but with so much going on, it may not be necessary.

I think the best way to end the working is to encourage everyone to pick one last piece of fruit or bread and take it with them back to the perimeter of the circle. Once they all are there, the High Priestess can lead everyone in a shared moment of thanksgiving.

HIGH PRIESTESS: *Let us one last time thank the gods and give thanks for our community and the blessings in our lives! All hail!*

ALL GATHERED: *ALL HAIL!*

Goodbyes to the Gods

HIGH PRIEST: *The Great Goddess has joined us in our rites, accepted our offerings, helped prepare our way forward, and bestowed upon us the blessings of the harvest season. Great Lady, walk with us in the darkening days ahead and forever remind us of your power and wisdom. Hail and farewell!*

HIGH PRIESTESS: *The Horned One has joined us in our rites, accepted our offerings, brought us closer to one another, and shared with us the magick and wonder of autumn. Great Lord, be a part of our days and nights as we head toward the colder turn of the wheel. Hail and farewell!*

Releasing the Circle and the Elements

Each quarter caller should approach the altar one by one and then walk to their particular compass point. As they walk widdershins around the circle, they should release the circle and dismiss the elements.

EAST QUARTER CALLER: *By the power of air and fallen leaf, I charged and consecrated this circle. Spirits of the east, we thank you for attending these our rites and sharing with us your magick and blessings. Go from this place and may our circle be open!*

SOUTH QUARTER CALLER: *By the power of fire and wine, I charged and consecrated this circle. Spirits of the south, we thank you for attending these our rites and sharing your sacrificial power. Go from this place and may our circle be open!*

WEST QUARTER CALLER: *By the power of water and rain, I charged and consecrated this circle. Spirits of the west, we thank you for attending these our rites and washing away the obstacles between us. Go from this place and may our circle be open!*

NORTH QUARTER CALLER: *By the power of earth and grain, I charged and consecrated this circle. Spirits of the north, we thank you for preparing us for the darker times ahead. Go from this place and may our circle be open!*

HIGH PRIESTESS: *With our circle released and the quarters dismissed, it is time to end our rite. May the blessings of the harvest ever be upon you! Until next we meet, merry meet, and merry part, and merry shall we meet again!*

FIN

CHAPTER 34
MABON COVEN RITUAL
Harvest Divination

Culturally, the autumn has been a time of new beginnings for several centuries. It's when the new school year starts, and for those of us who still remember network television, it was when new TV shows would premiere after a summer of reruns. In September, the vacations end and the mundane world kicks into overdrive, and it's a pace that usually doesn't let up until after Yule and the secular new year.

At Mabon, my coven honors this change by doing some personal harvesting, while also doing a bit of divination to see what is to come in the near future. For this ritual you'll need several flat stones and a big pot filled with loose soil. The stones should be big enough to comfortably write on, and for the writing you'll need a quality marker. (My wife likes glitter-infused Sharpie markers, but anything will work.) The type of stones you'll need for this rite can easily be found at most craft stores and also outdoors if you're willing to do some serious scavenging.

In this ritual you're going to have everyone in the coven dig into the dirt and pull a rock up out of the earth. Upon each stone will be one word indicating potential outcomes for this coming fall. The words on the rock will reveal what you're likely to harvest (bring into your life this fall), and knowing this ahead of time will give everyone in the coven time to prepare and be aware of the potential possibilities soon to arise.

A week or so before the ritual, you'll want to make sure you have one stone for every coven member (and maybe an extra or two just in case). Upon each stone there should be one written word. Keep the words simple but pertinent for the individuals in the coven. Words you could write on the stones include success, money, love, opportunity, travel, abundance, family, magick, change, relationship, growth, caution, and danger. (They don't all have to imply good news.) Once you've written something on each stone, place them all on your altar or in a spot where they can absorb some moon and sunlight.

The day of your ritual, place all the stones in your container of earth. I like to do this with my eyes closed so I have no idea where any of the stones are in the dirt. Before you place the stones in the dirt, ask the Goddess and God to bless your work.

> *Lady of the Autumn, Lord of the Harvest, bless this my coven's work, and may each stone be grasped by the hand it was meant for! So mote it be!*

Once all the stones have been placed in the earth, move your container to the site of your ritual space. It's best to keep the dirt here fairly loose, so the stones aren't too hard to get out of the soil. Keep your dirt damp but not overly wet; nobody wants to go fishing in the mud. Our coven brings a pitcher and bowl of water into our ritual space so people can clean up after getting their hands dirty. (Alternatively, you could have people dig into the soil with a spoon, but getting your hands dirty is much more fun!)

Instead of cakes for cakes and ale, I've included apple slices, cut in ritual with an athame or white-handled knife. It just adds a little something different to the ritual, and apples are usually in season just about everywhere by the fall equinox. The apple can either be cut on a cutting board during the ritual or can be pre-cut and then cut ceremonially during the rite.

Ritual Roles

- High Priestess
- High Priest
- Four quarter callers
- Circle caster

Materials Needed

- Standard altar setup
- Pot full of loose soil

- One flat stone for each coven member, written upon (see above)
- Athames (for the High Priestess and High Priest)
- An apple (or apples, depending on the size of your coven and apples) and a knife sharp enough to cut one
- Small cutting board for the apples
- Ale

The Ritual: Harvest Divination

Start with everyone gathered in a circle around the altar. When all are quiet and focused, the High Priestess should start the ritual.

HIGH PRIESTESS: *This night of the Autumn Equinox we gather once more as a chosen family. Tonight we will receive the blessings of the earth and peer into our futures to see what the autumn and winter have in store. In perfect love and perfect trust, this coven meets once more. Witches all, be welcome.*

Cleansing

HIGH PRIEST: *Close your eyes for a moment and let your muscles relax. Now take a deep breath and hold it for a moment (maybe twenty seconds or so) and now release that air. As the air escapes from your nose and mouth, imagine all the tension you carry with you, as well as your problems, moving out and through you. Continue to breathe, letting go of any mundane concerns every time you exhale. As you breathe, begin to live only in this moment, with your thoughts turning to ritual and the love of this coven. When you feel refreshed, open your eyes and return to us all here. By the power of this world, we are cleansed and ready for this rite.*

The High Priestess picks up her athame and then sets a dish of water upon the pentacle. She places her athame into the water to cleanse it.

HIGH PRIESTESS: *Great Mother, Goddess of the Harvest and Lady of the Autumn, I ask that you bless and cleanse this water before us. May it charge and sanctify this space and serve as a reminder of your love for us. Blessed be!*

The High Priestess moves the dish of water off the pentacle and replaces it with a bowl of salt. She then sticks her athame into the salt to cleanse it.

HIGH PRIESTESS: *Great Mother, I ask that you bless and cleanse this salt before us. May it charge and sanctify this space and serve to protect us from all harm. Blessed be!*

The High Priestess sprinkles some salt into the water, using either her fingers or the blade of the athame. She then holds the mixture of salt and water aloft in thanks and praise of the Goddess.

HIGH PRIESTESS: *Praise to our Lady!*

The High Priestess sprinkles the salted water around the perimeter of the circle, on all who are in attendance, and then finally in the middle of the circle to rid the sacred space of the negative energy exhaled earlier. When she's done, the High Priest blesses the flame and incense.

HIGH PRIEST: *God of the Sun, Harvest Lord, bless this flame that shall burn bright in our rite. May it guide us ever closer to you and your Lady. Blessed be!*

The High Priest lights a candle and places it in the middle of the altar. When that's done, he picks up the coven's incense and places it and its holder upon the altar's pentacle.

HIGH PRIEST: *Harvest Lord, bless this creature of air that shall charge all within this circle with your wisdom and that of your Lady. Blessed be!*

He then raises the burning incense aloft and praises the God.

HIGH PRIEST: *Praise to our Lord!*

The High Priest lights a taper from the candle lit earlier and uses it to light the incense. Once the incense is lit, the High Priest walks it around the perimeter of the circle, shares its smoke with all in attendance, and then takes it through the middle of the ritual space. When he's finished, the circle should is cast.

Circle Casting/Calling the Quarters

Starting in the east, the circle is cast with an athame, sword, or wand.

CIRCLE CASTER: *I cast and consecrate this circle in the names of the Lord and the Lady. May we now enter a time that is not a time and a place that is not a place, and walk in the realms of the Mighty Ones. This circle shall protect and transform all those within its magickal boundaries on this sacred night of autumn. The circle is cast. So mote it be*

Call the quarters, beginning in the east and moving clockwise. After each quarter has been called, a candle can be lit and an invoking pentagram drawn.

EAST QUARTER CALLER: *All hail the watchtower of the east, the element of air. Stand guard over our circle, and if it be your will, protect all within it from harm. Hail and be welcome!*

SOUTH QUARTER CALLER: *All hail the watchtower of the south, the element of fire. Stand guard over our circle, and if it be your will, protect all within it from harm. Hail and be welcome!*

WEST QUARTER CALLER: *All hail the watchtower of the west, the element of water. Stand guard over our circle, and if it be your will, protect all within it from harm. Hail and be welcome!*

NORTH QUARTER CALLER: *All hail the watchtower of the north, the element of earth. Stand guard over our circle, and if it be your will, protect all within it from harm. Hail and be welcome!*

Calling to the Goddess and God

HIGH PRIEST: *Great Mother, Goddess of the Grain, and Lady of the Autumn, join us in our circle tonight. Surround us with the energy of the harvest as we seek to reap that which you have sown for us, and bless us with your wisdom as we look toward the road ahead. Smile upon your children and be here with us once again in this sacred space. Hail and welcome!*

HIGH PRIESTESS: *God of the Sun, Harvest Lord, join us in our rites tonight. Let us taste and revel in your gifts as we celebrate the autumn. Share with us your patience and your love as we gather in the gifts of this season. Walk with us in this space between the worlds so we might know your mysteries. Hail and welcome!*

The Working: Harvest and Divination

Before having everyone reach into the pot of earth containing the stones, ask for the blessings of the Lord and Lady upon the stones in the earth and the night's working. Start with the High Priest placing his athame into the earth, blessing it, and calling to the Goddess.

HIGH PRIEST: *Lady of the Autumn, we ask that you guide our hands this night and allow us to reap what you have sown for us. Share with us the bounties, sacrifices, and opportunities to come. In your name do I bless this earth and all that lies within it. So mote it be!*

The High Priestess places her athame in the soil, blessing it, as she calls to the God.

HIGH PRIESTESS: *Harvest Lord, help us to ascertain what it is that lies in the darker days ahead. Let our eyes see with your wisdom and let our hearts be open to the possibilities that lie ahead of us. Let us receive your gifts of earth, stone, and sun this night! In your name do I bless this earth and all that lies within it. So mote it be!*

Moving clockwise, take the pot of earth around the circle, allowing all to place their hands within it and draw up a stone. Instead of interpreting each stone as it's pulled up, we think it's best to give everyone some time with their stone to feel its energy and try to interpret its message. So go around the circle once and let everyone choose a stone before trying to figure out their various meanings. If you want to raise a little more energy while the pot of earth is moving around, the coven can softly chant this together:

> *Harvest night, harvest night,*
> *Witches magick burning bright.*
> *Earth and stone, earth and stone,*
> *Let our future to us be known!*

When everyone has pulled their stone from the earth, instruct them to place it between both their hands and to feel the stone's energy there. Let everyone take a few moments to interpret that power and energy and piece together what their personal message might be. When everyone has spent a minute or two with their stone, go around the circle and give anyone who wants to share what was on their stone an opportunity to do so. There's no need to make anyone feel like they have to talk; many Witches prefer to keep such portents of the future to themselves. As a coven, we try to piece together the various messages received by everyone in the circle.

If there are more rocks than people, the coven can also pick a stone at the end of the ritual. If this is done, place the pot of earth in a central location and have everyone stand around it, then instruct everyone to begin pushing energy into the earth.

HIGH PRIESTESS: *And now, as a coven, we shall harvest what is left in the fertile earth. May what we find here guide us in wisdom in the months ahead. So that this stone represents all of us, let us all place our energy into this container. We shall tone and push our energy into this earth.*

The High Priestess begins the toning ("Ohhhhhhhhh"), with everyone slowing moving their hands closer and closer to the soil. When she feels as if enough energy has been summoned, the High Priestess should indicate to someone that they should pull up a stone, or she can do it herself. In our coven, our High Priestess will often just ask, "And who will draw a stone for us this night?" and wait for a volunteer. The moment a hand dives into the soil, the toning should stop and the coven should let out a big "So mote it be!"

Place the coven stone upon the altar's pentacle and have everyone take a moment to interpret its message. Often the stone that's picked will let the coven know if it's due to grow (or contract) in the coming months. After everyone is satisfied with the readings of the stones, allow them to get the dirt off their hands for cakes and ale.

Cakes and Ale

HIGH PRIESTESS: *The days grow shorter and the nights colder, but we know that the Lord and Lady continue to walk with us. For they have blessed this world, and the signs of their blessings are everywhere.*

The High Priestess picks up the apple.

HIGH PRIESTESS: *And here in the simple apple we see their blessings most clearly, for the apple is the fruit of the Witch. Behold the sign of our faith!*

The apple is cut in half through its middle.

HIGH PRIESTESS: *Here in the center is the five-pointed star of the Witch. The gods love and provide.*

The apple is now cut into pieces and shared with all who are gathered. We like sharing the fruits of the harvest with the words "May you never hunger" or "May all your hungers be satisfied." As the apple slices go around the circle, the High Priest picks up the cup of wine/juice from the altar and holds it in the air.

HIGH PRIEST: *The cup of the gods is ever overflowing with the gifts of the harvest. Earth, vine, field, and sun all gather in this cup so that we might enjoy life and the blessings of the Mighty Ones. Lord and Lady, we thank you.*

The cup is shared with all in the circle. Like the apples, we often share our drinks with the phrases "May you never thirst" or "May all your thirsts be quenched." Be sure to leave some apple pieces and drink for the gods and the fair folk in your libation bowl to be taken outside later.

HIGH PRIESTESS: *And now our feasting is at an end and the time has come to end our rite until next we meet.*

Goodbyes to the Goddess and God

HIGH PRIESTESS: *Great Goddess, Lady of the Autumn, we thank you for being in our circle tonight and being a part of our lives. Hold us close in the long nights to come and may we ever grow closer to you and your wisdom. Blessed be!*

HIGH PRIEST: *Harvest Lord, God of the Sun, we thank you for being in our circle and shining down upon us this turn of the wheel. We are grateful for your gifts and your sacrifice in the autumn. Be ever with those who honor you. Blessed be!*

Dismissing the Quarters/Releasing the Circle

Starting in the north and moving widdershins, dismiss the watchtowers. Banishing pentagrams can be drawn, and candles should be extinguished if lit.

NORTH QUARTER CALLER: *All hail the watchtower of the north, the element of earth. You have stood guard over our circle, and we thank you for your watch. Hail and farewell!*

WEST QUARTER CALLER: *All hail the watchtower of the west, the element of water. You have stood guard over our circle, and we thank you for your watch. Hail and farewell!*

SOUTH QUARTER CALLER: *All hail the watchtower of the south, the element of fire. You have stood guard over our circle, and we thank you for your watch. Hail and farewell!*

EAST QUARTER CALLER: *All hail the watchtower of the east, the element of air. You have stood guard over our circle, and we thank you for your watch. Hail and farewell!*

Starting in the east and moving deosil, the circle caster releases the circle with an athame, sword, or wand.

CIRCLE CASTER: *I cast this circle in the names of the Lord and the Lady. Within we stood in the realms of the Mighty Ones and were transformed by the circle's power. And now I release the power we have gathered here and declare that all is once more as it was. Our autumn circle is open but our fellowship never broken. So mote it be!*

The High Priest takes the candle lit earlier and picks it up while everyone else in the coven holds hands.

HIGH PRIEST: *The autumn has come, the wheel has turned, but still we stand, Witches all united in perfect love and perfect trust. Until next we meet, hide away our secrets and may the gods preserve the Craft!*

The candle is blown out.

FIN

CHAPTER 35

MABON SOLITARY RITUAL

Welcoming Persephone to the Underworld

Persephone has long been one of my favorite goddesses, and she's been a part of my ritual life as a Witch for the last twenty years. She's the goddess we most associate with death and Samhain in my house, and she's a frequent visitor in our spring revels too, returning life to the land at the conclusion of winter. In addition to Persephone, my wife and I have attachments to several other Greek deities, and two of them, Demeter and Dionysus, also show up in this ritual.

This rite features a "burning away" of the things that trouble us (via flash paper), along with the reminder that without death, there can be no new life. Persephone provides the magick to help ease our burdens, burning away the things that no longer serve us so that we may transition to something better. The gifts of Dionysus (wine or grape juice) and Demeter (grain) are both joyous but also require death. Mabon is a time of balance and an opportunity to honor both sides of the realities we face in this world.

This ritual does require a few extra tools, most notably flash paper, which burns quickly and with much less smoke than regular paper.[82] It also requires something to put that burning paper in. My recommendation is a small iron cauldron, which can be purchased relatively inexpensively at most metaphysical stores and online. I like using a cauldron here for

---

82. Flash paper can easily be found online and in many discount stores. Some Witch shops carry it as well.

its symbolism: cauldrons are vessels of rebirth and transformation, two things that are a part of this ritual.

Because Mabon is a harvest ritual, wine (or grape juice) and bread feature prominently. For those with gluten sensitivities, any type of food will work. Demeter is not just a goddess of the grain, she's also a goddess of abundance. I like to ceremonially pour my wine and break my bread during the ritual itself, which is how the rite is written, but if that's not possible, it's nothing to worry about.

Many Witches once marked out their circles with physical substances such as chalk, flour, and salt. Those who do so tend to make sure their salt (or other substance) forms a perfect, easy-to-see circle. For me, it's more about the ceremony than a perfect circle (and I don't want to sprinkle that much salt on my flour), but do what feels best to you. If you want to create a near-perfect circle, this can easily be done by securing a cord in the center of your circle and holding it taut as you sprinkle or pour your salt.

Materials Needed

- Regular altar setup
- Dish of salt (You'll need a lot if you want to create a visible circle.)
- Bottle of wine or grape juice
- Bread (or other seasonal food)
- Flash paper
- Pen or pencil
- A candle to light for Persephone

The Ritual: Welcoming Persephone to the Underworld

The best time for this ritual would be sunset, where night and day meet, and where the night once more overtakes the day in length. If you're outdoors, great. If you're indoors, start the ritual by looking up at the sky. Notice the sun and moon (if applicable) and the orange glow that kisses the horizon at sunset. Reflect for a moment on the balance between day and night, and how from now until Ostara there will be more darkness than light.

Take a deep breath and imagine the powers of the sun and the nighttime sky both entering your body. Feel the power of the sun within you, the power that ripens the grain, gives life to fruit and vegetables, and warms the skin. Now feel the cool power of the nighttime world within you. Notice the maternal energies of the moon, the timelessness of starshine, and the promises of new tomorrows that come with every sunset. As you breathe out, let go of any mundane problems that might disrupt you in your work. When you feel settled and in touch with the world around you, return to your altar and begin the evening's work.

Casting the Circle/Calling the Quarters

Pick up your bowl of salt and starting in the east, sprinkle salt around the entire perimeter of your circle. As you let it fall from your hand, imagine its magickal energy shielding you from all harm and any negative entities. I generally picture the salt forming a sphere of blue fire around me as each crystal hits the ground. Words aren't necessary here, but they can be said if you choose.

> *Salt of the circle, salt of earth,*
> *Magickal space of death and birth.*
> *By my hand this circle is cast,*
> *Place beyond time, future and past.*
> *By my will and power, this be done.*
> *My circle is cast, the ritual begun!*
> *So mote it be!*

After you return the salt to your altar, take one last pinch and place it upon your tongue. Before eating the salt, I usually state my intention behind this act, which is simply "to cleanse the self." Salt is one of the simplest and most powerful tools that a Witch can keep in their toolbox or upon their altar. Once you've had a pinch of salt, begin calling the quarters, starting in the east. If you have a candle for each of the quarters, they can be lit at this time.

Hail thee spirits of the east, caretakers of the air. Be present in this circle.

Hail thee spirits of the south, caretakers of fire. Be present in this circle.

Hail thee spirits of the west, caretakers of water. Be present in this circle.

Hail thee spirits of the north, caretakers of earth. Be present in this circle.

After each call, blow a kiss to the elements to honor them for being in your ritual. I like to put the flat part of my athame's blade to my lips, kiss it, and then salute the elements.

Calls to Persephone, Demeter, and Dionysus

Start by lighting a candle for Persephone and saying, "To light your way," acknowledging her journey from this realm to the land of the dead. Once your candle is lit, call to her to be a part of your ritual.

Great Persephone, Queen of the Dead and Goddess of the Living, join me in my Mabon rite. May your magick be a part of my circle, filling it with endings, beginnings, death, and life anew. Though I mourn your journey from this realm to that of the Summerlands, I take solace in knowing all who die shall be reborn through your love and grace.[83] As we transition to the dark half of the year, I honor you and ask that you will help me in my wish to change myself this night. Hail Persephone!

Take your loaf of bread and break it in half. Remove a generous chunk of bread and place it in your libation bowl in honor of Demeter.

Mighty Demeter, Earth Mother, Goddess of the Grain, to you I give thanks this night. You are she who tends the fields and watches over the children of this world. Be a part of my magick this night as I celebrate the blessings of the harvest. Hail Demeter!

Place a generous pour of wine in your libation bowl in honor of Dionysus, then call the wine god into your circle.

Great Dionysus, God of the Vine, Cultivator of Madness and Ecstasy, join me in my rite this evening. Let me see the powers of life, death, and rebirth as reflected in your gifts, and may your magick and power fill this circle and stay with me this turn of the wheel. Hail Dionysus!

---

83. This is not a traditional understanding of Persephone, but as a believer in reincarnation, I feel like someone has to open the gates that let the dead return to the land of the living. At our house, we look toward Persephone to fill that role.

The Working: Into Persephone's Cauldron

Take a moment to think about the things you wish to remove from your life. This could be an unhealthy relationship, a bad habit, or a problem that's been vexing you. Once you've decided on what you'd like to be rid of, write that trouble down on a piece of the flash paper.

> *Great Persephone, it is you who transforms the dead back into the living. As you journey this night to the Summerlands, take these my burdens with you and transform them into something that no longer causes me suffering or pain. Energy cannot be destroyed, only transformed, and you have forever been an agent of change! Hear my pleas this autumn night! So mote it be!*

Using your candle lit in honor of Persephone, light your first written-upon piece of flash paper and then place it (quickly and carefully) into your cauldron or bowl. As you do so, say, "Persephone, take this (name of problem) from me! So mote it be!" and imagine her transforming your problematic thing into something healthy and whole. Imagine your pain being turned into the energy that ripens the grain and gives life to the grape on the vine. Repeat this process until you've gone through all the written-upon pieces of flash paper you set aside for this task.

Pick up your bread and break off a piece to eat. Before eating it, thank Demeter and remember what had to die for your bread to be made. There was the grain that was harvested and all the nutrients in the soil, much of which came from the energy of decomposition. From life to death to life once more.

> *Demeter, Lady of the Earth, I eat this bread thanks to your love and grace. From death you have given birth to this bread. What was once unwanted and unneeded found new purpose through your power and magick. To new journeys for me in this life! So mote it be!*

As you eat the bread, think of Demeter and the gifts of the harvest. Envision the endless wheat fields that shine in the autumn and our ability to store that wheat in the dark of winter. In honor of Dionysus, pour some wine into your chalice. Think of the vineyards where he rules, and the annual journey of the grapevines and their fruit, contemplating how the natural world moves from life to death to life again. Raise a toast to Dionysus and thank him for the gift of the grape and the transformative power of the earth.

Dionysus, Lord of the Field, I drink this wine thanks to your magick and might. What dies has been transformed into wine, and I thank you for your gift. May that which was taken from me this night be reborn and serve this world anew. Here's to life!

Before closing up your circle, eat and drink for a while, thinking about the balance of life and death and the changes that grip the world every autumn. Reflect on the abundance of the gods and how they provide even in the coldest and darkest of times. Be sure to pour some wine and leave some bread for Persephone in your libation bowl as a thanks to her.

Goodbyes to the Gods

Now say:

My cares now transformed from anguish to wine. For this gift I thank you, great Dionysus. May I feel your presence in the months to come and know joy, peace, and contentment. I honor you within and without this circle. Hail and farewell!

Through the power of Demeter, that which is unwanted is turned into the bread that nourishes us. Great Mother, thank you for your gifts this night and this Mabon season. And thank you most of all for your daughter Persephone. May your abundance flow long after the final grains are gathered. I honor you within and without this circle. Hail and farewell!

Lady Persephone, Queen of the Dead, thank you for being a part of my rite as you have journeyed this night. Cast out that which no longer serves me and let that energy be reborn in your cauldron. As the veil thins in the autumn, I know you will be watching over me and my fellow Witches. I honor you both within and without the circle. Hail and farewell!

End your goodbyes by blowing out the candle lit for Persephone.

Dismissing the Quarters/Releasing the Circle

Starting in the north, move widdershins around the circle, dismissing the quarters. At the conclusion of each quarter dismissal, blow out any candles you may have lit.

Hail thee, spirits of the north, caretakers of earth! I salute your presence in my rite and now wish you hail and farewell!

Hail thee, spirits of the west, caretakers of water! I salute your presence in my rite and now wish you hail and farewell!

Hail thee, spirits of the south, caretakers of fire! I salute your presence in my rite and now wish you hail and farewell!

Hail thee, spirits of the east, caretakers of air! I salute your presence in my rite and now wish you hail and farewell!

At the conclusion of each call, blow the quarters a kiss as a sign of respect, using the flat of your athame blade or your index and middle fingers. To clear the circle, start in the east and begin walking widdershins. As you walk, break up the circle of salt with your foot (if outside or on carpet) or sweep it away using your besom (ideal for wood or tile floors). As you break up the circle, imagine the blue flame that surrounded you during your rite extinguishing and your ritual space transitioning back to its normal state.

Salt of the circle, salt of earth,
Magickal space of death and birth.
By my hand this circle was cast,
A place beyond time, future and past.
Power raised, spells woven and spun,
The circle is now open, my ritual done.
So mote it be!

At the conclusion of your rite, be sure to leave your offerings to Persephone, Demeter, and Dionysus and thank them one last time for being a part of your ritual.

FIN

CHAPTER 36

SAMHAIN

When the Veil Is Thin

Name of Sabbat: Samhain (sometimes also spelled Samuin, Samhainn, Samain, and Samhuinn; also known as Hallowmas, November Eve, All Hallows, and Calan Gaeaf)

Date: October 31 (celebrated by some Witches on the evening of October 30)

Pronunciation: "SOW-in"

Samhain was originally an ancient Irish-Celtic holiday, but we know very little about how it was celebrated thousands of years ago. What we do know is that how it is celebrated today is radically different. Long ago, there were no glowing vegetables, trick-or-treating, Witches, Druids, or visits from the dead. Most of the trappings we associate with Samhain date only from the Christian era, though that doesn't make any of them less real or witchy.

The holiday of Samhain shows up with some frequency in Irish mythology. In myth, Samhain was generally a time of high magick. Enchanted gifts were given to kings that night, and just as often, magickal items were stolen from those kings. Heroes died or met destinies influenced by magick, and sometimes monstrous beings attacked castles and keeps. The supernatural features prominently in myths that name-drop Samhain, and sometimes that magickal influence could even be positive. Samhain was often a rather amorous time thanks to the use of love spells and other enchantments.[84]

---

84. Hutton, *The Pagan Religions of the Ancient British Isles*, 177.

What's probably most important about ancient Samhain is the feeling of dread it brought to most people. It was a holiday to be feared, not embraced. Bonfires would have been built to keep malevolent fairies at bay. There's nothing in the historical record suggesting that ancient Samhain had anything to do with the dead, though the dividing line between humans and fey was indeed very thin that night.

There are also mundane goings-on in Samhain mythology that shed light on how the holiday might have been celebrated. It was apparently a time for the making of laws, as tribal assemblies were said to meet on the holiday.[85] From this, it's possible to infer that there might have been a lot of food consumed at Samhain, making it perhaps something of a harvest festival. The trappings of Halloween have always been related to the harvest, making this even more likely.

The modern celebration of Halloween most likely has something to do with the Irish-Celtic celebration of Samhain, though just how much will never be known with certainty. Many people believe that the Catholic holidays of All Saints' Day (Nov. 1) and All Souls' Day (Nov. 2) are related to the original celebration of Samhain, though this is historically problematic. Both holidays were established centuries before Ireland converted to Christianity and were originally celebrated in the spring, before being moved in the eighth century. (This is about a hundred years after Ireland and the rest of the British Isles had effectively been "Christianized."[86])

For Witches, the person most responsible for connecting Samhain with the dead is the English anthropologist Sir James Frazer. In his multivolume work *The Golden Bough*, Frazer wrote of "the souls of the departed hovering unseen" over ancient celebrations, an inference reached due to Samhain's proximity to All Souls' Day. (Alas, Fraser had it backward.) Frazer's interpretation of Samhain comes across more as Halloween than an ancient Irish-Celtic festival. In his writings, he also makes mention of "Witches ... sweeping through the air on besoms, others galloping along the roads on tabby-cats, which for that evening are turned into coal-black steeds. The fairies, too, are all let loose, and hobgoblins of every sort roam freely about."[87] Frazer was certainly onto something long before the first Modern Witches would add Samhain to their calendars!

---

85. Hutton, *The Pagan Religions of the Ancient British Isles*, 177.

86. Ibid., 280.

87. Frazer, *The Golden Bough*, 634.

The placement of All Souls' Day and All Saints' Day at the start of November is not an accident. There's just something about late October/early November that brings us closer to those we have lost. Mexico's Day of the Dead is celebrated from October 31 to November 2, and its origins predate the arrival of Christianity. While the Irish-Celts may not have celebrated Samhain as a festival involving the dead, it most certainly feels appropriate to us.

Divination was a popular pasttime at Halloween celebrations beginning in at least the seventeenth century in England, and might have been the most popular one. Games like bobbing for apples were originally designed to reveal a young person's true love. For those who wanted to avoid getting wet, it was said that slicing an apple and eating the slices at midnight would result in the image of a future lover being revealed in a mirror. No apples? Throw some nuts into a fire instead and look into the flames, and maybe you'll see who you're destined to marry.[88]

Knowing how the ancient Celts might have celebrated Samhain can inform our own rituals and rites, but what's most important is what Samhain means to us today as Witches. We know that it's the time of year when the veil between the worlds is thin because we can feel it! Since the beginning of the Modern Witchcraft revival, Samhain has held a place of high importance in the rites of Witches.

Ways to Celebrate Samhain

Samhain is essentially a harvest celebration, though it's rarely celebrated that way anymore. Rituals featuring apples, pumpkins, sunflowers, squash, and pomegranates work well at Samhain, and even when these foods aren't specifically used in ritual, they often decorate altars and shrines. I've always found it funny that many Christian groups like to host "harvest parties" instead of Halloween ones, since both types of parties have Witch and Pagan overtones.

Rituals involving the sacrificial god are not all that common at Samhain, but the energy of the season makes this type of ritual especially powerful. In October, death is in the air, and it's an easy time of year to get swept up in the drama involving a dying deity. The death of the sacrificial god might also serve as a window in which to mourn the deaths of loved ones.

For many Witches, Samhain is a celebration of the new year, and a Samhain ritual might open with an activity designed to initiate a fresh start or to burn away unwanted

---

88. Skal, *Death Makes a Holiday: A Cultural History of Halloween*, 31–32.

things from the past year. (If your ritual is outside, some sort of fire will help you connect to our distant ancestors who celebrated Samhain all those centuries ago.) Even when my Samhain rituals don't include specific activities commemorating a new turn of the wheel, I'll often use language that refers to it, since so many Witches expect it at this time of year.

The myth of Demeter and Persephone remains a popular one among many Witches, and a ritual detailing the descent of Persephone into the Underworld is appropriate at Samhain. When this story is combined with the pain of Persephone's mother, Demeter, and the wisdom of the goddess Hecate, it can become a multifaceted ritual that touches upon a variety of emotions and magickal themes. Other goddesses often honored at Samhain include the Morrigan, Freya, and Santa Muerte. Before honoring any deity at Samhain, be sure that you or someone in your coven has a personal relationship with them first.

The idea of reuniting with deceased loved ones is the most common theme at Samhain, and makes Samhain unique among all the other sabbats. I've found that this type of working generally ends up incorporating everything else commonly found at Samhain. My wife often works with Persephone at Samhain, and the sacrificed Harvest Lord has now become the Lord of Death and Rebirth. Our ritual space is usually decorated with jack-o'-lanterns and pomegranates, and we usually mention the turning of the wheel toward a new cycle. At public Samhain rituals, I've found that many people are disappointed if the ritual neglects to include some sort of acknowledgment of those who have gone before.

Divination is a powerful Samhain activity, and many of the games we associate today with Halloween, such as bobbing for apples, were originally forms of divination. It's something probably best suited for solitary rites, or perhaps before or after coven rituals, but it's not something that should be overlooked. Take advantage of the powerful energies flowing through the world in late October/early November and get a sneak peek at what the new year has in store.

While we'll never quite know for sure just how much of the modern celebration of Halloween was a part of ancient Samhain practices, the trappings and customs associated with the holiday today are welcome in nearly all Samhain circles. The most popular symbol of Halloween is the Witch on her broomstick, and while the caricature isn't always the most flattering, it's still about us. Samhain rituals that utilize dressing up, trick-or-treating, and everything else associated with the secular Halloween are fair game for Witches.

CHAPTER 37

SAMHAIN CIRCLE RITUAL

Through the Gate: A Journey
to the Edge of the Summerlands

I love all the rituals in this book, but this one is probably my favorite because it captures so many of the things I value in large public rituals. There's a lot for people to do during the course of the ritual, and the people participating in the rite get to experience things on their own terms. We all process death differently as Witches, and we all have our own interpretations on what happens after we die. This ritual allows for a multitude of interpretations instead of dictating a certain point of view.

This is a rather complex ritual and requires the use of two spaces. When I've presented it in the past, I've either used two separate rooms in the same building or partitioned off a large room that contains two separate entrances (figures 9 and 10). Ideally you want the participants of the ritual to "journey" from one space to the other, which is why the two entrances are important. Alternatively, the ritual could start outdoors, with people being led indoors. Because this ritual was explicitly designed for large groups of about a hundred or so people, I have only presented it in the sanctuary of a Unitarian Universalist church and a Masonic hall.

The focus of this ritual is reuniting with our beloved dead. Everyone participating in the ritual should be encouraged to bring a picture of a deceased loved one (or loved ones), and this most certainly includes pets. Before the ritual starts, those pictures are placed in a room dedicated to the dead (the "room of the dead"). I recommend bringing some extra pictures to hang, including those of mentors and influences in Witchcraft (people like Doreen Valiente or Margot Adler), as well as literary, political, and musical influences (for my wife and me, this means rock stars like John Lennon, David Bowie, and Janis Joplin, along with figures such as Dr. Martin Luther King, Matthew Shepard, and suffragette Matilda Joslyn Gage).

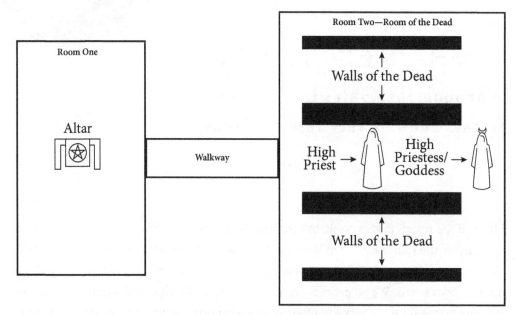

Figure 9. Samhain Circle Ritual Setup 1:
Masonic Hall, Two Rooms

During the course of the ritual, the Goddess of Death and the Dread Lord of Shadows are drawn down into the High Priestess and High Priest. The High Priest then goes off and opens a portal between the world of the living and the world of the dead, with the High Priestess then leading all those in attendance to him and the dead. Once in the room of the dead, those participating in the ritual scatter out to find the pictures of those they've lost, with the hope of reuniting with them, however briefly. Participants can also speak to the Goddess if they wish while in the room of the dead.

When I've presented this ritual, we've generally built "walls" in the middle of our spaces to hang the pictures of the deceased. Our walls are generally black tarps or sheets placed in the middle of the room, and remind me of the Vietnam Memorial in Washington DC. I often think of this as our "avenue of the dead," and the more walls that can be built, the better. Alternatively, pictures can simply be taped to the walls of the room you're using. This ritual works best when people have to search for a bit to find their pictures, which is one of the reasons I like the cloth walls set up in the middle of the room. (Just how a group chooses to build the walls will vary. We used the cloth backdrops of a local photographer once, and a clothesline or two works well too. Since the walls exist only to hold taped-on pictures, they don't have to be especially strong or durable.)

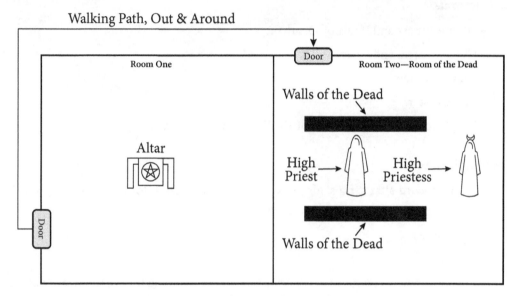

Figure 10. Samhain Circle Ritual Setup 2:
Unitarian Universalist Church, One Room

Because the High Priestess and High Priest actively draw down the Goddess and God (for an extended period of time to boot), there's a second set of ritual leaders to make sure they come back to themselves after that experience. In the ritual, I call the second set of leaders the "High Priestess and High Priest of Life."

This ritual is also presented in "High Witch" style, with a whole lot of "summon, stir, and call you up" type of language. I think witchy-sounding language creates a more magickal atmosphere and lends a lot of gravity to ritual. For ambience, the room of the dead should be lit in large part with candlelight. Generally, I've used electric tealights for this in order to avoid fire dangers. It also offers a take-home keepsake for those participating in the ritual.

This ritual calls for tissues because most people cry at some point while in the room of the dead. One box may not be enough, so be prepared! We strategically place boxes of tissue around the room of the dead, and send the quarter callers to pass them out as needed. Because this is a rather intense ritual, everyone presenting it should be prepared to help anyone at the rite who might need assistance.

Participants

- High Priestess and Priest of Death
- High Priestess and Priest of Life
- Quarter callers
- Circle caster
- People to distribute the foods of the living and the dead

Materials Needed

- Two standard altar setups, ideally with a black altar cloth for the altar in the north and a red altar cloth for the altar in the south
- Six chalices
- Sword
- Lots of candles (one for each participant if you're planning to give them away at the end)
- Black veil for the High Priestess of Death
- Circlets, crowns, or horned helmets for the High Priestess and Priest of Death
- Cauldron with salted water
- Bell or chimes
- Stang
- Food of the dead: pomegranate seeds, dark chocolate
- One whole pomegranate (pre-sliced but looking intact)
- Food of the living: cakes/cookies and apple cider (or other fall comfort food)
- Cakes and ale (bread and wine or sparkling apple juice)
- Baskets of flowers for offerings

- Autumn decorations (pumpkins, corn, wheat, etc.)
- Music player or musicians
- Boxes of tissue

The Ritual: Through the Gate: A Journey to the Edge of the Summerlands

The ritual opens in dim, but not dark, light. There are two altars set up in the circle, one toward middle north and one toward middle south. Both pairs of Priests and Priestesses stand in the middle of the circle. Those representing death are toward the north, and the other pair more toward the south. The circle caster stands in the center of the circle, with the quarter callers near their assigned positions, on the inside edge of the circle.

Statement of Intent/Purification of the Circle and the Participants

HIGH PRIESTESS OF DEATH: *We gather here tonight to celebrate the passing of the old year and to welcome in the new. We are here to celebrate Samhain, the final harvest, that time when the veil between the worlds is at its thinnest and those who have departed this world may return to it once more. We journey this sacred night to the edge of the Summerlands to honor our ancestors and our dearly departed dead. So mote it be!*

HIGH PRIESTESS OF LIFE: *And now we prepare the circle and those who seek the dead. We cleanse our circle and those who would witness our rites. Ready yourselves for the journey to come.*

Beginning in the east, salted water from a bowl or cauldron is sprinkled upon the participants and the circle itself. This is followed by a candle carried from east to north, its flame burning away any negativity. A bell or chime is then rung at each of the cardinal points as a final sweeping away of unwanted energies. The quarter callers of the west and north sprinkle the salted water, the south quarter caller carries the candle, and the east quarter caller uses the bell.

Casting the Circle

Using a sword, the circle caster casts the circle beginning in the east and moving clockwise. The circle is cast "thrice," with special emphasis placed on keeping out any unwanted entities.

CIRCLE CASTER: *I conjure thee, O circle of power, that thou may be a meeting place of love and joy and truth and as a shield against all wickedness and evil. Thou art a boundary between the world of mortals and the realms of the Mighty Ones, and an entryway to the realm of spirit. Tonight we cast thee so that we might journey to the world between the worlds, where the living can meet with the dead. Wherefore do I bless thee and consecrate thee in the names of the Lord and the Lady.*

Calling the Watchtowers

An invoking pentagram should be drawn in the air at each of the cardinal points during the invocations to each watchtower. I like to draw the pentagram with my athame just before saying "Hail and welcome!" but this is just a personal preference. As always, quarter candles can be lit if desired, but they aren't necessary.

EAST QUARTER CALLER: *Ye guardians of the watchtower of the east, powers of air, spirits of inspiration and delight, I do summon, stir, and call you up to witness our rites and to guard our circle. Hail and welcome!* (Participants repeat "Hail and welcome!")

SOUTH QUARTER CALLER: *Ye guardians of the watchtower of the south, powers of fire, spirits of clear will and desire, I do summon, stir, and call you up to witness our rites and to guard our circle. Hail and welcome!* (Participants repeat "Hail and welcome!")

WEST QUARTER CALLER: *Ye guardians of the watchtower of the west, powers of water, spirits of initiation and death, I do summon, stir, and call upon you to witness our rites and to guard our circle. Hail and welcome!* (Participants repeat "Hail and welcome!")

NORTH QUARTER CALLER: *Ye guardians of the watchtower of the north, powers of earth, spirits of hearth and home, I do summon, stir, and call upon you to witness our rites and to guard our circle. Hail and welcome!* (Participants repeat "Hail and welcome!")

Calls to the God and Goddess of Life

HIGH PRIEST OF LIFE: *We call to the Lord of the Forest, the Horned One, the seed of the crops, the quickening of the grain, the one who sows and the one who is himself reaped! Your yearly journey has begun anew, but before you slip behind the veil between this world and the next, we ask that you might witness and be with us in our rites. Lend your waning energies to us this blessed Samhain night. We summon, stir, and call you forth! Hail and welcome!*

HIGH PRIESTESS OF LIFE: *We call to the Goddess of Life, wise woman, nurturer, bringer of flowing love and illuminating abundance! From deep within the waters of your womb, thee we invoke! As we journey through the gates of the Dark Times, may we be reminded of your gifts of rebirth, regeneration, and fertility! Lend your growing energy to our sacred rites this night. We summon, stir, and call you forth! Hail and welcome!*

Drawing Down the Moon/The Fivefold Kiss

The High Priest of Death approaches his High Priestess and humbly bows before her. Then he begins the fivefold kiss, with the intention of drawing down the Goddess of Death. Though she's unnamed in this ritual, my wife tells me that the goddess drawn down is the Greek Persephone.

HIGH PRIEST OF DEATH:

Blessed be thy feet, which have brought thee to these ways. (The High Priest of Death kisses the feet of the High Priestess of Death.)

Blessed be thy knees, which shall kneel upon the sacred earth. (kisses knee)

Blessed be thy womb, from which all life is born. (kisses womb)

Blessed be thy heart, source of eternal strength. (kisses breasts)

Blessed be thy lips, which shall speak the words of our Lady. (kisses lips)

The High Priest of Death draws down a black veil to cover the face of the High Priestess of Death.

HIGH PRIEST OF DEATH: *I invoke and call upon thee, O Great Lady of Death. You are the doorway from this world into the next and the way back home for those we have lost. You are a goddess of love, beauty, and truth, and though we often fear you, we also know that you are the Mother of Us All, and the power to see and do all things. By leaf and blade, and bud and blossom, I do invoke thee to descend into this the body of thy servant and Priestess here.*

Hail the Lady of Death from the world beyond! We bend our knees before thee and adore thee without limit. Hear our cries lifted by our trembling and our awe! O Mighty One, descend and aid us this sacred Samhain night, for without thee, we are lost!

Drawing down the moon can have a chaotic effect on ritual. It's possible that the Goddess drawn down here won't want to read the Charge of the Lady of Death (below) or participate in the ritual as outlined. Before trying this ritual, I suggest that the person doing the drawing down have an agreement in place with the Goddess they serve before the ritual starts, and that both mortal and deity work together to ensure a smooth ritual.

If you decide not to do a full drawing down in the ritual, I suggest skipping the five-fold kiss and having the High Priest of Death simply read the invocation as an invitation for the Goddess to attend the rite, removing the lines about descending into the Priestess's body. Drawing down the moon at a public ritual should be attempted only by experienced Witches!

After the drawing down, it might take a few moments for the Goddess to truly settle into the body of the Priestess. This is fairly normal, so be prepared for a bit of a pause here before the Charge is read.

Charge of the Lady of Death

HIGH PRIESTESS OF DEATH: *I am she who is feared yet she who would bring comfort. I am the end of all things and the beginning of all else. I would give you peace, freedom, and reunion with those who have gone before you. My gifts are rarely sought, yet freely I offer them. I am she who embraces every woman and every man. None shall escape my touch, but fear not, for I hold the cauldron of life within my hands, the power of immorality for all those who would be reborn in your world.*

I am feared, yet I am the balance in this world without end. Without me, thou would not live again. I am the end of suffering, the release from all pain. I gather the spirits who have left your world and offer them a place in it once more. I am the mystery of the end and the wonder of beginnings.

The Food of Death and Preparing the Priest

HIGH PRIESTESS OF DEATH: *Tonight we shall journey together and come to the edge of my realm. We shall lift back the veil and experience reunion with our ancestors and those we loved in this world. But before we can feel those souls close to us once more, we must prepare the one who would open the portal.*

On this night of Samhain, we mark the passing of the old year and the start of the new. The sun slips into twilight, awaiting once more to be reborn in the land of the young.

The Priestess of Death walks toward the altar in the north and picks up her sword and raises it high in the air.

Now, my servant, I have need of thee. (She gestures to the High Priest of Death).

The Priest of Death approaches his Lady, stang in hand, and comes before her and bows on one knee. She lightly touches his brow and then raises her sword up high before laying it upon his back.

High Priestess of Death: *Dread Lord of Shadows, God of Death, Giver of Life, open wide, I pray thee, the gate through which we all must pass. Let our dear ones who have gone before return to us this night to share their love and wisdom. And when our time comes, as it must, O thou comforter, counselor, giver of peace and rest, we will enter your realms gladly and unafraid. For we know that when rested and refreshed among our dear ones, we will be reborn by your grace and the grace of me who art Queen of the Dead and the Great Mother of us all. Let it be in the same place and the same time as our beloved ones, and may we meet, and know, and remember, and love them again. Descend, O lover and loved, into this thy servant and Priest.*

The Priestess of Death puts a circlet, crown, or horned helm upon the High Priest of Death.

He then rises and stands next to the Priestess of Death. She sets down her sword and takes up a pomegranate from the northern altar. She holds it up in one hand for all to see, and grabs her athame or white-handled knife with the other.

High Priestess of Death: *Behold the fruit of life!*

The High Priestess of Death plunges her athame into the pomegranate, cutting it in half. (We generally pre-slice our pomegranate to make this part of the ritual easier on the Priestess.)

High Priestess of Death: *And now behold the seeds of death.*

Picking up one of the seeds, she places it upon the tongue of the High Priest of Death.

> *Before beginning your journey, you must eat of the food of the Summerlands. And now go and do your duty and prepare our way.*

Stang in hand, the High Priest of Death leaves the circle and heads out to whatever room or location will serve as the gathering point for the spirits of the deceased. The job of the High Priest of Death is to open a crack in the veil between the worlds. When I "open the portal," as we call it in this ritual, I tend to envision a very dark and angry layer of clouds, with all of my energy going into opening a small crack in them. Piercing the veil is intense work, and the person who succeeds in this task might be pretty strange for a while afterward. I don't tend to say anything while opening the portal, which works well in this ritual since the High Priest of Death opens it while alone.

HIGH PRIESTESS OF DEATH: *I am she who gives birth to the fallen and teaches all who love her that in the time of greatest darkness, there is also the greatest light. I am the gracious Goddess who offers reunion with those who we keep in your hearts.*

> *Our journey tonight is not long but might still be treacherous. We walk to the edge of the Summerlands; we travel the road of those who have left this world. When we have reached our destination, seek out those spirits that you wish to commune with. Find them all in their appointed place, and share with them your tears and your thanks. Console those around you and pay your respects to all who have departed your world. If you have need of me, you may approach me and ask me for a blessing.*

> *While I can lead you on our journey in, I need others to lead us on our journey out.*

The High Priestess of Death walks toward the High Priest and Priestess of Life and looks them in the eye. They should meet her gaze.

HIGH PRIESTESS OF DEATH: *Will you lead us home? Bring us back when our time of reunion is at an end?*

HIGH PRIESTESS AND HIGH PRIEST OF LIFE: *Yes, we will, my Lady.*

HIGH PRIESTESS OF DEATH: *Good. And now before you can make this journey, all must eat of the food of death. Prepare your minds and bodies. We leave for the portal, the veil between the worlds.*

The High Priestess of Death leads everyone out of the circle, and in the hallway between rooms, all participants eat the food of the dead (pomegranate seeds and dark chocolate). You could have people holding these things and whispering to all of the participants, "Eat of the food of the dead," or you could simply have the food sitting on a table. This task is probably best handled by either the quarter callers or others specifically chosen for this part of the ritual.

In order to give the people holding the food of death time to set up, they should probably slip out and set up where you want them to be immediately after the High

Priest of Death goes to prepare the portal. Instead of using the pomegranate sliced by the High Priestess of Death, you'll want the seeds and chocolate ready before the ritual starts. I usually keep it on a large tray covered with a dark cloth.

Entering the Room of the Dead

When the participants enter the room of the dead, they see a space bathed in dim light, most of it coming from individual candles. In the center of the room, stang in hand, stands the High Priest of Death. The portal to the Summerlands lies in front of him, hovering over the area where the High Priestess of Death will soon stand. His back faces those entering the room, and his entire focus lies on keeping the door between the living and the dead open.

Silence at this juncture of the ritual is not advised. When my group has presented this ritual, we've used recorded music to fill the quiet. Background noise is essential, as it takes away the self-consciousness of crying and keeps conversations between the Goddess of Death and those in attendance a bit more private. When it comes to music, everyone's idea of Samhain music is going to be different. During our ritual we used two songs by English artist Kate Rusby ("Canaan's Land" and a cover of the Sandy Denny song "Who Knows Where the Time Goes") and two by Loreena McKennitt ("The Dark Night of the Soul" and "Dante's Prayer"). Before those songs played, we had a group of local singers perform a couple of songs.

How long this part of the ritual should last will probably depend on the size of the ritual and those in attendance. I think you should count on this part of the rite lasting at least twenty minutes, and as long as forty if the ritual is especially large. Everyone directly involved in the staging of the ritual should keep an eye out on all the attendees to make sure they understand the intent of the ritual and to assist them with any problems they might have.

This is a time for everyone participating to feel the power and presence of the souls of the dead and to have their own personal experience. Those who believe in the immortality of the soul may feel their deceased loved ones near them. Those who don't might simply find comfort in remembering those who have gone before them. What people get out of this ritual will vary depending on how they interpret what happens after death. Be sure to have plenty of tissues on hand for this part of the ritual. If your ritual is really large, you may want to set up a dais or some other special place for your High Priestess of Death to stand.

Just how you create sacred space in the ritual's second room is a personal decision. When I've done this ritual, I've called the quarters specifically into the second room privately before the rite's real beginning. I usually cleanse it too, and get it charged up with as much energy as possible before everything starts. We also generally cast the circle during the ritual with the idea that the circle is going to encompass all the space we're using that night, both indoors and out, and all the rooms we might be using. This means we don't have to cut doorways in or out of our circle and keeps things running smoothly.

At the Edge of the Summerlands

HIGH PRIESTESS OF DEATH: *And now I bid you all to walk the avenues of the dead and reunite with lost loved ones once more. Tokens of flowers are available to you if you wish to leave a gift for our dearly departed. If you would ask a favor of me, the Lady of Death, I will await you here.*

People stroll through the realm of the dead and perhaps feel their loved ones near once more. Most participants will kneel near the pictures of their loved ones, and often those in attendance will comfort both friends and strangers. Expect tears at this point in the ritual, and keep an active lookout for those who might end up a bit overcome.

Baskets of flowers are spread along the avenue of the dead, and other spots are decorated with dried corn and other signs of the season. At the end of the room, the High Priestess of Death stands ready to offer comfort, hugs, and whispers for those who might need them. It's best to keep someone near the High Priestess of Death to shoo away ritual participants trying to monopolize her time or acting inappropriately.

If there is a large receiving line for the Lady of Death, she may be forced to walk quickly through it at the end, stopping only to touch hands and give assurances. Encourage everyone at your ritual to share in the experience of grief, and be ready to hug and comfort those who might need it. Share the experience of grief and the joyful emotion of reunion.

Toward the End of Our Time at the Portal…

The High Priest of Life approaches the High Priestess of Death and kneels before her. Rising slowly, he places his hands upon her shoulders.

HIGH PRIEST OF LIFE: *It is time, my Lady, time to leave this place, to close the portal and return to the realm of the living. You may say goodbye to those who need your touch or voice.*

The High Priest of Life leads the High Priestess of Death back toward one of the exits, going through the middle of the room. If there are people waiting to receive her in line, she may stop to squeeze their hands, hug them, or offer a few brief words, but the point is to move quickly out toward the other room being used in the ritual. The space once occupied by the High Priestess of Death is then occupied by the High Priestess of Life.

HIGH PRIESTESS OF LIFE: *And now we must journey back to the realm of the living and close the portal. We thank the spirits who have joined us and bid them farewell as they journey back toward their realm. We feel them in our hearts and know that through the power of the Lord and Lady, we can always reach out to them.*

Before we leave, I would ask all of you to take a candle with you to light your way in the coming dark of the year, and as a reminder of those who have gone before us. May the light of your candle always lead the souls of those you love back to you.

A lot of groups like the participants to leave the ritual with a token. If this is true of your group, candles make a great token for the reasons outlined earlier. We used electric votive candles in our ritual so there was no danger of anyone getting burned. I'm not sure lit candles would work so well.

HIGH PRIESTESS OF LIFE: *As we walk the passageway between the worlds, we eat this time of the food of life, which prepares us to once more walk upon our mortal coil. The time has come, my friends, the time to go back from where we came.*

The High Priestess of Life descends and begins to walk out of the room, escorting the High Priestess of Death with her. When she comes across the Priest, she stops behind him and places her hands upon his shoulders. Quietly she whispers in his ear, "It is time."

HIGH PRIEST OF DEATH: *And now I prepare to close this portal. All spirits and loved ones, those who dwell in the Summerlands, the lands of death, we bid you all farewell. Your home and place of existence calls to you. Go back to your shadowy realms, but dwell ever in our hearts and our minds until we meet again once more. I close this portal, this passageway from life to death. I seal this portal so that all who remain now are of flesh. The portal is closed.*

Having the High Priest of Death say something about closing the portal is done so that everyone in the ritual knows that the portal is being closed. I don't think words are really necessary, but they do provide a bit of closure.

As before, whoever is holding your food should slip away before the High Priestess of Life tells everyone to leave the room of the dead. We used cakes/cookies and apple cider for our food of the living, but that's just a personal preference.

Here's to Life/Cakes and Ale

Both Priestesses and Priests return to the center of the original circle. The High Priest and Priestess of Life stand closest to the altar in the south, with the servants of death in front of them: the High Priestess of Life before the High Priest of Death, and the High Priest of Life before the High Priestess of Death.

HIGH PRIESTESS OF LIFE: (Bows.) *Thank you for your service, my Lord.* She removes the circlet from the head of the High Priest of Death and lightly kisses him on the lips.

Kisses are not absolutely necessary here, but if your ritual group is comfortable with them, it does help with grounding.

HIGH PRIEST OF LIFE: (Bows.) *Thank you for your service, my Lady.* He removes the veil from the head of the High Priestess of Death and lightly kisses her on the lips.

The High Priestess and Priest of Death retire to the north, preferably to some comfortable chairs.

HIGH PRIEST OF LIFE: *While Samhain is a time to reunite with those we have lost, it also allows us to look inward and to find the things there worth celebrating. The fields may lie fallow, but the touch of the Lord and Lady are always with us. The heart quickens, the pulse races, and we celebrate what it means to be alive. While we have journeyed to the edge of the soul's rest, that rest is not yet for us. Even in the time of the greatest darkness, there is also the time of greatest light. Blessed be!*

HIGH PRIESTESS OF LIFE: *The days grow shorter and the nights grow colder, but the gods have not forgotten us. Life is ever present, even when the darkness grows.*

HIGH PRIEST OF LIFE: *Life is more than a gift; it is a promise. All that dies shall be reborn.*

HIGH PRIESTESS OF LIFE: *We now shall bless this bread and this drink as it was done in days of old, when Pagans and Witches were forced to hide their art.*

HIGH PRIEST OF LIFE: *The athame is to the sky,*

HIGH PRIESTESS OF LIFE: *As the cup is to the earth.*

HIGH PRIESTESS AND HIGH PRIEST OF LIFE: *United in life and abundance. Blessed be!*

The athame is plunged into the chalice.

The quarter callers come forward with both cakes and ale ready to distribute. The High Priestess of Life touches each plate and cup containing food/drink with her athame while the High Priest of Life asks the Lord and Lady for their blessings.

HIGH PRIEST OF LIFE: *In the names of the Lord and the Lady, we bless this bread and bless this drink. So mote it be!*

Bread and juice are passed out quickly. If there is a deep exhale here or even a laugh, all the better, for such things remind us of life!

Goodbyes to the Lady and Lord

HIGH PRIESTESS OF LIFE: *We thank the Lady, the Great Mother, the Eternal Goddess, for being with us tonight in our circle. Remind us of your beauty and your love in the days ahead. Help us to find the strength to honor you as much in the darkness as we do in the light. Hail and farewell!*

HIGH PRIEST OF LIFE: *Lord of the Forest, we thank you for your shadowed presence during these sacred rites! Please continue your journey now, Beautiful One. As the God of Death, you trod in the darkness. As the God of Rebirth, you dwell ever in the light. Hail and farewell!*

Dismissing the Watchtowers

This is done just like the beginning calls to the watchtowers, but in reverse order and with the banishing pentagram made before saying "Hail and farewell!"

NORTH QUARTER CALLER: *Ye guardians of the watchtower of the north, ye powers of earth, spirits of hearth and home, you have joined us in our rites and have guarded our circle well. We thank you for joining us this sacred night. Hail and farewell!*

WEST QUARTER CALLER: *Ye guardians of the watchtower of the west, powers of water, spirits of initiation and death, you have joined us in our rites and have guarded our circle well. We thank you for joining us this sacred night. Hail and farewell!*

SOUTH QUARTER CALLER: *Ye guardians of the watchtower of the south, powers of fire, spirits of clear will and desire, you have joined us in our rites and have guarded our circle well. We thank you for joining us this sacred night. Hail and farewell!*

EAST QUARTER CALLER: *Ye guardians of the watchtower of the east, powers of air, spirits of inspiration and delight, you have joined us in our rites and have guarded our circle well. We thank you for joining us this sacred night. Hail and farewell!*

Taking Down the Circle

CIRCLE CASTER: *I conjured thee, O circle of power, as a meeting place between the worlds and to keep from us all wickedness and evil. Thou has served us well, and now we undo this boundary between the worlds of mortals and those of the Mighty Ones. We seal forth the entryway from the realm of spirit. All will now be as it once was, and what was once here has been dismissed in the names of the Lord and the Lady. So mote it be!*

Closing

HIGH PRIESTESS OF LIFE: *The circle is open but never broken. Another year has passed us and another year full of promise and hope stands before us. With the blessings of the Lord and Lady, the love of those around us, and the memories of those who have left us, we go from this sacred place knowing of the bounty yet to come in our lives. Blessed be!*

FIN

CHAPTER 38

SAMHAIN COVEN RITUAL
The Dread Lord of Shadows

The circle ritual for Samhain in this book focuses on the Lady of Death. She's the one who leads her people to the entrance of the Summerlands and interacts with those who seek her out. This ritual changes the focus of Samhain toward the Horned God, here called the Dread Lord of Shadows. The term *Dread Lord of Shadows* is one commonly used in British Traditional Witchcraft traditions, and while it sounds rather ominous, he's a benign figure (though in my experience not very talkative).

The Dread Lord of Shadows guards the portal between the worlds of the dead and the living. He is the god of both beginnings and endings, for we cannot be reborn in this world unless we've died. The Dread Lord of Shadows has one foot in the mortal world and one in the world beyond; he embodies the magickal maxim "As above, so below." He is a "dread" lord only because we have been taught to fear death.

This ritual calls for the Dread Lord of Shadows to be drawn down and interact with those in the coven. Once drawn down, he opens a portal to the Summerlands so people may feel their beloved dead close to them once again. After their moment of reunion, they are embraced by the Dread Lord and given a token to remember their experience, along with the promise that "all that dies shall be reborn." In this ritual, each covener approaches the portal to the Summerlands alone, with only the Dread Lord standing nearby. This means the ritual will take a bit of time, which is why it's best for covens and small groups.

Because words often fail us when interacting with the dead, before seeking the portal to the Summerlands, each covener is encouraged to write down a few words expressing their feelings toward those they have lost. This gives coveners something to do while waiting for their time before the portal, and helps them to best express their emotions. Once the ritual is over, I generally burn the letters we've written and give them up to the realm of spirit.

Since many Witches celebrate the new year at Samhain this rite also includes a mini tarot card reading to prepare for the next turn of the wheel. This part of the ritual is done while people are waiting to visit and/or have returned from the portal to the Summerlands. A deck of tarot cards is spread out upon the altar, and each Witch in the room picks one when they feel the time is appropriate. The meaning of each card is then interpreted by those in the room.

This ritual requires two separate spaces. In our coven, we held the main part of the ritual in our usual working space and then used a hallway as the entryway to the Summerlands. Because we wanted reunion with the coven's beloved dead to be an intimate personal experience, coveners had to walk through a curtain to reach our portal and altar to the dead. The dead altar was rather simple, with just a few candles, a statue of the Horned God, and a basket to place the letters written by those in the coven. Taped to the wall above the altar were pictures of the coven's beloved dead.

The cleansing in this ritual utilizes a bowl and pitcher for a ritual hand washing. In my coven, we add two or three drops of essential oil (either a cleansing oil, such as ylang-ylang, or a welcoming one, such as rose oil) to a pitcher of warm water and pour that over each convener's hands into a bowl. The person carrying the bowl generally places a clean towel over one of their arms so coveners can dry their hands after the cleansing.

Because there are many spirits and entities out and about near Samhain, this ritual calls the elements twice. The first go-through is an invitation to the powers of the elements to join us at ritual and features a ritualized candle lighting. This is often known as "lighting the temple" and can be done by the individuals leading the ritual or by each of the quarter callers. This is then followed by the more common calls to the watchtowers. In my coven, we utilize both of these steps at every ritual.

There are not a lot of bodies required for this ritual, but whoever casts the circle will probably get a bit of a workout, as they have to let people in and out of the circle to visit with the Dread Lord of Shadows.

Ritual Roles

- High Priestess
- High Priest
- Four quarter callers
- Circle caster

Materials Needed

- Standard altar setup
- Tokens to be handed out by the Dread Lord of Shadows (We used a variety of stones.)
- Tarot cards
- Cakes and ale (For Samhain, I prefer bread and hard apple cider.)
- Paper, pen, and string (to tie around the rolled-up paper)

THE RITUAL: THE DREAD LORD OF SHADOWS

Before beginning the ritual, make sure everything is set up, including your altar to the beloved dead and the curtain guarding it (figure 11). If coveners have brought pictures of their beloved dead with them, they should be placed upon the altar of the dead or taped to the wall/area around it.

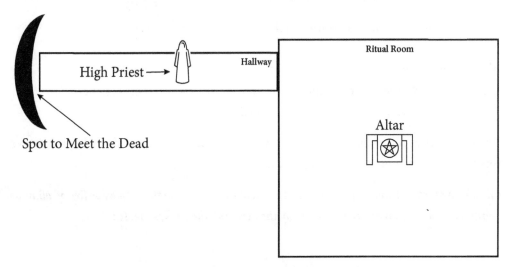

Figure 11. Samhain Coven Ritual Setup

Cleansing/Statement of Intent

The High Priestess and High Priest bless and cleanse all the coveners using the pitcher of water and the bowl. Whoever is pouring the water upon the coveners hands should say, "We bless and cleanse you in the names of the Lord and the Lady." Coveners generally reply with "Blessed be," which is then repeated by the High Priestess and Priest. Most coveners will anoint themselves with the purifying water, but they don't have to. The High Priestess and Priest are the last to be cleansed and will need another covener to assist them either to use the pitcher or hold the bowl.

HIGH PRIEST: *We gather here tonight to celebrate the passing of the old year and welcome in the new. We are here to celebrate Samhain, the final harvest, that time when the veil between the worlds is at its thinnest and those who have departed this world may return to it once more. So mote it be!*

Many covens choose to represent spirit, or the center, upon their altar with a large central candle. This is something we do in my coven, and we look upon that candle as representing the cosmic glue that unites everything in the universe. We then use this candle to light the temple and the candle that is symbolic of fire.

HIGH PRIESTESS: *Blessed be we who gather this night, and blessed be all who have come before us and will come after us. Blessed be the powers that will join us, and blessed be this time and this place and all who would walk in the Old Ways.*

The High Priestess lights the spirit candle.

Blessing the Elements

HIGH PRIEST: *I cleanse and consecrate this creature of water so that it my be free of all impurities and uncleanliness. In the names of the Lord and the Lady, so mote it be!*

The High Priest removes the bowl of water from the pentacle, and the High Priestess sets a bowl of salt upon the altar's pentacle.

HIGH PRIESTESS: *I cleanse and consecrate this creature of earth so that it may be free of all impurities and uncleanliness. In the names of the Lord and the Lady, so mote it be!*

The High Priestess takes her athame and places it in the salt, removing three measures of "earth" and placing it in the water. She then stirs the salt into the water with her athame.

HIGH PRIESTESS: *Thrice measured, thrice taken, thrice given. So mote it be!*

The salted water is set aside. The High Priest takes an unlit candle and lights it with a taper lit from the spirit candle. He places the candle (in a holder) on the pentacle and touches it with his athame.

HIGH PRIEST: *I cleanse and consecrate this creature of fire so that it may be free of all impurities and uncleanliness. In the names of the Lord and the Lady, so mote it be!*

The High Priest removes the candle from the pentacle, and the High Priestess takes the incense and sets it upon the pentacle, placing her athame on or in it, depending on the type of incense used.

HIGH PRIESTESS: *I cleanse and consecrate this creature of air so that it may be free of all impurities and uncleanliness. In the names of the Lord and the Lady, so mote it be!*

The High Priestess lights incense with the fire candle (or at taper lit from the fire candle) and then walks the incense around the circle deosil. The High Priest picks up the salted water and follows the High Priestess, sprinkling the water around the perimeter of the circle. For me, the incense and salted water are about cleansing the circle, and not so much the participants. With that in mind, I tend to fling the salted water into every corner of my ritual room.

Casting the Circle, Lighting the Temple, Calling the Watchtowers

To cast the circle, start in the east and move deosil three times.

CIRCLE CASTER: *I cast and conjure thee, O circle of power, that thou may be a meeting place of love, truth, joy, and reunion. This circle is a boundary between the world of the living, that of the dead, and the realms of the Mighty Ones. May this circle serve as a protection from any and all that might seek harm upon this coven or would attempt to join our rites uninvited. I bless and consecrate this circle in the names of the Lord and the Lady. So mote it be!*

To light the temple, candles should be set up at each of the four quarters. In our coven, those candles are placed in sconces on the walls of our ritual room. Alternatively, altars can be set up for each quarter, or the coven can choose to simply place a candle on the floor or somewhere near the quarter to represent it. Once each element has been summoned, the candle representing it should be lit with a taper whose light comes from the spirit candle. Once the element candle has been lit, the taper should be blown out and passed to the next quarter caller.

EAST QUARTER CALLER: *I bring air and light in at the east to illuminate this temple and bring to us a sense of belonging.*

SOUTH QUARTER CALLER: *I bring fire and light in at the south to illuminate this temple and bring to us our true will.*

WEST QUARTER CALLER: *I bring water and light in at the west to illuminate this temple and bring to us the promise of hope.*

NORTH QUARTER CALLER: *I bring earth and light in at the north to illuminate this temple and bring to us a feeling of power.*

Once the elements have been summoned, the watchtowers should be called, again going deosil. Coveners generally repeat the greeting "Hail and welcome!" at the end of each call. Additionally, each of the four quarter callers can draw an invoking pentagram while summoning their watchtower.

EAST QUARTER CALLER: *Ye guardians of the watchtower of the east, powers of air, spirits of intuition and insight, in the name of the Craft we summon, stir, and call you up to bear witness to our rites and watch over our circle. Hail and welcome!*

SOUTH QUARTER CALLER: *Ye guardians of the watchtower of the south, powers of fire, spirits of devotion and ecstasy, in the name of the Craft we summon, stir, and call you up to bear witness to our rites and watch over our circle. Hail and welcome!*

WEST QUARTER CALLER: *Ye guardians of the watchtower of the west, powers of west, spirits of memory and beginnings, in the name of the Craft we summon, stir, and call you up to bear witness to our rites and watch over our circle. Hail and welcome!*

NORTH QUARTER CALLER: *Ye guardians of the watchtower of the north, powers of air, spirits tradition and place, in the name of the Craft we summon, stir, and call you up to bear witness to our rites and watch over our circle. Hail and welcome!*

Calls the God and the Goddess/Charge of the Lady of Death

HIGH PRIEST: *I call to the Great God, Lord of the Underworld, the Horned One, Master of the Great Hunt. We ask you to be with us tonight and join us in our circle. Help us to understand the mysteries of the Underworld. Help us to reunite with loved ones who are now a part of your realm. Give us the courage to face the coming of the new year, and help us to learn the lessons we received in the last turn of the wheel. Hail and welcome!*

HIGH PRIESTESS: *We call to you, Great Goddess, she who is Maiden, Mother, and Crone and all that lies between. Join us, Lady of Death, as we celebrate the passing of the old year and the coming of the new. Great Lady, smile down upon us and illuminate our rite with your power, compassion, and grace. Allow us to feel the touch of those who have left us this night. Stir our souls with passion and fire as we gather here tonight to celebrate the sacred Samhain festival. Hail and welcome!*

HIGH PRIEST: *O Gracious Goddess, Eternal Mother, you who gives birth to the fallen, teach us all to know that in the time of the greatest darkness there is the greatest light. Share your wisdom with us this night as explore the mysteries of Samhain.*

What follows is what we call in our coven the "Charge of the Lady of Death."

HIGH PRIEST: *Now listen to the words of the Great Mother, the Lady of Death, who was once called Diana, Hecate, Kali, Ariadne, Persephone, and by many other names.*

HIGH PRIESTESS: *I am she who is feared yet she who would bring comfort. I am the end of all things and the beginning of all else. I would give you peace, freedom, and reunion with those who have gone before you. My gifts are rarely sought, yet freely I offer them. I am she who embraces every woman and every man. None shall escape my touch, but fear not, for I hold the cauldron of life within my hands, the power of immortality for all those who would be reborn in your world.*

I am feared, yet I am the balance in this world without end. Without me, thou would not live again. I am the end of suffering, the release from all pain. I gather the spirits who have left your world and offer them a place in it once more. I am the mystery of the end and the wonder of beginnings.

And all will come to know me, for I am death, and none can escape my grasp. But remember, I reach for thee because I also love thee. For I was with thee at the start of your journey and will be there again at the end. I exist both in this world and in the world beyond, and offer love and comfort to all who enter my realms. Blessed be!

Drawing Down the God

HIGH PRIEST: *The Lady of Death dwells ever around us and is a part of this life's journey.*

HIGH PRIESTESS: *But to see the Summerlands this night, we must call down he who is the Dread Lord of Shadows. He is the god of both this world and the next, and through his power we shall be granted reunion with those who have gone before us. My love, are you ready to be his vessel?*

HIGH PRIEST: *Yes, I will stand for him.*

The High Priestess stands before the High Priest. She looks him square in the eye, and he raises his hands above his head to draw forth the power of the Dread Lord of Shadows. At this point she may choose to embrace the High Priest in order to direct the God into the body of his servant, or she may stand in front of the High Priest, using her will to help manifest the drawing down.

HIGH PRIESTESS: *Dread Lord of Shadows, God of Death, Giver of Life, open wide, I pray thee, the gate through which we all must pass. Let our dear ones who have gone before return to us this night to share their love and wisdom. And when our time comes, as it must, O thou comforter, counselor, giver of peace and rest, we will enter your realms gladly and unafraid. For we know that when rested and refreshed among our dear ones, we will be reborn by your grace and the grace of me who art Queen of the Dead and the Great Mother of us all. Let it be in the same place and at the same time as our beloved ones, and may we meet, and know, and remember, and love them again. Descend, O lover and loved, into this thy servant and Priest.*

Blessed be thy feet, which stand in this world and the realm beyond. (The High Priestess kisses the High Priest's feet.)
Blessed be thy knees, which kneel in promise to the dead. (kisses knees)
Blessed be thy sex, which brings us again to this life. (kisses area above the genitals)

Blessed be thy heart, source of strength and courage. (kisses between breasts)

Blessed be thy lips, which shall speak only truth. (kisses lips)

I Invoke and beseech thee, O Father of us all, Dread Lord of Shadows, God of Death and Giver of Life. By root and tree, by petal and bud, by steam and life, by my life and love, do I invoke thee to descend into the vessel of your servant and Priest here.

Arrival of the God / The Charge of the God of Death

HIGH PRIESTESS: *Let all come forward now and show proper respect and reverence to he who is the Dread Lord of Shadows, God of Death, Giver of Life.*

The High Priestess bows to the God, and the coveners follow suit, with everyone coming up to where he stands in the circle. Alternatively, the God may choose to walk around and greet each covener individually. What a deity chooses to do, especially in a coven rite, can never truly be controlled. If the drawing down is successful, the God may choose to address the coven. If it's not successful, the High Priest can read this short "Charge of the God of Death." I've also seen fully drawn-down deities prefer to read whatever charge has been prepared for them.

HIGH PRIEST / DREAD LORD OF SHADOWS: *I stand at the end of all things and the beginning of all that is new. I take and I give. I am the spark of life and he who extinguishes all. I stand with you in this journey and will walk with you upon the next. I am he who gives release from pain and brings to you all that is pleasurable. My touch is feared, yet my hand is readily grasped. I rend, I rip, I tear. I love, I lift, I embrace.*

The Gates of Death / Into the Summerlands

HIGH PRIEST: *I go now with the power of the Dread Lord of Shadows to open the portal to the Summerlands so that we might all experience reunion with those who have gone before. My Priestess will guide you when each of you are ready.*

The High Priest leaves the ritual space and prepares to open the portal. How each of us envisions the land of the dead is a personal one, and I'm not sure there's any one right way to open a gate between this world and the Summerlands. My own method is to reach out with my being and seek the veil that keeps the dead mostly apart from us. Once I discover that veil, I focus on opening a small rift in it. I picture all of this in my mind's eye while concentrating on a space near the coven's altar of the dead. To then keep that rift open requires continuous concentration.

When my coven has done this ritual, the Dread Lord often challenges each covener as they walk into the hallway, generally asking them how they choose to approach the veil between the worlds. Answers often vary, with "in perfect love and perfect trust" and "with courage" being the most common. After each covener leaves the altar of the dead and the spirits of those they have lost, they are given a small token by the High Priest/Dread Lord. In our experience, he often whispers words of advice and encouragement to our coveners. Even if the drawing down hasn't truly "taken," he's often present, and the High Priest may find himself saying things that will surprise him.

There's a lot to balance here for the High Priest, as he must focus on keeping the portal open, interacting with coveners, and containing the Horned God. But who said Witchcraft was easy?

After the High Priest leaves, the High Priestess should address the coven.

HIGH PRIESTESS: *There are always so many things we wish to say when reuniting with those who have gone before us, but words often fail us. Our speech is replaced by tears, our emotions over-powering nearly all else. Before we all stand before the veil, I ask that you take a moment to write a few words to your beloved dead. Tell them that you love them, that you miss them, and that a part of them lives in this world, because nothing and no one is truly gone if they are but remembered.*

When you're done writing down those things within your heart that you wish to share, roll up your letter and tie it with a string. Before finishing, you may wish to reflect upon those you have lost or whisper a prayer to our Lady and Lord at our altar. When I see that you're ready, I shall lead you to the portal and you shall be let out of our temple by they who cast our circle.

The idea behind writing the letters is to limit a mad rush to the door, and since each person writes at a different pace, this has worked well for our coven. However, if you have a lot of coveners and feel like the journey to the portal is not quite enough, you can supplement this rite by adding the tarot divination rite below. This should be used once everyone is done writing letters but while there is still a line to seek the beloved dead.

In order to retain the power and energy present in the circle, the circle caster will have to cut everyone out of the circle and then back in when they go to and depart from the altar of the dead. Alternatively, the circle can be cast around both the coven's regular working space and the altar of the dead.

HIGH PRIESTESS: *Before reunion with your beloved dead, you may be challenged by the God at the outside of the veil. Remember always our password, "In perfect love and perfect trust," and if he were to ask a question of your heart, remember to always reply true.*

Slowly, all the coveners write letters to their dead and then approach the God and the portal. Because this process can take quite a while (I think in our coven it once lasted over an hour), I created an optional tarot rite that coveners can participate in if they desire. This is optional, but it does help keep everyone engaged as each covener has their individual moment with the Dread Lord of Shadows and their beloved dead.

Tarot for the New Turn of the Wheel (Optional)

HIGH PRIESTESS: *Upon this Samhain night, we begin a new turn of the wheel and begin another year, one tinged with the feelings of joy, hope, sadness, and promise. To see what may lie ahead of us on this journey, I invite you to come forward and pick a tarot card that we will then read together as a coven.*

The High Priestess lays down the deck of tarot cards, spreading them upon the altar's pentacle and perhaps around it too if it's not particularly big. One by one, coveners come forward and pick a card if they so choose, allowing their intuition to guide their hand. All present are allowed to remark upon the card and offer their interpretation of it.

Because there's so much going on, this should be done quietly and with the knowledge that some coven members may need to be consoled after touching their loved ones across the veil. Once all who want to participate have drawn a card and all have gone to the altar of the dead and passed the Dread Lord of Shadows, the High Priestess should leave the circle and indicate to the High Priest that it's time to rejoin the coven. Before making his way back into the circle, he must close the portal and bid farewell to the spirits who remain.

HIGH PRIEST: *I now close this entryway from the land and realm of spirit. What was torn asunder is once more whole. So I say this in the names of the Lord and the Lady. So mote it be!*

The High Priestess leads the High Priest back to the circle.

HIGH PRIESTESS: *Well have you done, our servant and Priest. You have opened the door to the Summerlands and led our journey this Samhain night. With the portal now closed, we welcome you back to us.*

The High Priestess kisses the High Priest on the lips.

HIGH PRIESTESS: *While Samhain is a time to reunite with those we have lost, it also allows us to look inward and find the things there worth celebrating. The fields may lie fallow, but the touch of the Lord and Lady are always with us. The heart quickens, the pulse races, and we celebrate what it means to be alive. While we have journeyed to the edge of the soul's rest, that rest is not yet for us. Even in the time of the greatest darkness, there is also the time of greatest light. Blessed be!*

The Great Rite/Cakes and Ale

The High Priest holds the cup, while the High Priestess holds her athame. At the end of the rite, the athame is placed into the chalice.

HIGH PRIESTESS: *The days grow shorter and the nights grow colder, but the gods have not forgotten us. Life is ever present, even when the darkness grows.*

HIGH PRIEST: *We shall now celebrate the promise given to us by the Lord and Lady and all that lies between.*

HIGH PRIESTESS: *The athame is to life,*

HIGH PRIEST: *As the cup is to death.*

BOTH: *All that dies shall be reborn!*

HIGH PRIESTESS: *We now shall bless this bread and this drink as it was done in the days of old, when Pagans and Witches were forced to hide their art.*

The High Priest picks up a tray of cakes and holds them up in front of the High Priestess.

HIGH PRIEST: *In the names of the Lord and the Lady, we bless these cakes.*

The High Priestess touches her athame to either the cakes or the plate they are being served upon. She then takes a cake and eats it. The High Priest does the same before passing the tray around to the rest of the coven.

The High Priest picks up the coven's chalice and holds it in front of the High Priestess.

HIGH PRIESTESS: *In the names of the Lord and the Lady, we bless this drink.*

The High Priestess touches her athame to the top of the cup and then takes a drink before passing the cup to the High Priest. He takes a drink and then passes it on so the rest of the coven may drink. Be sure to reserve some cakes and ale for the libation bowl.

Goodbyes to the Gods and the Beloved Dead

HIGH PRIESTESS: *We thank the Lady, the Great Mother, the Goddess of Death, for being with us tonight in our circle. Remind us of your beauty and your love in the days ahead. Help us to find the strength to honor you as much in the darkness as we do in the light. Hail and farewell!*

HIGH PRIEST: *We thank the Horned One, Dread Lord of Shadows, God of Birth and Death, for being with us tonight in our circle. We thank you for opening your realm to us. As death comes to our lands, help us to remember that you are a god of beginnings as well as endings. The Wheel turns, and as you sink down into the shadows; we say to you hail and farewell!*

HIGH PRIESTESS: *Dearest Ancestors, Beloved Death, those who have departed this world, thank you for joining us this night. Let us never forget what you mean to us as you retreat once more into the veil that separates the two worlds. Hail and farewell!*

Dismissing the Watchtowers / Closing the Circle

The watchtowers and the powers of the elements are dismissed starting in the north and working counterclockwise back to the east. After the entire coven has said "Hail and farewell!" the quarter caller should blow out the candle of the element they have dismissed.

NORTH QUARTER CALLER: *Ye guardians of the watchtower of the north, powers of air, spirits of tradition and place, in the name of the Craft we called you up to witness and watch over our rites, and in this you have served us well. We thank you for your service and for being a part of our journey this sacred night. Hail and farewell!*

WEST QUARTER CALLER: *Ye guardians of the watchtower of the west, powers of water, spirits of memory and beginnings, in the name of the Craft we called you up to witness and watch over our rites, and in this you have served us well. We thank you for your service and for being a part of our journey this sacred night. Hail and farewell!*

SOUTH QUARTER CALLER: *Ye guardians of the watchtower of the south, powers of fire, spirits of devotion and ecstasy, in the name of the Craft we called you up to witness and watch over our rites, and in this you have served us well. We thank you for your service and for being a part of our journey this sacred night. Hail and farewell!*

EAST QUARTER CALLER: *Ye guardians of the watchtower of the east, powers of air, spirits of intuition and insight, in the name of the Craft we called you up to witness and watch over our rites, and in this you have served us well. We thank you for your service and for being a part of our journey this sacred night. Hail and farewell!*

The circle is taken down by walking around it three times widdershins, with sword outstretched.

CIRCLE CASTER: *I cast and conjured thee, O circle of power, to be a meeting place of love, truth, joy, and reunion. You were a boundary between this the world of the living and that of the dead and the realms of the Mighty Ones. But now all will be as it was once before, and what has been changed shall only exist within us. I release this circle and prepare us all to stand once again in our mortal realm. In the names of the Lord and the Lady, the circle has been opened and that which was once within it has been dismissed in their names and by our power. With courage we return to our world. So mote it be!*

Closing Statement

HIGH PRIESTESS: *Another year has passed us and another year full of promise and hope stands before us. With the blessings of the Lord and Lady, the love of those around us, and the memories of those who have left us, we go from this sacred place knowing of the bounty yet to come in our lives. Merry meet, merry part, and merry meet again! And may the gods preserve the Craft!*

FIN

CHAPTER 39

SAMHAIN SOLITARY RITUAL

Through the Cauldron

I have always been intrigued by the rites of Traditional Witchcraft, and I believe that in many ways they work best in a solitary context. Just what Traditional Witchcraft *is* will vary from Witch to Witch, but in my experience many of its ideas and techniques are designed to transport the Witch back in time. The practices of many Traditional Witches echo those of cunning folk from centuries ago, individuals who most likely practiced their magickal craft alone and in isolation.

At Samhain especially, I can imagine these individuals visiting a liminal space—such as a cemetery, crossroads, or perhaps under the boughs of a tree whose leaves have almost all drifted away—and while in that space utilizing the unique energies of the season to catch a glimpse of a deceased love one or perhaps of their own future. Many of the tools of the Traditional Witch are simple tools commonly found in rural settings, such as brooms and pitchforks. Many Traditional Witchcraft rites require very few tools and often forgo the usual altar.

This ritual makes use of the stang, a tool that can be used for transformation (in the same way one might use an athame or wand) but is most commonly used as the focal point of ritual. A stang is basically a staff with "horns" or points at the top of it. A common substitute is the pitchfork, though you'll probably attract less attention when using a stang cleverly disguised as a walking stick instead. If you don't have a pitchfork or a traditional stang available, a small (fallen) tree branch will also work. This ritual also calls for a broom (or besom, if you want to use the fancy Witch word). If one is unavailable, a leafy branch or bundle of twigs is an acceptable substitute. Many Witch stores also sell mini brooms that are no more than six or seven inches tall, which also work pretty well.

Samhain is traditionally associated with the harvest, the dead, and prophecy. This ritual focuses (again) on the latter two and utilizes a cauldron or bowl of water to facilitate those experiences. For this rite I generally use a mini iron cauldron (again available at most Witch stores), but a regular kitchen bowl or cup will work just fine as well. Instead of utilizing a sword or athame to cast the Witches' circle, the Witches' Compass is created by crafting three physical circles using water, ash, and dried grain. (Rice is probably the easiest to come by today.)

The *Witches' Compass* is the name given to the area where a Traditional Witch creates their sacred space. Many Trad Witches see this space as something that exists not simply between worlds but in another world entirely. Within the compass, the individual Witch is truly in the world of the gods and spirits. It's almost like a vessel that enables a Witch to journey between realms.

Most Traditional Witch rituals are held outdoors, and this rite is no different. But I don't believe it should be enacted just outdoors; it should be performed in a liminal space. Crossroads and graveyards (especially on Samhain) can be problematic, but most of us should be able to find a tree to work under. If all you've got is a backyard, that can work too. Just place a few fallen leaves on a patch of still-living grass.

This ritual works best when it's accompanied by a bit of a journey. Grab a backpack and fill it with the supplies you'll need, and be prepared to carry your broom and stang. As you journey toward your ritual space, take some time to think about your time as a Witch, what it is you wish to accomplish in the coming turn of the wheel, and who it is that you most miss when the veil is thin.

Materials Needed

- Stang
- Broom
- Bottle of water (and a small bowl)
- Ashes (and a bowl to place them in; incense ashes work well, as do ashes from charcoal)
- Rice or other grain (and a small bowl)

- Offerings for the dead and the gods
- Cauldron (or bowl)
- Compass

The Ritual: Through the Cauldron

The rite should begin the moment you step upon the path to the location of your rite. While walking under the light of the moon, think about your life as a Witch and what you've accomplished during that time. As you walk, be aware of any signs from the Witch Father and Witch Mother, the fey, and the spirits of those you have lost. Breathe in the crisp, cool night air, and take joy in simply being a Witch.

When you've reached your ritual spot, take a few moments to tidy it up if necessary. Unless you're doing your rite in a place where a lot of people visit, there should be no need to cleanse it. Trust in the powers of nature to do that part of the ritual for you. Set your broom and stang upon the ground and remove your supplies from your backpack. Using a compass, mark the directions of north, east, south, and west on the ground around you. Your Witches' Compass need not be large. A few feet in diameter will work just fine.

Starting in the north, begin to create your compass by sprinkling water upon the ground. The sprinkled water is the first of three physical circles you'll create, each one representing a separate phase of our existence. Water is for life, ashes for death, and grain for rebirth. As you sprinkle the water, say:

> This circle is for the life I lead,
> A witch in both thought and deed.
> I travel the compass round
> To create hallowed Witches' ground!

As you sprinkle the water, imagine the ground you're standing on changing around you, becoming more than just a spot in the woods. See it becoming a place that exists only for Witches, where mortals might truly walk with the gods! Do the same as you sprinkle the ashes, while saying:

> This circle is for the lives I've lost,
> For mortality comes with cost.

> *I travel the compass round*
> *To create hallowed Witches' ground!*

Lastly, pick up the rice or grain and create the third circle, this one symbolic of rebirth.

> *This circle is for life yet to come,*
> *Death does not mean we are done.*
> *I travel the compass round*
> *To create hallowed Witches' ground!*

Once the three circles have been marked upon the ground, take your stang and approach the northern edge of your circles. Hold the stang aloft and take a deep breath of the night air. When you're centered and ready, drive it into the ground so that it will stand up on its own and is touching at least a small portion of the rice, ash, and/or water you previously sprinkled. (If the ground is hard, you may have to prepare in advance for this part of the ritual.) As you plunge your stang into the ground, say:

> *By earth and stang, I create!*
> *To be a Witch, my chosen fate!*
> *By forest and moon of night,*
> *Bless my sacred Samhain rite!*

After your stang is securely in the ground, move your remaining ritual implements under it but inside the circle. From here on out, your stang will serve as the ritual's altar.

To call the elemental powers, start in the north and begin moving around the circle clockwise. While moving, chant your invocation to the four powers and feel their energy enter your compass. Note that Traditional Witchcraft often utilizes different configurations for the cardinal points, which I use here. In addition, the powers aren't called in order. Instead, the invocations are done in the following order: north, south, east, and finally west. This means you'll have to walk around the circle twice.

> *From the north, wind and gust of air,*
> *To tread where only Witches dare.*

> *From the south, earth and stone,*
> *Place of rest for flesh and bone.*

From the east, fire and flame,
The mantle of the Witch I claim.

From the west, water and sea,
By these powers may it be!

Repeat the invocation as much as is needed until you feel the power of the elements in your compass. Many Traditional Witches visualize these energies as "walls," so you may feel the four powers fold in around you (imagine a pyramid with four sides). Where the four walls touch in the center of your circle is the place of greatest power in your compass, and this energy can be used for magickal purposes. This spot is often called the *castle*, and is seen as a gateway to other worlds and dimensions.

Once the elements have gathered around you, look up in the sky and focus on the moon. (If it's the night of a new moon, direct your attention to the brightest star in the sky.) As you look up, imagine an ancient Witch staring up at that same sky and thinking of Diana, Queen of the Witches. Set your senses free and try to feel her, the Mother of Witches, around you. Most likely you'll feel her energy radiating downward from the sky, or perhaps in the center of your compass, the castle. When you feel her near, speak to her, thanking her for her presence.

Queen of the Witches, Mother of those who walk the crooked path, be with me this Sam-
hain night. Aid me in my work, draw close the realm of spirit unto me, and help me to see
what may yet transpire. I call to you on this sacred night of Witchery to assist me in my
magick as you may desire. By moon and tree, so shall it be!

Before calling the Horned God, the Witch Father, take a moment to reach out to your surroundings. Feel his power in the wind and in the trees around you. Reflect on the Witches long ago who might have possibly called to the Horned God as a man dressed all in black to thank him for another successful harvest. Imagine him stepping out of the shadows and coming to greet you in your compass. When you feel him near you, speak to him and ask him for his assistance this Samhain night.

Witch Father, Horned One, god of death and life! Join me in my rites this night as I cele-
brate your sacred night of Samhain. Lend your powers to my rites and allow me to peek
through the veil! Bring those who have left me close once more, and allow me to get a

glimpse of what tomorrow might bring. Bring your magick to my work if you so will it so
that I might embrace the mysteries of the Craft. By moon and tree, so shall it be!

Take your cauldron and some water out from under your stang and bring them back to
the center of your compass. Next pour your water into the cauldron. As you do so, call
to the Witch Father and Mother for assistance with your rite.

> *Witch Father, Witch Mother,*
> *In this may I see another.*
> *Those who have past and that to be,*
> *Hear my sacred Samhain plea!*

Once the water is in your cauldron, position it so that the moon is reflected upon its surface (if possible). Stare at the water and the image of the moon in your cauldron and let
your eyes loose focus. Take the index finger of your dominant hand and move it through
the water several times. As you do this, ask for whatever you wish to see to appear in the
cauldron's waters. Look for images of lost loved ones, Witches of old, or perhaps
glimpses of your own future. If you don't see anything in the cauldron, extend your
senses outward and be aware of any powers or spirits that might be in your compass
with you.

When you're done peering into the cauldron's waters, leave a few gifts in the center
of your circle as offerings for any souls you have seen. If I'm doing this and I see both of
my grandparents, I leave two offerings instead of expecting them to share just one. If
you've caught any glimpses of your future, leave a bit extra for the gods as thanks too.

When you're through with your scrying, refocus your eyes and focus on your surroundings. Take out whatever you brought with you for cakes and ale and eat and drink
quietly, enjoying the dark of the night and contemplating anything you may have seen.
Leave a bit of your cakes and ale as thanks to the spirits of place who inhabit the space
you built your compass in. Before letting the elemental powers go and releasing your
compass, thank the Witch Mother and Witch Father for being with you on Samhain.

> *Goddess and God of Witcheries,*
> *You who have revealed your mysteries,*
> *Thank you for your magick and aid*
> *In catching glimpses of future and shade.*

Walk beside me always and ever,
In the way of the Witch I endeavor.
By moon and tree, so shall it be!

Now starting in the north at your stang, begin to move counterclockwise around your compass. As you move, imagine the walls of the castle collapsing and your compass returning to the waking world. Feel the elemental powers begin to depart and move around the circle, repeating the following chant until you feel the intensity of their energies dissipate. (Their power will never completely go away, since we know such powers are always about us, but they should at least subside a bit.)

Powers of air, earth, fire, and water, depart,
My thanks for your contribution to the art.
To the mortal world I now return,
From the Witches' Compass away I turn.

After the elements have been let go, take your broom and sweep away the three circles you built at the beginning of the rite. As you sweep, visualize all the energies you have gathered dissipating and all returning as it once was. When you're done sweeping, pick up your stang and declare the rite to be at an end.

By moon and tree, so shall it be!
My rite ended, this world transcended.
Long hail the Old Craft!

Before leaving, pour your cauldron water upon the ground where you think it will most be appreciated (such as at the base of a tree). Thank the gods and the spirits of the land one last time before departing, and feel the souls still stirring on the breeze around you.

FIN

ACKNOWLEDGMENTS

Writing books is a rather solitary endeavor. While friends and family can offer support and encouragement, it's not like assembling a table; at the end of the day it's up to the writer to write and convey their experiences in some sort of understandable way to their readers. The solitary work of writing is the exact opposite of my Witchcraft practice, which often involves several hundred (if not thousands of) people every year. Those hundreds and thousands are the people I'm lucky enough to speak in front of and share ritual space with.

The most important of those people is my wife, Ari Mankey. Ari is thirteen times the Witch I am, and as you might have gathered from this book, she's an equal partner in everything I do. She's responsible for dozens of ideas that have ended up in this book, and almost all of my best work has been with her by my side. I'm sure you're tired of getting called out in these books, dear wife, but it's all the truth.

This book exists only because my coven, the Oak Court, is an amazing group populated with even more amazing people. Several of them contributed ideas that ended up in this book, most notably Amanda Moonflower, who worked with Ari to come up with the working in the Mabon coven ritual. The Ostara circle ritual was highly influenced by a ritual I did with Scottie (I can't use her last name in this book) for Imbolc several years ago. Scottie, all of us in the Oak Court miss you terribly and hope you move back to the Bay Area one of these days.

Angus McMahan is my pretty hair twin from another county, and he and his wife, Karen Broughton, have been the nexus point for so many of the great people Ari and I have met in California. Amber, Stephanie, and Sharyle, the Oak Court works today because you were all such integral cornerstone pieces. Matt, you are my brother in the truest sense of the word and have made both my rituals and magick stronger. Michael Harris in Santa Cruz, thanks for always giving me something to aspire to in life. When Ari and I "grow up," we want to be you and Margie. Ankhira, your perfectionism is something I aspire to, and the Brigid Imbolc rite is much stronger because of your work. I don't have room to thank all of the Oak Nuts past and present, but I think you know how I feel about you all.

I want to thank the Patheos Pagan Illuminati for their encouragement (and for letting me vent) during the writing of this book. John Beckett, Laura Tempest Zakroff, Phoenix LeFae, Astrea Taylor, Gwion Raven, Misha Magdalene, Kelden Mercury, Mat Auryn, and Heron Michelle, it's amazing to me that I get to call such amazing Witches and Druids peers, and it's even cooler that you are all my friends. Thanks to my extended writing community too: Chas Bogan, Storm Faerywolf, Thorn Mooney, Devin Hunter, Dorothy Morrison, Christopher Penczak, Mickie Mueller, Lilith Dorsey, and Deborah Blake (plus the other three dozen I don't have room to mention). I feel incredibly lucky to be writing alongside you all.

My first experiences with Witchcraft were through books, and those books had a tremendous impact on me as a young person. So thanks to Silver RavenWolf, D. J. Conway, Ray Buckland, Amber K, Janet and Stewart Farrar, Pauline and Dan Campanelli, Margot Adler, Starhawk, Scott Cunningham, Chas Clifton, and Doreen Valiente for taking the time to write some amazing stuff over the decades. It was life-changing.

I am always indebted to the folks at Llewellyn not only for letting me write books but for doing such a great job editing, sharing, and marketing them. You are also all fantastic people and I'm glad Llewellyn is my book-writing home. My editors at Llewellyn, Elysia Gallo and Andrea Neff, both truly have the Midas touch and make everything they work on that much better.

I've been blessed to have some truly great artists as a part of my books over the years, but nothing prepared me for the amazing cover art and illustrations by Kjersti Faret that grace this book. Kjersti's contributions have been just tremendous, and I'm so grateful to her for lending her talents to this endeavor.

Away from Paganism, I'm grateful for my Tuesday Night Trivia team at Fibbar Ma-Gee's in Sunnyvale. I realize how weird this sounds in a Pagan book, but without a break from Paganism, I probably couldn't write these things. To Bert, Alex, Sarah, Payton, Andy, Lesley, Jody, and the many others who have graced our table over the years, I really do appreciate you. Also, Missy, Ben, Irene, Laramie, and everyone at Fibb's over the years, thanks for the home away from home. Love always to my dad and mom and the rest of my extended family.

Last but not least, thanks to Roger Clyne and the Peacemakers, Rhett Miller and the Old 97s, and Butch Walker for continuing to give me new things to listen to, and reminding me that in my forties I'm not quite dead yet.

Ramble On,

Jason Mankey

September 2018

GLOSSARY

altar: The focal point of most Witch rituals, and where a great deal of spellwork is performed. At its simplest, an altar is simply where Witches put their stuff.

asperge: The process of sprinkling blessed and consecrated (salted) water around the circle for purification purposes. If an object other than the fingers is used to sprinkle the water (such as a mini broom or a feather), the object is called an *asperger.*

athame: A ceremonial knife or dagger used to project magickal energy. Athames are most commonly used to cast magick circles and for the rites of cakes and ale and the Great Rite. Traditionally the athame is a double-sided steel blade about five inches long, with a wooden handle. Athames are rarely used for physical cutting.

Beltane: A holiday celebrating the fullness of life, generally celebrated on May 1.

besom: A fancy name for a ritual broom. Besoms in ritual are generally used to sweep away negative energy.

boline: A knife exclusively used to tend to a Witch's magickal garden. Bolines are used to harvest vegetables, fruits, and herbs. The boline is often confused with the white-handled knife, and for that reason it often has a white handle. The blade of a boline can be either straight or curved like a sickle.

Book of Shadows: A book containing the spellwork, rituals, thoughts, and dreams of a Witch. If it's sacred and important to you, it can go into a Book of Shadows (BoS). The earliest version of the BoS was reserved exclusively for Witch ritual and instruction. Since then, many Witches have begun keeping their own personal Book of Shadows.

chalice (or cup): A cup or wine glass reserved for Witchcraft ritual. The chalice is generally used during the ceremonies of cakes and ale and the (symbolic) Great Rite.

charge: To "charge" an item is to infuse it with your own magickal energy. In ritual, a *charge* is a firsthand written revelation from deity itself (such as the Charge of the Goddess). The term *charge* in this context is originally Masonic and indicated a set of instructions.

circle: A Witch's working space, generally created with personal and natural energies. A circle exists between the mundane world and that of higher powers. Circles can be cast anywhere. The term *circle* often indicates an open ritual group that performs Witch rites. The term *circled* is used by many Witches to indicate the people they practice ritual with. ("I circled with Phoenix and Gwion.")

coven: A Witch ritual group that acts in perfect love and perfect trust. Some Traditional Witch groups use the term *cuveen* as an alternative.

covenstead: The territory of a Witch coven. A coven's convenstead is their base of operations.

cowan: A term for a non-Witch. This word was originally Masonic and referred to non-Masons.

(the) Craft: An abbreviation of the word *Witchcraft*. The term the *Craft* originally referred to Freemasonry.

creative visualization: A mental picture used in magickal work in order to apply intent to energy. Creative visualization (or CV) is one of the building blocks of magickal practice.

degree: A symbol of rank and/or accomplishment in many initiatory Witchcraft traditions.

deosil: To walk or move clockwise. Clockwise is the default direction that energy moves in and is how most Witches operate in sacred space.

downline: The initiates of an initiated Witch.

drawing down: The willful surrendering of consciousness to a higher power (generally a deity) so that higher power can interact with the people around them.

elements: The powers of air, fire, water, and earth. Most substances on earth can be broken down into these four broad categories, and contain attributes generally associated with one of these powers.

esbat: A Witch ritual performed on or near a full or new moon. Alternatively, the word *esbat* might be used as shorthand for "Witch ritual not connected to a sabbat."

fey: A name used for the unseen folk who share this world with us, sometimes also known as the fair folk, fairy folk, or fairies. Despite Disney's claims to the contrary, the fey aren't always nice.

Great Rite: The ritual celebration of union and the consequences of it. The Great Rite is often performed alongside cakes and ale.

greater sabbats: Shorthand for the cross-quarter holidays of Samhain, Imbolc, Beltane, and Lammas. The first Modern Witches celebrated only these four holidays, with the lesser sabbats celebrated at the equinoxes and solstices coming later. These are perhaps called "greater" because they were the first sabbats celebrated by Modern Witches and were the holidays celebrated by the Celts of Ireland.

initiation: A ritual designed to bring a Witch into a specific tradition, coven, or practice.

intent: The specific, desired outcome in a magickal working.

invoke: An invitation to a higher power to be present at a ritual or magickal working. In some instances, *invoke* is used as a synonym for drawing down the moon.

Lammas: Another name for *Lughnasadh,* originally used by Anglo-Saxon pagans and later by Christians.

lesser sabbats: The four sabbats celebrated at the solstices and equinoxes: Yule, Ostara, Midsummer, and Mabon.

Like attracts like: A magickal philosophy that encourages the use of items and ideas that are similar to the magician's end goal. For instance, to attract love, you'd want to use ideas and items associated with love instead of the opposite. It also suggests that Witches will attract and find Witches similar to them because "like attracts like."

lineage: The family tree of an initiated Witch. Most lineages can be traced to the specific founder of a Witchcraft tradition.

Lughnasadh: The celebration of the first harvest, generally observed between July 31 and August 2. Spellings of Lughnasadh will vary, and the sabbat is also called *Lammas* by some Witches.

Mabon: The name used by many Witches to indicate the Autumn Equinox sabbat. The term *Mabon* was first used by American Witch Aidan Kelly in the early 1970s and means "son of the mother." It's essentially a Modern Witch holiday. There were no ancient Mabon celebrations, though harvest celebrations were common enough.

magick: Energy that is given a specific intention. Many Witches spell *magick* with a *k* to differentiate it from stage magic.

Midsummer: A sabbat celebrating the Summer Solstice, usually around June 21. Some Witches also call this sabbat *Litha*, which was first suggested by American Witch Aidan Kelly in the early 1970s.

(the) Mighty Ones: A phrase used to indicate divine beings, generally deities. Some Witches also use the term *Mighty Ones* to indicate the watchtowers who are invoked at the quarters.

Pagan: Someone who practices a spiritual tradition that emphasizes the sacredness of the earth and calls upon pre-Christian deities. Because most Pagan traditions today utilize both modern and ancient ideas, practitioners are sometimes called *Neo-Pagans*.

pentacle: A round disc inscribed with a magickal symbol traditionally used to invoke spirits, angels, or demons. In most Modern Witchcraft traditions, the pentacle is viewed as a tool of earth and inscribed with a pentagram. It's generally used to bless the elements and serves as a gateway for both deity and magickal energy.

pentagram: A five-pointed star. The pentagram is most often depicted with one point facing upward, which represents the triumph of the spiritual over the material. Many left-hand-path traditions use the star with two points facing upward. In certain Wiccan traditions, the upside-down pentagram (with two points facing upward) is used to indicate the second degree.

perfect love and perfect trust: The ideal coven is said to operate in a state of perfect love and perfect trust. Because of this, *perfect love and perfect trust* is often used as a password in Witchcraft rituals.

sabbat: A Witch holiday. The sabbats are most often associated with the solstices and equinoxes, and the cross-quarter days that occur between them.

sacred space: The interior of a magick circle. Alternatively, a room set aside specifically for ritual or magickal workings or an extremely powerful place in the natural world.

Samhain: A sabbat celebrated on October 31 commemorating the year's final harvest. Many Witches celebrate Samhain as the Witches' New Year. The modern Halloween is a descendent of the Samhain celebrations of the Irish-Celts.

stang: A wooden stick, pole, or pitchfork used in many rituals by Traditional Witches. Stangs often function as the focal point of ritual, acting much like an altar, and can be decorated to represent the change of the seasons.

Summerlands: A place where souls go after death before reincarnating in this world. The term *Summerlands* comes to us via the Theosophical Society.

sword: The tool that is generally used to cast the magick circle. Anything one can do with a sword they can also do with an athame, and vice versa (though using a sword to bless cakes and ale can be challenging due to its size!). Swords are often shared by a coven, while athames almost always belong to the individual Witch.

tradition: A specific Witchcraft subgroup that generally requires an initiation for membership. Traditions often have their own Book of Shadows, and members can trace their lineage to a specific individual, such as Gerald Gardner (Gardnerian Wicca) or Cora Anderson (Feri Tradition).

Traditional Witchcraft: A Modern Witchcraft tradition most often focused on ideas found in magickal traditions such as cunning-craft. Any Witch group not related to Wiccan-Witchcraft is often included in this category.

upline: A Witch's upline consists of those who initiated the individual Witch, along with the initiators of their initiators. When thought of like a family tree, it's all the Witches above the initiate going all the way back to the tradition's source.

(the) watchtowers: Four powers that are invoked at the compass points of east, south, west, and north. The watchtowers are generally associated with the elemental energies of air (east), fire (south), water (west), and earth (north). In the grimoire tradition, the term *watchtowers* referred to the angels Raphael (east), Michael (south),

Gabriel (west), and Uriel (north). The energy provided by the watchtowers is generally thought to be protective.

white-handled knife: A knife with a white handle generally used for cutting or inscribing candles while in ritual space. It's sometimes known as a *kirfane* or *kerfan*. The traditional white-handled knife is often confused with the boline.

Wicca: A Modern Witchcraft tradition that generally utilizes some form of the ritual structure first revealed by Gerald Gardner in the early 1950s. Wicca is probably best defined by its ritual structure and not by theological ideas.

widdershins: To walk or move counterclockwise. Widdershins energy is most often used for banishing or aggressive magickal workings.

Yule: The name for the holiday celebrated at the winter solstice. Many Christmas traditions actually stem from ancient pagan holidays celebrated near the winter solstice. Some Pagans call the holiday *Midwinter*, as it falls between Samhain and Imbolc (seen by some as the start dates of winter and spring, respectively).

BIBLIOGRAPHY

This is mostly a list of resources I used while putting together this book, though it barely scratches the surface when it comes to books that have influenced me as a ritualist over the years and decades. For those looking for more information on the sabbats and related holidays, the history books listed here should be helpful. For those more interested in other general works about Witchcraft and rituals, everything else should be right up your alley.

Bowler, Gerry. *The World Encyclopedia of Christmas*. Toronto, Ontario: McClelland & Stewart, 2000. This giant book lives up to its title.

Brand, John. *Brand's Popular Antiquities of Great Britain: Faith and Folklore, Vol. 1*. London: Reeves and Turner, 1905. There are many books like this one listed in this bibliography, and all of them contain great tools to build rituals around.

Campanelli, Pauline and Dan. *Ancient Ways* (1991) and *Wheel of the Year* (1989). St. Paul, MN: Llewellyn Publications. Both books are full of great ideas and crafts for the sabbats. The history in them doesn't hold up very well, but I still love them.

Carmichael, Alexander. *Carmina Gadelica, Vol. 1*. Edinburgh: T. and A. Constable, 1900. This is an amazing collection of Scottish customs and rituals from the countryside. Many of them definitely have Pagan overtones.

Conway, D. J. *Celtic Magic*. St. Paul, MN: Llewellyn Publications, 1990. I can't say this book has any good history in it; however, it was the first Witch-related book I read as an adult, and as a result, it influenced me a great deal. I still find myself saying some of the things I first read in this book in ritual.

Cotterell, Arthur. *The Encyclopedia of Mythology.* New York: Smithmark, 1996. This book has been in my library since it was first released and is still a handy reference work.

Cunningham, Scott. *Wicca: A Guide for the Solitary Practitioner.* St. Paul, MN: Llewellyn Publications, 1989. For many Witches of my generation (and beyond), this was their first Witch book. It has guided all sorts of solitary Witches over the last thirty years.

Curott, Phyllis. *Book of Shadows: A Modern Woman's Journey into the Wisdom of Witchcraft and the Magic of the Goddess.* New York: Broadway Books, 1998. Though this is a memoir, Curott's recollections of ritual are so powerful and transformative that it almost reads as a how-to book. It's one of the best Witch books ever written. Curott later wrote her own guide to Witchcraft in 2001, with the title *Witch Crafting,* also highly recommended.

Forbes, Bruce David. *America's Favorite Holidays: Candid Histories.* Oakland, CA: University of California Press, 2015. This book includes Forbes's *Christmas* history, along with histories of Easter, Halloween, Thanksgiving, and Valentine's Day.

———. *Christmas: A Candid History.* Berkeley, CA: University of California Press, 2007. I love this book, and Forbes's history of Christmas includes the holiday's Pagan ancestors.

Frazer, Sir James George. *The Golden Bough.* 1890. Reprint, New York: Macmillan, 1922. Frazer's magnum opus has been incredibly influential in the Witch and Pagan worlds.

Gardner, Gerald. *The Meaning of Witchcraft.* London: Aquarian Press, 1959. *Witchcraft Today.* London: Rider & Co., 1954. Gardner's books don't hold up all that well today, but they've been super influential over the decades. Also, while reading them you'll find yourself stumbling into some parts that look really familiar and you'll realize why they still have value outside of their historical worth.

Gary, Gemma. *The Devil's Dozen: Thirteen Craft Rites of the Old One.* London: Troy Books, 2015. Gary is one of the most influential Traditional Witchcraft writers today, and her aesthetic is inspiring.

Graves, Robert. *The White Goddess: A Historical Grammar of Poetic Myth*. 1948. Reprint, New York: Farrar, Straus and Giroux, 2001. Along with Frazer, Graves is responsible for many of the modern myths that populate the Witch's Wheel of the Year. The idea of Maiden, Mother, Crone can be found in the pages of *The White Goddess*, along with the Oak and Holly King stories. Reading Graves is challenging but worth the effort, even if it's not a good representation of history.

Guiley, Rosemary Ellen. *The Encyclopedia of Witches & Witchcraft*. New York: Facts on File, 1999. I was lucky enough to meet Rosemary in New Orleans in 2018. I'm not sure what she thought about me, but her book is fabulous and a valuable reference tool. Sadly, her publisher is no longer updating this book, so I'll never be in it.

Hutton, Ronald. *Pagan Britain*. New Haven, CT: Yale University Press, 2013. Another great Hutton book, this one looking at what we might actually know about the Pagans who resided in Great Britain before the conversions to Christianity.

———. *The Pagan Religions of the Ancient British Isles: Their Nature and Legacy*. Cambridge, MA: B. Blackwell, 1991. Much of what's in this book Hutton covers again in *Pagan Britain*, but I've had this one longer, so I know where certain pieces of information are hiding!

———. *Stations of the Sun: A History of the Ritual Year in Britain*. New York: Oxford University Press, 1996. This is a treasure trove of historical information, much of it going directly back to the rituals of the Irish-Celts. Highly recommended for anyone interested in holiday history.

———. *The Triumph of the Moon: A History of Modern Pagan Witchcraft*. New York: Oxford University Press, 1999. Twenty years after its initial publication, this remains the go-to book on early Witch and Pagan history in Great Britain.

Kelly, Aidan A. *Hippie Commie Beatnik Witches: A Social History of the New Reformed Orthodox Order of the Golden Dawn*. Tacoma, WA: Hierophant Wordsmith Press, 2015. Aidan's book isn't referenced in this work, but if you're interested in what might have helped him come up with Mabon, Ostara, and Litha outside of the blog article in my footnotes, this is a good place to start.

———. *A Tapestry of Witches: A History of the Craft in America, Vol. 1*. Tacoma, WA: Hierophant Wordsmith Press, 2014. Kelly's book provides a quick overview of the earliest Modern Witch traditions in the United States.

Mankey, Jason. *Transformative Witchcraft: The Greater Mysteries.* Woodbury, MN: Llewellyn Publications, 2019. I realize it's rather self-serving to put myself in my own bibliography, but this book will be one I borrow from when it comes to ideas and information for the rest of my life. Also worth mentioning: *The Witch's Athame* (2016), *The Witch's Book of Shadows* (2017), and *The Witch's Altar* (with Laura Tempest Zakroff, 2018), all published by Llewellyn.

Nissenbaum, Stephen. *The Battle for Christmas.* New York: Vintage Books, 1996. This is not a quick read, but it's totally worth the investment in time. Nissenbaum makes Christmas even more Pagan than most people believe it to be.

O'Donovan, John, trans. *Cormac's Glossary.* Edited by Whitley Stokes. Calcutta: Printed by O. T. Cutter for the Irish Archeological and Celtic Society, 1868. This book is fascinating for history nerds.

Otto, Walter, F. *Dionysus: Myth & Cult.* Translated by Robert Palmer. Bloomington, IN: Indiana University Press, 1965. One of my favorite academic books on the patron deity of my home.

Pearson, Nigel, G. *Treading the Mill: Workings in Traditional Witchcraft.* London: Troy Books, 2016. Though Pearson barely touches on treading the mill, his writings are influential in the Traditional Witchcraft world.

RavenWolf, Silver. *To Ride a Silver Broomstick.* St. Paul, MN: Llewellyn Publications, 1993. Sometime in the early 2000s it became fashionable to slag on Silver RavenWolf, and many have dismissed her books as a result. Silver is a gifted writer, ritualist, and Witch, and I love this book.

Rhys, John. *Manx Folklore & Superstitions.* Edited by Stephen Miller. Onchan, Isle of Man: Chiollagh Books, 1994. Originally published as *Celtic Folklore: Welsh & Manx* in 1901. Rhys's book has so much stuff in it to inspire rituals. Most of the material is Christian on the surface, but I can't help but wonder just how much of it possibly has pre-Christian Pagan origins.

Shaw, Philip A. *Pagan Goddesses in the Early Germanic World.* London: Bristol Classical Press, 2011. Instead of presenting Eostre as a Maiden goddess, Shaw argues that she was probably a matronly Mother goddess. His version of Eostre was not the one I was expecting, which makes his work even more fascinating!

Skal, David, J. *Death Makes a Holiday: A Cultural History of Halloween.* New York: Blooms-bury, 2002. Those who truly love Halloween owe it to themselves to read this book.

Starhawk. *The Spiral Dance.* San Francisco, CA: Harper & Row, 1979. Starhawk's book is one of the most influential Witch books ever. Her version of Witch ritual is quite in-teresting when compared to what came after.

Wallis, Faith, trans. and ed. *Bede: The Reckoning of Time.* Liverpool, UK: Liverpool Uni-versity Press, 1999. Wallis makes Bede readable. If Aidan Kelly had had this transla-tion, maybe he would have gone with *Halig* for the Autumn Equinox instead of *Mabon.*

West, M. L. *Indo-European Poetry and Myth.* Oxford: Oxford University Press, 2007. West brings to life the connections that run through Slavic, Greek, Celtic, and Indian my-thology that stem from the language and myth of the Indo-Europeans.

INDEX

GET MORE AT LLEWELLYN.COM

Visit us online to browse hundreds of our books and decks, plus sign up to receive our e-newsletters and exclusive online offers.

- **Free tarot readings • Spell-a-Day • Moon phases**
- **Recipes, spells, and tips • Blogs • Encyclopedia**
- **Author interviews, articles, and upcoming events**

GET SOCIAL WITH LLEWELLYN

Find us on  🐦 **@LlewellynBooks**

www.Facebook.com/LlewellynBooks

GET BOOKS AT LLEWELLYN

LLEWELLYN ORDERING INFORMATION

 Order online: Visit our website at www.llewellyn.com to select your books and place an order on our secure server.

 Order by phone:
- Call toll free within the US at 1-877-NEW-WRLD (1-877-639-9753)
- We accept VISA, MasterCard, American Express, and Discover.

 Order by mail:
Send the full price of your order (MN residents add 6.875% sales tax) in US funds plus postage and handling to: Llewellyn Worldwide, 2143 Wooddale Drive, Woodbury, MN 55125-2989

POSTAGE AND HANDLING

STANDARD (US):(Please allow 12 business days)
$30.00 and under, add $6.00.
$30.01 and over, FREE SHIPPING.

CANADA:
We cannot ship to Canada. Please shop your local bookstore or Amazon Canada.

INTERNATIONAL:
Customers pay the actual shipping cost to the final destination, which includes tracking information.

Visit us online for more shipping options. Prices subject to change.

FREE CATALOG!

To order, call
1-877-
NEW-WRLD
ext. 8236
or visit our
website